The Truth about Conservative Christians

The Truth about Conservative Christians

What They Think and What They Believe

Andrew Greeley
& Michael Hout

THE UNIVERSITY OF CHICAGO PRESS • CHICAGO AND LONDON

ANDREW GREELEY is on the staff of the National Opinion Research Center at the University of Chicago and is professor of social science at the University of Arizona. He is the author of numerous books, most recently *Priests: A Calling in Crisis.*

MICHAEL HOUT is professor of sociology and chair of the joint program in demography and sociology at the University of California, Berkeley. He is coauthor of *Inequality by Design.*

The University of Chicago Press, Chicago 60637
The University of Chicago Press, Ltd., London

Printed in the United States of America

15 14 13 12 11 10 09 08 07 06   1 2 3 4 5

ISBN-13: 978-0-226-30662-9
ISBN-10: 0-226-30662-3 (cloth)

Library of Congress Cataloging-in-Publication Data
Greeley, Andrew M., 1928–
The truth about conservative Christians : what they think and what they believe / Andrew M. Greeley & Michael Hout.
p. cm.
Includes bibliographical references and index.
ISBN 0-226-30662-3 (cloth : alk. paper)
1. Christian conservatism—United States. 2. Conservatism—Religious aspects—Christianity. I. Hout, Michael. II. Title.
BR526.G75 2006
277.3′083—dc22

2006015672

∞ The paper used in this publication meets the minimum requirements of the American National Standard for Information Sciences—Permanence of Paper for Printed Library Materials, ANSI Z39.48-1992.

Dedicated to the honored memory of
OTIS DUDLEY DUNCAN
teacher, colleague, friend.

Who among the well educated will
speak well of Evangelicals? It's like
standing up for the Crusades.

CHRISTIAN SMITH

Contents

Acknowledgments ix

ONE Introduction 1

TWO The Religion of Conservative Christians: A Return to the Reformation? 11

THREE Conservative Christians in American Politics 39

FOUR The Politics of Conservative Christianity in Black and White 69

FIVE Freedom, Inequality, and Conservative Christianity 76

SIX A Social Portrait of Conservative Christians 91

SEVEN Conservative Christian Growth: Membership Begins at Home 103

EIGHT Conservative Christians in the "Sexual Revolution" 113

NINE The Conservative Christian Family and the "Feminist Revolution" 136

TEN Happiness and Lifestyle among Conservative Christians 150

ELEVEN The Pentecostals: Ultimate Conservative Christians 162

TWELVE Conservative Christians and Catholics: Too Estranged for Alliance 172

THIRTEEN Conclusions 178

APPENDIX Regression Results for Models of Vote and Party 184

NOTES 189

REFERENCE LIST 199

INDEX 203

Acknowledgments

We are grateful to the colleagues who read this manuscript in various stages of development and commented on it: Henry Brady, Mark Chaves, Claude Fischer, Martin Marty, William Shea, Peter Rossi, Tom Smith, and especially, Tom Reese.

ONE

Introduction

Conservative Christianity, as a religious movement, could hardly be more straightforward. Members seek a religious practice consistent with a relatively small number of basic principles that are rooted in scripture. Such a straightforward approach apparently offers little protection against misapprehension, though. Insiders and outsiders alike misperceive, misrepresent, and stereotype this large and diverse segment of American culture.

To insiders, Conservative Christianity is—in Christian Smith's memorable phrase—"embattled and thriving." That is, Conservative Christians defend the core values of both America and Christianity against the onslaughts of a secular and vulgar culture that will, if unchecked, undo both nation and religion. Conservative Christians alone can be trusted to accomplish this, and in pursuing it, they become stronger.

Conservative Christians are a dangerous juggernaut bent on undoing liberty, equality, and the fraternity of nations. Power-mad hypocrites, they mask hate with love, a judgmental streak with pieties, exclusion with appeals to inclusion, and monoculture in the name of diversity.

Neither the insider nor outsider portrait does justice to the variety, complexity, and subtlety of Conservative Christianity. How could it be otherwise? No collection this large—by our count just under one American in three identifies with a Protestant denomination affiliated with one of the Conservative Christian traditions—could possibly be as monolithic in their opinions as this group is made out to be. Both insiders and outsiders have an interest in exaggerating. Movement leaders gain political clout by pumping up their numbers. Movement critics bring in more political contributions and sell more magazines by broad-brush caricature.

We have no stake in either the insider or outsider rendition of Conservative Christianity.[1] As social scientists we not only resist stereotyping on principle, but we also have the tools to counter stereotypes with facts. And that is our goal here in this book. We hope to deliver facts about Conservative Christians.

The first thing to remember is that the last two Democratic liberals to be president of the United States were Southern Baptists—and by their lights devout ones! The skeptical reader should start there and ask where Presidents Carter and Clinton fit into the stereotypes about Conservative Christians.

OUR APPROACH

We began our project with an op-ed article for the *New York Times* that appeared on the Saturday of Labor Day weekend before the 2004 election. In that piece we argued for fairness for the fundamentalists. They are, we contended, far too varied in their political views to be President Bush's political base, as everyone seemed to think. White Protestants from conservative denominations contributed only a minor increment to the Republican coalition over that already provided by other Protestants. In our own research on American religion (spanning the past several decades) we have been impressed by the variety and pluralism among those who call themselves "Christians." Our reading of the extensive academic literature reinforces that view. Yet the journalists and public intellectuals who form and reform and re-form again the conventional wisdom of the United States, it seems to us, are monumentally ignorant of the faith and behavior of the citizens who fit under the rubric of "Conservative Christians"—a label we will here apply because there seems to be little agreement on what "fundamentalist" and "evangelical" mean. They live someplace else—in the red states.[2] They are invisible in the global cities of the country—Boston, New York, Chicago, Los Angeles, San Francisco. We don't know them. We rarely meet them. We judge them by enthusiastic preachers, militant spokespeople, speakers at national meetings, and the occasional person who asked us whether we've been saved.

Fortunately we have at our disposal a wealth of data gathered over a span of over thirty years—enough time to add some historical perspective to our up-to-date information. We do not deny partial truth in some of the stereotypes.[3] In many cases we replace absolutes with qualified statements about tendencies. For example, we replace the absolute statement that Conservative Christians are the Republican base with the observation that 7 percent more of them vote Republican than Mainline Protestants. Conservative religion, we argued in our *New York Times* piece, cannot be equated with conservative politics. In the leisure activities their propensity to enjoy NASCAR racing reflects the stereotypes, and the tendency for one-fifth of them watch PBS every day flies in the face of it. They are more likely to oppose abortion than other Americans, but only 14 percent of them oppose abortion in all circumstances while 22 percent counter that with a consistently pro-choice stance.

Thus we present a sociodemographic study of Conservative Christians, which will attempt to understand them from within their own perspectives and to reveal them in all the variety and complexity that they—like all other large groups of people—display.

As we go about our task of describing and documenting the beliefs and practices of Conservative Christians, we take people at their word. When we tender an explanation, we do so with respect for the ideas they express. We take seriously William Shea's (2004) warning that explaining ought not become "explaining away." It is not acceptable to dismiss Conservative Christians with psychological explanations. To say that they are frightened and hence emotionally troubled or to say that they are insecure and hence resisting change insults their faith. And it begs the important social and political questions. Granted, Conservative Christians defend the "fundamentals" of the Reformation against modernity and the compromises with modernity that they think other Christians—Protestant and Catholic—have made. However, a dislike of modernity is a social attitude, not a psychological symptom. Conservative Christians insist that Darwin's findings go against the Christian faith and must be rejected. They criticize other Protestant denominations for compromising with Darwinism because compromise is only possible if one accepts a drastic reinterpretation of sacred scripture. Conservative Christians also firmly believe that their faith is the faith of the reformers that must be defended against modernity and those Protestants who make compromises with modernity. It is said that they need certainty in their worldview and hence hide from the obvious findings of modern science. However, it is our observation that the adherents of every worldview seek certainty, whether it be Mainline Protestantism or Catholicism or secular rationalism. There are some adherents of every worldview who find it difficult to be tolerant of other worldviews—whether they be agnostics or believers. We are ill-advised to see the mote in the eye of the Conservative Christians and ignore the beam in our own.

Conservative Christians' convictions may be living truth or misguided; it is not our ken to assess those kinds of claims. But as social scientists studying a religious subculture, we must respect the sincerity and integrity of its convictions, regardless of our own opinion. Otherwise fairness is impossible and so too is understanding.

We also note to those who are heavily invested in demonizing Conservative Christians for their alleged political stands that they might well consider the similarities we will report between Conservative Protestants and Afro-American Protestants.[4] If whites are emotionally troubled searchers for certitude in their Republican vote, how then do the critics account for the fact that African Americans, who are in nearly every respect as religiously conservative as whites, vote overwhelmingly for Democrats?[5] Belief, for example, in the key conviction of the Conservative denominations—the word-for-word inerrancy of the Bible—does not inhibit political liberalism among African Americans. The political dissimilarity of religiously conservative black and white Americans calls into question the equation of biblical Christianity and conservative politics. Both of us have long been concerned with the demonization of Conservative Christians in the higher media and the scholarly academy. It is unjust to dismiss anyone with pop-psychological putdowns. When a group is one-fourth of American society, bigotry against them is a dangerous threat to the fabric of that society.[6] Even if, as Smith argues, this adversity strengthens the Conservative Christian movement, it brings no credit to the critics or academics who sit by and let the errors prevail.

Neither of us is a Conservative Christian.[7] We do not believe in the literal word-for-word inspiration of the Bible. We have not been "saved." We have not pressured anyone to join our own denomination—though we are ready at the drop of a statistic to argue its merits.

Science is the quest for truth with no holds barred, in the inimitable phrase of Columbia sociologist Harrison White. Sociology, because it deals with the most complex phenomenon that we know—humans in society—has its own methods and its own limitations. Our style of sociology, the analysis of survey data, has many limitations and also many advantages. We must be transparent about our presuppositions, the probability samples we use for our estimates, the statistical rules for drawing conclusions (tests of statistical significance), the wording of our questions,[8] and the necessary restraints on our conjectures about the meaning of our findings.

One of the alleged weaknesses of our methods is in fact a strength. When we are told that our findings are mired in qualifications or that the world we describe is gray, we rejoice because we believe that therefore we have reflected the reality of a gray and qualification-worthy world, the world that exists outside our office windows and is not always visible in the neat ideological divides of the faculty dinner parties or the "balanced" television news interviews.

Our picture of the gray world is built up, alas for the reader who would like this book to read like an article in *Time* or the *New York Times Sunday Magazine*, by numbers, a succession of numbers more typical of the business and sports pages. There is no other way to put our gray portrait together. We try to keep tables at a minimum and use charts only when the story they tell is dramatic. Yet without our obsession with numbers we would never have discovered how many Conservative Christians watch PBS every day, that while they tend to be more pro-life than pro-choice more take an absolute pro-choice stand than an absolute pro-life stand, how many of them approve of maternal leave, how few of them support anti-pornography laws for adults, and how many of them vote Democratic.

DATA AND METHODOLOGY

Our work draws extensively on the General Social Survey (GSS), a broad-ranging inventory of behaviors and attitudes conducted by the National Opinion Research Center at the University of Chicago since 1972. Initially an annual survey, the data have been since 1994 collected in even-numbered years. A representative sample of U.S. households is drawn using full probability methods. An English-speaking adult is randomly selected from within the household. About 77 percent of persons thus selected choose to participate in a 75-minute face-to-face interview and 20-minute self-completion questionnaire. When surveys were done annually, the target number of interviews was 1,500; the new biennial design calls for samples of 3,000. The total number of interviews through 2004 was 46,510, including 707 African Americans in oversamples collected in 1982 and 1987. Nobody is asked to answer all the questions, even all the questions slated for a given year.[9] Only a few very basic questions are asked of all respondents. Fortunately one of them is, *What is your religious preference? Is it Protestant, Catholic, Jewish, something other religion, or no religion?* People who respond "Protestant'" are then asked, *What specific denomination is that, if any?*

The question about Protestant denominations has yielded the names of over 230 specific religious organizations over the years. A few researchers may have the expertise required to make use of the full complexity of these denominational distinctions, but most use one of two approaches to classify the denominations by type. The first was developed by Tom W. Smith, one of the GSS principal investigators, in a 1990 article. He referred to the three *sola* we discuss in chapter 2 and classified denominations as "fundamentalist" if they (or their fellows) showed a close affinity to three prescriptions: literal interpretation of the Bible, acceptance of Jesus Christ as personal Lord and savior, and spreading the good news. He classified as "liberal" the (mostly liturgical) denominations that did none of these and "moderate" the ones that were neither "fundamentalist" nor "liberal." A decade later Steensland et al. (2000) proposed some reclassification and a couple of additional categories.

In our research we have combined the two approaches. For the most part, we follow Smith (1990). But the Afro-American tradition is so distinct that we found it useful to follow Steensland et al. (2000) in giving it its own category. Also we only classify the Protestant denominations as "Conservative" and "Mainline. " Our "Conservative" denominations are Smith's "fundamentalists" with the Afro-American churches pulled out; our "Mainline" denominations are Smith's "moderates" minus the Afro-American moderates and the Catholics plus his "liberals" minus the Jews. Finally we reclassified the "Christians" and "Nondenominational or inter-denominational" parts of the "other religions" as "Conservative." These two groups within the "other religions" have much in common with the Conservative

Protestants who call themselves Protestants: half are Bible literalists compared to 55 percent of Conservative Protestants, 88 percent believe in God without doubt compared with 82 percent of Conservative Protestants, their distributions on church attendance and prayer frequency are indistinguishable, and they are more likely to think of themselves as "strong" Christians than Conservative Protestants are to think of themselves as, for example, strong Baptists or Pentecostals or members of the Church of Christ. The GSS has only reported these two categories since 1998.

We tabulate the current religion, classified according to our scheme, by decade in table 1.1. Conservative Protestants increased from 22 to 26 percent of adults between the 1970s and the 1980s, then leveled off (the one-point increase in the 1990s and one-point decrease in the 2000s are not statistically significant). Afro-American Protestants are between 6 percent and 10 percent of adults (the changes over time are not statistically significant). Mainline Protestants decreased from 34 percent to 23 percent of adults in thirty years. Catholics held steady at 25 percent; Jews held steady at 2 percent. People of other religions increased from 1 to 4 percent of adults, and no religion doubled from 7 to 14 percent of adults. The doubling of nonaffiliation is rooted in the demography of the 1990s and the politics of that decade. The cohort that was probably the most religious cohort in American history, the one born 1900–1914, passed away and was replaced by a much less religious one, born in the 1970s. Meanwhile the growing identification between organized religion and a conservative social

Table 1.1 Religion by decade

	Decade			
Religion	1972–1978 (%)	1982–1989 (%)	1990–1998 (%)	2000–2004 (%)
Conservative Protestant	22	26	27	26
Afro-American Protestant	9	10	6	6
Mainline Protestant	34	29	27	23
Catholic	25	25	24	25
Jewish	2	2	2	2
Other religion	1	2	3	4
No religion	7	7	10	14
Total	100	100	100	100
N	10,627	14,190	13,156	8,359

SOURCE: General Social Surveys, 1972–2004

agenda turned off casually religious liberals, some of whom dropped their religion identification (Hout and Fischer 2002).

Table 1.2 shows the breakdown of Protestants. Southern Baptists are the largest Conservative Protestant denomination—one-third of Conservative Protestants are in that denomination. The next largest segment among Conservative Protestants are the other conservative

Table 1.2 Specific denominations by religion category

Religion	Percent
Conservative Protestant	
Southern Baptist	32
Other Baptist	21
Missouri or Wisconsin Synod Lutheran	6
Churches of God / Assemblies of God	3
Pentecostal	9
Christian Scientist	1
Church of Christ	3
Jehovah's Witnesses	3
Latter Day Saints–Mormon	3
"Christian"	5
"Inter-denominational"	2
Other Conservative	10
Total	100
Afro-American Protestant	
American Baptist	14
National Baptist	10
Other Baptist	54
African Methodist Epispcopal / AME Zion	10
Other Methodist	3
Holiness	3
Sanctified	3
Church of God in Christ	2
Other Afro-American	2
Total	100
Mainline Protestant	
United Methodist	25
Other Methodist	4
Lutheran, other than Missouri and Wisconsin Synod	15
Presbyterian	11
Episcopal	9
United Church of Christ	5
Other Mainline	9
Protestant–no denomination	23
Total	100

SOURCE: General Social Surveys, 2000–2004.

Baptists (including people who identified as Baptists but could not say which kind they were). Pentecostals are 9 percent of Conservative Protestants; "Christians" are 5 percent.

The largest group among the Afro-American Protestants are various kinds of Baptists (including those who cannot name a denomination). The African Methodist Episcopal tradition is also important.

Mainline Protestants are the familiar Methodist, Lutheran (except Missouri and Wisconsin Synods), Presbyterian, and Episcopal denominations. They also include the elements of the United Church of Christ—the Congregational and Reformed churches—and the Quaker, Unitarian/Universalist, and Brethren traditions.

STATISTICS

We have tried to keep our statistical manipulations simple and transparent. But some questions require multivariate calculations to get an accurate answer. Most of the techniques we use are based on the standard social science tool of multiple regression: a statistical routine for assigning the relative weights to each of a set of independent variables thought to be important for some outcome. We use a special feature of this approach. In situations where three variables link up in what might be thought of as a causal chain, that is, *X* causes *Y* which in turn causes *Z*, then a regression that treats *Z* as the dependent variable and *X* as the independent variable, ignoring *Y*, will yield a large, significant regression coefficient for *X*. Then when a second regression brings *Y* into the analysis, *X* disappears, and *Y* carries all the explanatory weight. Otis Dudley Duncan spelled out how all this works in an important series of papers between 1963 and the late 1970s (e.g., Duncan 1966, 1969, 1970; Duncan and Hodge 1963; also see Alwin and Hauser 1975).

In most analyses in this book, religious denomination takes the role of *X*, the EVANGELICAL scale takes the role of *Y*, and we apply the method to a wide variety of *Z*s. We get a coefficient from the first regression of, say, the frequency of praying, on denomination, ignoring the EVANGELICAL scale. That represents the direct effect of denomination on praying and its indirect effect that operates through the components of the EVANGELICAL scale. When we do the second analysis, this time adding EVANGELICAL to the regression equation, EVANGELI-

CAL does its own work and the coefficient for denomination is just its direct effect (if any). If the coefficient for denomination was, say, .90 in the first regression and .10 in the second then we would say that the EVANGELICAL scale accounted for 1 − .10/.90 = .89 or 89 percent of the original (total) effect.

Ordinary multiple regression methods depend on some key assumptions that are likely to be violated unless the dependent variable has lots of possible scores. Some of the variables we are interested in approximate these conditions tolerably well; for them we use ordinary regression. But many of the variables we analyze have just two, three, or four categories. For them we make use of generalizations known as logistic regression and ordered logistic regression. Technical information is available in Long (1997; also see the appendix to Greeley and Hout 1999 for a short primer). We also use a statistic developed by Leo A. Goodman (1991) as an analogue to the regression coefficient. Hout, Brooks, and Manza (1995) modified Goodman's coefficient for these kinds of problems. We called it "kappa" and denote it with the Greek letter (κ). It works just like a regression coefficient in the sense that when we perform a logistic or ordered logistic regression with denomination as the independent variable we get a κ that represents the total effect of religion on the outcome; when we add EVANGELICAL scale to the equation, we get a smaller κ and the proportional reduction is, as in the ordinary regression approach, the proportion explained by the EVANGELICAL scale. Consult Hout et al. (1995) for the formulas and details about how to calculate κ.

CONCLUSION

There is a built-in conflict, we very much fear, between survey analysis and conventional wisdom. After all, we fashion the conventional wisdom in conversation with people we know. But "people we know" is a lousy sample. There is more variation in American society than we can sample in the circles of our acquaintance. Of course when the conventional wisdom stresses the otherness of some group, it usually turns out that what the intelligence gatherers overlooked were the similarities. Therefore we proceed to our study of Conservative Christians open to the possibility that they may very well emerge as men and women much like the rest of us—especially like the appropriate comparison group, Mainline Protestants.

TWO

The Religion of Conservative Christians

A Return to the Reformation?

INTRODUCTION

Conservative Christianity today inherits the religious doctrines and worldview of the social movement that swept through American Protestantism little more than a century ago. Our question is whether that initial formation survives as a religious system among contemporary Conservative Christians (our name for those who are otherwise called "evangelicals" or "fundamentalists"—a pair of misleading labels). Can one describe its key elements, its worldview, its beliefs, its spirituality, and its sense of moral obligations by interviewing American adults who identify with it? We will conclude that Conservative Christianity—in both its major contemporary forms—is a biblical religion in the tradition of the Reformation not only at the leadership level but also within the ranks of the faithful. We also find enough heterogeneity to challenge any facile generalization or stereotype. Importantly, though, our test is not uniformity of belief (in fact, we find that only a minority of Conservatives embrace all of Conservative Christianity's essential elements). Our test is whether those historically defined elements partially distinguish Conservative from Mainline Protestants today. They do.

Once we have established the evidence that Conservative Christians' approach to the Bible sets them apart from other Christians, we will turn to the political and social correlates of that distinction. But first things first. What do Conservative Christians believe and how do those beliefs set them apart?

THE REFORMATION LIVES!

Shea (2004) contends that Conservative Christians are in most respects the legitimate heirs of the Protestant Reformation. The three "*sola*" (alone) of the Reformation—*sola scriptura, sola gratia, sola fide*—exist in their pure and undefiled form among the Conservatives, with perhaps a single exception. They propose the inerrant Bible as the only legitimate authority against those denominations that place greater or lesser authority in churches and traditions of one sort or another. They propose faith in God's mercy against the temptation to think that mercy can be obtained by human works. They propose God's supervening grace against any human attempts to merit (earn) that grace.

Conservative Christians—or at least most of their writers and teachers—also have inherited, Shea says, the virulent anti-Catholicism of the Reformation, an anti-Catholicism that is only weakly reflected (if at all) in the attitudes of Mainline denominations. The Conservatives for the most part reject all attempts at ecumenism both among Protestants themselves and between Protestants and Catholics as a betrayal of the Protestant heritage. Conversations should be directed towards winning them as converts and thus saving their souls.

Shea observes, however, that Conservative Christians read the Reformation incorrectly if they think that the leading Reformers took inerrancy to be "word-for-word" inerrancy—that God personally inspired every word that the authors of the Bible wrote. In this respect the different understanding of inerrancy among Mainline Protestants may be closer to what the Reformers practiced—which is why the Conservatives are so constrained to denounce them for their questioning of the authority of the inspired word of God in the Bible. If they give that up, they believe that will be no different from other "compromisers" with Darwin and modernity. One either accepts Genesis as written word for word, or the game is lost. This passage from *The Fundamentals* (vol. 1, chap. 5) is illustrative:

> I think it is an essential element in a tenable doctrine of Scripture, in fact the core of the matter, that it contains a record of a true supernatural revelation; and that is what the Bible claims to be—not a development of man's thoughts about God, and not what this man and that one came to think about God, how they came to have the ideas of a Jehovah

> or Yahveh, who was originally the storm-god of Sinai, and how they manufactured out of this the great universal God of the prophets—but a supernatural revelation of what God revealed Himself in word and deed to men in history. And if that claim to a supernatural revelation from God falls, the Bible falls, because it is bound up with it from beginning to end.

While it is fair to say that contemporary Conservative Christians are repeating the theories of the Reformation, one must also remember that the context of this repetition is difference and that the difference in context means that Reformation doctrines take a different shape, however verbally similar they may be. Thus the original reformers—Luther, Calvin, and Knox, for example—were fighting against a Church that they perceived was overwhelming the scriptures with its political power and its claim that tradition gave it final authority in the interpretation of the scriptures. The contemporary "reformers" are much less threatened by Catholicism (though they don't like it very much, as we shall note in a later chapter) than they are by Darwinism and the Modernism compromise with it among the Mainline Protestant denominations. Hence the insistence on word-for-word inerrancy is necessarily much stronger today than it needed to be in the original *sola scriptura*. Would Luther, disciple of Augustine that he was, have as much trouble with Darwin as his successors do today? To engage in that sort of historical and theological discussion goes beyond our skills and our mandate.

Shea suggests that the Conservative Christians practice Biblical Christianity—a religion centered on the Bible as the sole (*sola*) source of authority without any need for a Church or for liturgy. Catholics on the other hand practice Liturgical Christianity—the Bible as understood within a worshipping Church. Mainline Protestants, with their own denominational structures and their own sacred liturgy, are somewhere in between.

We must note that the methods of the brand of social science we practice—analysis of survey data—have their strengths and weaknesses. They are powerful tools in drawing big pictures and refuting conventional wisdom—the major goals of this project. They often lack the precision necessary for intricate investigations of complex issues like religious decisions. We believe that our tools could become much more useful in these matters—as in the questionnaire items about basic worldviews we will turn to later in this chapter. However the resources necessary to support such efforts do not seem to be available in the present climate of research funding. We hope to add important clarifications to the understanding of Conservative Christian religion in this work, but we are aware that much mystery will remain.

At the very center of Reformation thinking—and of Conservative Christian conviction—is the belief that the Bible is the sole rule of faith. There is no need for an organized church so long as the individual Christian has the sacred book available for study. God speaks directly to the reader in the book and God's grace enables the reader to understand what He is saying. For the Conservative Christian the Bible is the bedrock of faith. The modernists view the Bible as a collection of stories, fables, law texts, religious instructions, history and poetry written by different authors with different intentions for different audiences in different times and places, and with different literary styles, a collection which was gathered together years, even centuries after the pieces of the collection were written. It can be understood properly only when the various components are read with an understanding of the context and the style in which it was written. The creation stories of Genesis are therefore to be understood as teaching profound religious truth about creation and human nature and destiny, but not as literal, scientific accounts. Mainline Protestantism has no problem now with such a literary view. For the Conservative Christian this construct destroys the possibility of faith. Thus one cleric, cited by Shea (2004, 32), argued in 1920:

> Every honest man knows that accepting evolution means giving up the inspiration of Genesis; and if the inspiration of Genesis is given up, the testimony of Jesus to the inspiration of the scriptures, goes with it; and if his testimony to the scriptures is given up, his deity goes with it and with that goes his being a real redeemer and we are left without a savior and in the darkness of our sin.

The movement which came to be called fundamentalism was born of the instinct that there could be no compromise with Darwinian evolution without the loss of Christian faith.[1] Between 1915 and 1920 a group of conservative scholars published twelve short volumes called *The Fundamentals*, which laid down the nonnegotiable requirements of Christianity. In 1919 the conservatives founded the World's Christian Fundamentals Association (in opposition to the Federal Council of Churches). During the 1920s the supporters of the Fundamentals tried and failed to take over the Northern Baptist Convention and the Presbyterian General Assembly. They charged that their adversaries were no longer Christians but founders of an entirely new religion. They claimed for themselves the title of "Evangelical" to which they denied that their opponents had a right. In 1942 a new generation of evangelical leaders founded the National Association of Evangelicals, which many claim has been responsible for the increase in members in the Conservative Christian churches (a claim we question in the "upsurge" chapter).

While the argument (in the finest tradition of apocalyptic Protestant controversy) between the Conservative Christians and their adversaries covers many topics, the Bible is still the critical issue. The touchstone question is whether one embraces the literal, word-for-word, inerrancy of the Bible.[2]

Since 1984 the National Opinion Research Center has asked the following question in its annual (more recently biennial) General Social Survey (GSS):

> *Which of these statements comes closest to describing your feelings about the Bible:*
>
> - *a) The Bible is the actual word of God and is to be taken literally, word for word.*
> - *b) The Bible is the inspired word of God but not everything in it should be taken literally, word for word.*
> - *c) The Bible is an ancient book of fables, legends, history and moral precepts recorded by man.*

Fifty-four percent of the Conservative Protestants and 59 percent of the Afro-American Protestants endorse the first response; 26 percent of the Mainline Protestants and 21 percent of Catholics choose this response. Four percent of Conservative Protestants and 7 percent of Afro-American Protestants say that the Bible is a book of fables, as do 13 percent of Mainline Protestants and 12 percent of Catholics. Conservative Christianity is thus firmly biblical but not unanimously so.[3] Moreover there is a notable (and statistically significant) decline in belief in word-for-word inerrancy across year of survey ($\kappa = .30$);

62 percent of Conservative Protestants in the earliest data, gathered in 1984, took a literal interpretation of the Bible; it was a minority view (47 percent) by 2002. Additionally there is a decline across birth cohorts from a high of 67 percent for those born before 1920 to 50 percent in the 1950s cohort followed by a modest rebound to 54 percent of those born since 1970s ($\kappa = .33$).

A statistical model that considers age, year of survey, and year of birth simultaneously reveals no age effect and independent influences for both year of survey and year of birth. Nonetheless half of Conservative Protestants born after 1980 believe in word-for-word inerrancy. Given the changes in society and in religion during the second half of the twentieth century, the conviction that God is responsible for every word in the Bible among Conservative Protestants remains remarkably robust. Without the data from twenty years ago we would be marveling at 50 percent orthodoxy. Conservative Protestants are twenty percentage points more likely to believe in word-for-word literalism than Catholics are to believe in the infallibility of the pope.

BORN AGAIN?

To be "saved" or (to "find the Lord" or to "find Jesus" or to be "born again") is an experience essential to the Conservative Christian creed. It is also often essential in relationships between Conservative Christians and others. To ask another whether she or he has been "saved" is to establish where one is in religious geography. The ranks of the saved will be rescued early in the end times. Others are, sadly perhaps, in the ranks of those who are destined for damnation. According to some Conservative Christian views, those not saved will be vaporized on the day of the Rapture. For Catholics at any rate the question of "finding the Lord" or "being saved" is a jarring experience. The words do not fit the Catholic's religious vocabulary. Unless one has had frequent contact with Conservative Christians it's not quite clear what they are talking about.[4] However, if the Conservative Christian believes that you have not been saved, then it is their duty to offer you the good news of salvation so that you can thus be reserved from hell fire and vaporization. Those Catholic prelates in Latin America who complain about the zeal of the "sects," as they are often called, to convert Catholics to "Christianity" do not understand that the goal of the missionaries is to guarantee the ultimate happiness of their converts, to save them from damnation. From the point of view of the Conservative Christians, the missionaries are risking their lives in the same cause for which the early Christian martyrs died. One might fairly compare the Conservative Christian missionaries to the Catholic missionary orders of priests and nuns who dedicated their lives to the conversion of "pagans" in Asia and Africa and indeed in South America. The theological and ecclesiological presuppositions and the techniques of the two kinds of missionaries might be very different, but the perspective—and the bravery—are similar.[5]

Thus the question arises as to whether the "born again" experience and the obligation to lead others to salvation are part of the religious perspective of all Conservative Christians. The GSS included the following question in its three special religious modules (1988, 1991, and 1998): *Would you say that you have had a "born again" experience—that is, a turning point experience in your life when you committed yourself to Christ?* Sixty-five percent of the Conservative Protestants report such experiences, as do 64 percent of the Afro-American Protestants; about half as many—36 percent—of Mainline Protestants have had experiences they describe this way. There is no trend over time or cohorts in this experience. Thus today's Conservative Protestants are even more likely to be "born again" than they are likely to believe in word-for-word inspiration of the Bible by God. In a similar question asked in an International Social Survey Program (ISSP) religion module (1998), *Did you ever have a religious or spiritual experience that chanted your life?*, 69 percent of the Conservative Protestants reported such experiences as did 66 percent of Afro-American Protestants; 45 percent of the Mainline Protestants affirm this variant of the question. With both the more expansive question and the more specific question, therefore, the Conservative Protestants are much more likely than the Mainline Protestants to report life-changing religious experiences. However, a substantial minority of Conservative Protestants apparently have never been "saved."

In the three religion modules (1988, 1991, 1998) a question was asked about spreading their faith to others:

- *Have you ever tried to encourage someone to believe in Jesus Christ or to accept Jesus Christ as his or her savior?*

Seventy-one percent of both the Conservative Protestants and the Afro-American Protestants replied that they had tried to spread the faith compared to 43 percent of the Mainline Protestants. Curiously, more Conservative Protestants report such efforts than report "reborn" experiences. Thirty-nine percent of those who had not "found Jesus" themselves nonetheless tried to lead others down the path to acceptance of Jesus as Savior. Nearly all of these apparently un-reborn proselytizers were raised in the same faith they now profess and report being active churchgoers as they were growing up. We infer that their negative response to the question about changing reflects this continuity in their religious background and current practice.

Taken together these three items—word-by-word inspiration, born again experience, and leading others to Jesus (belief, experience, and action)—are crude measures of the presence of the Reformation faith in the Conservative Protestants—*sola scripture, sola fides, sola gratia.* To what extent, one may ask, do the Conservative Protestants endorse all three? Two-fifths of Conservative Protestants endorse all three—40 percent (35 percent of Afro-American Protestants); 15 percent of Conservative Protestants reject all three (11 percent of Afro-American Protestants). However, only 15 percent of Mainline Protestants affirm all three "fundamental" items, as do a small 4 percent of Catholics. Forty-one percent of Mainline Protestants and 54 percent of Catholics reject all three.

How can it be that only one-third to two-fifths of those who one can legitimately call Conservative Protestant because of their denominational background live up to the full requirement of the Reformation pure and undefiled? Orthodoxy is tricky, and propositional orthodoxy even trickier. No one can reasonably expect everyone who embraces a religious heritage to conform to all of its doctrines. Arguably we could end this exposition of Conservative Protestant religion at this point and consider only those who are its perfect exemplars. While the Conservative Protestants are almost a quarter of the American population (one-third when we add Afro-American Protestants to the tally), those who measure in on all three of the "fundamental" items are a more modest 18 percent of the population—hardly the mass of Reformation zealots that both the enemies and the friends of Conservative Christianity pretend to see.

However, it would seem more useful to ask how the differences among the Conservative and Mainline Protestants can be explained by the EVANGELICAL scale as we will hereinafter call it. Are the Conservative and the Mainline Protestants different one from another precisely because they embrace the EVANGELICAL scale to differing degrees?

Half of both the Conservative Protestants and Afro-American Protestants read the Bible at least every week (21 percent every day) as opposed to a third of Mainline Protestants (14 percent every day). Fourteen percent of Catholics read the Bible once a week (just 3.5 percent every day). This corresponds to Shea's (and others') characterization of Conservative and Afro-American Protestants as Bible Christians, Catholics as Liturgical Christians, and Mainline Protestants as a mixture of the two style. The EVANGELICAL scale completely accounts for the differences in Bible-reading frequency among Protestant denominations, but Catholics read the Bible significantly less than Protestants, even at the same EVANGELICAL value.[6]

In conclusion to this section, Conservative and Afro-American Protestants can reasonably claim to be the legitimate heirs of the Reformation. Americans who identify with these two Christian traditions are more likely than other American Christians to adhere to the three solas—scripture, faith, and grace. However, even among the Conservative and Afro-American Protestants, full embrace eludes the majority. Mainline Protestantism and Catholicism are significantly different Christian traditions. Catholics emphasize liturgy and community over the lone believer encountering the word of God alone in Bible study (see Greeley 2000). The Mainline Protestant denominations (in the United States at least) blend Biblical and Liturgical Christianity.

WORLDVIEW

Religion, in the definition of Clifford Geertz, is a symbol system that seeks to explain reality and especially the suffering in human life—death, sickness, injustice. In the archives of the General Social Survey there are a number of items that seek to probe the worldview of the respondents. In general they suggest that in keeping with the ethos of the Reformation, Conservative Protestants tend to have a harsh picture of God and a negative view of both the world and human nature.

Two items are based on David Tracy's (1981) view of a Catholic "analogical imagination" and a Protestant "dialectical imagination." Both items ask respondents to place themselves on a seven-point continuum between these poles:

- *On a seven-point scale, where would you place your image of the world and human nature between these two contrasting images: "The world is basically filled with evil and sin" and "There is much goodness in the world which hints at God's goodness"?*
- *Where would you place your image of the world and human nature between these two contrasting images: "Human nature is basically good" and "Human nature is fundamentally perverse and corrupt"?*

Twenty-four percent of both Conservative Protestants and Afro-American Protestants lean to a view of the world as evil compared to 13 percent of Mainline Protestants. Twenty-three percent of Conservatives and 27 percent of Afro-Americans also see human nature as fundamentally evil and corrupt in comparison again with 13 percent of the Mainline Protestants. Conservative Protestants and their partners, Afro-American Protestants, are much closer to the Reformation's grim view of the world and human nature than are the Protestant Mainline. Adding the two items together to form a simple scale, we find that the Conservative and Afro-American Protestants get a score significantly closer to the "evil" pole than Mainline Protestants do. Protestants of any denomination who are high on the EVANGELICAL scale incline more to the "evil" side of the scale; differences on EVANGELICAL account for 54 percent of the difference between Conservative and Mainline Protestants.

Another series of questions asks people to think about God as more like *mother* or *father, master* or *spouse, judge* or *lover,* and *friend* or *king.*

The Conservative and Afro-American Protestants generally have a much harsher image of God than do Mainline Protestants. Either Conservative or Afro-American Protestants are more likely to view God in the harsher term; Mainline Protestants are least likely to take the harsher alternative in each case (table 2.1).

Table 2.1 Image of God by Protestant denomination

	Protestant Denomination		
Image	Conservative (%)	Afro-American (%)	Mainline (%)
Father	66	47	47
Master	62	56	48
Judge	46	46	35
King	28	33	18

SOURCE: General Social Surveys, 1996–2002.

When these four items are combined into a single scale, Conservative Protestants score almost one-third of a standard deviation higher than the Mainline (the difference is .30, to be precise). The EVANGELICAL scale accounts for 51 percent of that gap; the residual difference is .15 standard deviations.

Thus Conservative Protestants hold starker images of the world, human nature, and God than Mainline Protestants do. The three solas, as captured by our EVANGELICAL scale, explain just over half of that propensity.

Finally, there are seven items in the ISSP religion modules of 1991 and 1998 that also might be considered indicators of worldview[7]:

- *There is a God who concerns himself with every human being personally.*
- *To me life is meaningful only because God exists.*
- *The course of our life is determined by God.*
- *In my opinion life does not serve any purpose.*
- *People can't change the course of their lives.*
- *Life is only meaningful if you provide meaning for yourself.*
- *We each make our own fate.*

Three factors[8] emerge from analysis of these items. The first factor includes the first three variables and seems to measure dependence on God; the next two are somewhat pessimistic; and the third emphasizes personal control. Only on the first scale are there any differences between Conservative Protestants and Mainline Protestants.[9]

Conservative and Afro-American Protestants view God as a more active agent in their lives than other Christians do. Thus 65 percent of Conservative Protestants and 62 percent of the Afro-American Protestants "strongly agree" about God's personal concern, and another

24 and 26 percent, respectively, merely agree. Fewer Mainline Protestants see God in such active terms; 40 percent agree strongly and 32 percent just agree that God has personal concerns.[10] While most Christians would, we speculate, ascribe some of the meaning they find in life to their faith that God exists, the ISSP question imposes a much stiffer condition in the form of the word "only." Nonetheless, 36 percent of Conservative Protestants and 38 percent of Afro-America Protestants strongly agree that "life is meaningful only because God exists"; another 32 percent of Conservative Protestants and 29 percent of Afro-American Protestants just agree. Mainline Protestants find meaning in other spheres of life; 20 percent strongly agree and 25 percent just agree.

The doctrine of predestination divided Protestants in the sixteenth century and, though the ISSP "predetermination" item is an imprecise expression of that doctrine, it appears that it continues to do so in the United States today. Afro-American Protestants are most likely to agree that "the course of our lives is determined by God"; 67 percent agree (36 percent do so strongly). Conservative Protestants are significantly less likely than Afro-Americans to agree—48 percent (26 percent strongly)—but significantly more likely than Mainline Protestants, of whom only 36 percent agree (16 percent strongly).

Combining the three items into a scale, we find that Conservative Protestants and Afro-American Protestants are indistinguishable while Mainline Protestants are less theistic by one-half of a standard deviation on this scale.[11] The EVANGELICAL scale accounts for 61 percent of the difference between Mainline and other Protestants; after statistically adjusting for differences on the EVANGELICAL scale Mainline Protestants are only .18 standard deviations less theistic than Conservative and Afro-American Protestants.

In summary, Conservative and Afro-American Protestants tend, in comparison with Mainliners, to emphasize dependence on God, the depravity of the world and of human nature, and the harshness of God. This emphasis is strongly reflective of the degree to which Protestants in different denominations and traditions accept and practice the three-point core of conservative belief, experience, and action. This, one assumes, is what the original Reformers meant by sola gratia, by grace alone.

BELIEFS

Conservative Protestants, as might be expected, are strongly orthodox in their beliefs. Regarding some beliefs, for example, in God's existence or life after death, there is little difference among the three Protestant groups we are studying. More than nine out of ten believe in God and more than four out of five believe in life after death. Even so, there are some discernible shades of belief. Conservative and Afro-American Protestants are more likely to express their belief in God without doubt (83 percent and 81 percent, respectively) than Mainline Protestants (60 percent), while Afro-American Protestants are less sure about the afterlife (81 percent believe) than Conservatives (87 percent believe) and Mainline Protestants (86 percent believe). The EVANGELICAL scale accounts for half of the greater doubt found among the Mainline Protestants but none of the difference between Conservative and Afro-American Protestants regarding the afterlife.

On other matters there is considerable difference of belief. The 1991 and 1998 ISSP religion modules included questions about heaven, hell, and religious miracles; the 1991 religion module also had a question about believing in the devil. Overall, more Protestants believe in heaven than in hell, more believe in hell than in religious miracles, and more believe in religious miracles than in the devil. As we see in table 2.2, Conservative Protestants have not only the highest belief in all four ideas but also the least drop-off from one belief to the next. Afro-American Protestants are indistinguishable from Conservative Protestants except regarding views of the devil. Mainline Protestants are less likely to believe in each of the four; they also are the group most likely to believe in heaven but not in hell.

We combined the three items that appear in both ISSPs into a scale.[12] Conservative Protestants and Afro-American Protestants were indistinguishable in 1998 (the year in which the EVANGELICAL scale items are also available); their means are 4.38 and 4.48. Mainline Protestants score significantly lower at 2.99. The EVANGELICAL scale accounts for 60 percent of the difference between Mainline and Conservative Protestants in beliefs about heaven, hell, and miracles; the difference with EVANGELICAL held constant is .55 (compared with the initial difference of 1.39).

Table 2.2 Beliefs about supernatural subjects by Protestant denomination

	Protestant Denomination		
Subject	Conservative (%)	Afro-American (%)	Mainline (%)
Heaven	91	89	80
Hell	82	79	62
Miracles	77	77	67
Devil[a]	78	61	58

[a] This item was only asked in 1991.

SOURCE: International Social Survey Program modules, 1991 and 1998.

One cannot be sure of the direction of causality in these matters. It may be that Conservative Protestants are more likely to believe in the devil, hell, and miracles because they also believe in literal interpretation, have experienced salvation, and have tried to win someone for Jesus. Or it may be that the relative orthodoxy of the Conservatives attracts others who hold similar interpretations of Christian dogma. However, as we show in chapter 7, we have no evidence of massive conversions of Mainline Protestants (or Catholics) to the Conservatives, despite contrary claims by the Conservatives. This suggests that few people adjust their affiliation to accommodate their beliefs. The interpretation more consistent with the bulk of the evidence is that most people are socialized to a broad spectrum of beliefs in the context of their religious heritage—in short, denomination constrains belief.

SPIRITUALITY

Conservative Protestants are very devout. Thirty-seven percent attend services every week—almost half of the weekly attenders go more than once a week. Afro-American Protestants are only slightly less devout; 28 percent attend weekly and one-third of them go more than once a week. Mainline Protestants practice their religion significantly less; 23 percent attend weekly and only one-fourth of the weekly attenders go more than once a week. The Conservatives also pray often—71 percent at least daily (37 percent several times a day)—as do Afro-American Protestants—69 percent daily (33 percent several times a day). Mainline Protestants pray less; 54 percent daily (25 percent several times a day). The EVANGELICAL scale completely explains these differences; significant as we have described them, the differences among the three denominational groups are not statistically significant after controlling for EVANGELICAL.

Three other questions were asked in the religion modules that might indicate the strength of one's relationship with religion or God—strength of religious preference, feeling religious, and engaging in religious activities:

- *Are you a strong ___ or not a very strong ___? {fill blanks with name of denomination}*
- *Would you describe yourself as extremely religious, very religious, somewhat religious, neither religious nor non-religious, somewhat non-religious, extremely non-religious?*
- *How often do you take part in the activities and organizations of a church or place of worship other than attending religious services?*

Conservative and Afro-American Protestants have stronger, more religious identities, and they participate more than Mainline Protestants. Over half of Conservative and Afro-American Protestants identify as "strong" members of their churches compared with just over one-third of the Mainline Protestants. Thirty-eight percent of the Conservative and 43 percent of the Afro-American Protestants compared to 25 percent of the Mainliners consider themselves either "extremely religious" or "very religious." Over one in five Conservative and Afro-American Protestants participate in church-related activities other than services on a weekly basis, but only one in seven Mainline Protestants do. Multivariate analyses of each of these measures of identity and activity show that our EVANGELICAL scale explains the differences. Thus the evangelical orientation (Bible, rebirth, convert) is a notable part of the proclivity of the Conservatives and Afro-

Table 2.3 Religiosity by Protestant denomination

	Protestant Denomination		
Indication of religiosity	Conservative (%)	Afro-American (%)	Mainline (%)
Strong identification	52	53	37
"Very religious"	38	43	25
Participates in activities	23	21	14

SOURCE: International Social Survey Program modules, 1991 and 1998.

Americans to feel more religious and participate in church-related activities other than services.

The world often seems to be evil and human nature bad. God is stern and demanding. In response Conservative Protestants are devout, feel religious, and engage in more religious organizational activity than anyone else (save for Afro-American Protestants). How then do they experience their relationship with God in the midst of the problems of life? What sort of spirituality emerges in times of stress? Several responses in the 1998 health and religion module provide some clues:

> *Think about how you try to understand and deal with major problems in your life. To what extent are the following involved in the way you cope:*
>
> - *I look to God for strength, support, guidance.*
> - *I work together with God as partners.*
> - *I try to make sense of the situation and decide what to do without relying on God.*
> - *I feel that God is punishing me for my sins or lack of spirituality.*
> - *I think about how my life is part of a larger spiritual force.*
> - *I wonder whether God has abandoned me.*[13]

Two items that immediately follow these are also relevant:

> - *I believe in a God who watches over me.*
> - *I try hard to carry my religious beliefs over into all my other dealings in life.*

The first three "coping" items plus the two that follow are hallmarks of Afro-American spirituality; the Afro-Americans rank highest on all five. Conservative responses are different from those of the Mainline on the first four "coping" items and the two that follow. Fifty-nine percent of Conservative, 68 percent of Afro-American, and 42 percent of Mainline Protestants look to God for strength, support, and guidance "a great deal." Denominational differences are almost as large on working together with God as partners; 28 percent, 42 percent, and 21 percent of Conservative, Afro-American, and Mainline Protestants, respectively, do that a great deal. They also differ on trying to make sense of the situation without relying on God (47 percent, 54 percent, and 35 percent of Conservative, Afro-American, and Mainline Protestants, respectively, do that "not at all").

The other large differences come in believing in a God who watches over people; 77 percent, 81 percent, and 57 percent of Conservative, Afro-American, and Mainline Protestants, respectively, share that belief strongly. Conservative Protestants then seem more likely to have a vivid sense that God is with them in their troubles, though African-Americans are even more likely to have that sense. Clearly this sense of the support of God is nearly as essential to the Conservative spirituality as it is to Afro-American spirituality. We formed a scale from the first three "coping" items and the two follow-up items. Afro-American Protestants score almost one point or one-fifth of a standard deviation higher on the eighteen-point scale than Conservative Protestants do; Mainline Protestants score a point and a half (one-third of a standard deviation) lower than Conservative Protestants. African Americans of all denominations score higher on this spirituality scale, so we include race as well as scores on the EVANGELICAL scale in our statistical adjustments. We find that race and the EVANGELICAL scale together account for all significant denominational variation, and the EVANGELICAL scale accounts for one-third of the racial difference within denominations too. Thus this form of God-in-action spirituality is a reflection of the Reformation core of Conservative Protestantism. It is tied in a special way to African Americans' spiritual lives whether they are in the Afro-American denominations or elsewhere.[14]

Another set of questions probes more deeply into the question of the Conservative Protestant spirituality—what is the nature of the presence of God that Christians experience.

The following questions deal with possible daily spiritual experience. To what extent can you say that you experience the following: [15]

- *I feel God's presence.*
- *I have strength and comfort in my religion.*
- *I desire to be closer to or in union with God.*
- *I feel God's love for me, directly or through others.*
- *I am spiritually touched by the beauty of creation.*
- *I feel deep inner peace and harmony.*

These items certainly measure a dimension of the spiritual tradition to which all Christian traditions would subscribe. Fifty-five percent of the Conservative Protestants report that they feel God's presence every day, as do 66 percent of the Afro-American and 43 percent of the Mainline Protestants. The numbers for "strength and comfort" are 55 percent, 65 percent, and 42 percent for Conservative, Afro-American, and Mainline, respectively; for the desire to be closer to God: 62 percent, 63 percent, and 46 percent; for feeling God's love: 60 percent, 59 percent, and 44 percent; for "beauty": 65 percent, 67 percent, and 59 percent; and finally for "harmony": 41 percent, 39 percent, and 32 percent. Summing the number of daily experiences we get a scale that ranges from zero to six. Among Protestants, the scale has a mean of 3.1; for Conservatives it is 3.4, for Afro-Americans it is 3.6, and for the Mainline it is 2.7. These differences are completely explained by the EVANGELICAL scale; at an average value of the EVANGELICAL scale (a score of 1.67), the adjusted means on the scale of daily religious experiences are trivially different—3.13, 3.19, and 3.09 for Conservative, Afro-American, and Mainline Protestants, respectively.

Conservative Protestants confront the problem of evil in life with intense religious conviction. When asked (in 1988) where on a scale from one to seven they would place the freedom of their faith from doubts, 63 percent of the Conservative Protestants choose 1 or 2 on the end of the continuum that asserts that their *faith is completely free of doubt;* only 43 percent of Afro-Americans and 38 percent of the Mainline Protestants are as free of doubt. Some might wonder whether complete freedom from doubt is a sign of strong faith or whether the other end of the continuum (*My faith is mixed with doubt*) is the more realistic and human stand. However, there can be no question that the Conservative Protestant faith is firm—perhaps in great part because they can call on a direct experience of salvation in Christ. The EVANGELICAL scale accounts for 81 percent of the difference between Conservative and Mainline Protestants, and the remainder is not statistically significant. Both an extra sense of closeness to God and an extra confidence in one's faith, therefore, are closely linked to commitment to the "fundamentals" of Reformation religion.

It would appear therefore that there is an authentic Conservative Protestant spirituality that the Christian tradition can hardly reject. It combines religious devotion, a strong faith, trust in God's active intervention to assuage life's difficulties (especially but not exclusively among African Americans inside and outside the Afro-American denominations), and an awareness of God's presence in the world and in the love of others. Moreover, these characteristics of spirituality are integrated around the three core items of the Conservative Christian faith—literal interpretation, spiritual rebirth, and a need to share the good news with others; our EVANGELICAL scale, composed of measures of these concepts, accounts for between 70 and 99 percent of denominational differences in spiritual issues. It hardly seems possible to deny that this is a Reformation spirituality and that it is admirable, though one may not like the words and the deeds with which it is propounded. Conservative and Afro-American Protestants share its most profound elements in a way highly distinct from the spiritual expressions favored by Mainline Protestants.

DUTIES AND RESPONSIBILITIES

A system of faith and spirituality arising from that faith creates duties and responsibilities for the faithful. If the faith and spirituality are in the tradition of the Lord's Prayer, then one duty is certainly forgiveness. Three items in the health and religion module of 1998 attempt to measure a person's willingness to forgive.

- *I have forgiven myself for the things that I have done wrong.*
- *I have forgiven those who hurt me.*
- *I know that God forgives me.*

On all three items the Conservative and Afro-American Protestants are more likely to choose forgiveness than are the Mainline Protestants, though the margins are smaller than in other aspects of religion we have investigated in this chapter. Afro-American Protestants are more likely to say they almost always forgive themselves (61 percent), and Conservative and Mainline Protestants are harder on themselves (only 46 percent have always or almost always forgiven themselves). Fifty-five percent of both the Conservatives and the Afro-American Protestants say that they almost always forgive those who hurt them as do 50 percent of the Mainline Protestants. Both the Conservative and Afro-American Protestants are somewhat more likely than are Mainline Protestants to say they know that God has forgiven them (88 percent and 90 percent compared with 79 percent). Only on this last item is the difference between Conservative and Mainline Protestants significant.

One measure of how serious this forgiveness may be is whether it correlates with willing to forego the death penalty. Forgiving self and others does not matter for how Protestants feel about capital punishment, nor does knowing that God has always forgiven them change Afro-American and Mainline Protestants' feelings about the death penalty. However, Conservative Protestants who feel they know God has forgiven them are significantly more likely than other Conservative Protestants to oppose the death penalty for murderers; 25 percent versus 8 percent.[16]

There is also a responsibility to be concerned about the influence of your religious faith on your daily life. With data on the relative influence of religion and other factors over important decisions, one can begin to address the issue of at a general level religion's place in people's life decisions. Four questions from 1988 ask respondents to place each of these influences on a five-point scale from very important to not very important when weighing decisions:

the Bible;
your family and friends;
the teachings of your church or synagogue;
your own personal judgment.

As one might expect, Conservative and Afro-American Protestants are more likely than Mainline Protestants to say that the Bible has a very important influence on decisions—59 percent and 65 percent versus 28 percent. They also, perhaps surprisingly, are more likely to list the teachings of the Church as very important—45 percent and 41 percent versus 22 percent. This second finding may be surprising because in Reformation theory one ought not to *need* a church, much less use its teaching in decision making. In an even more surprising outcome, Conservative Protestants are twenty percentage points more likely than are Catholics to say that the teachings of the Church are very important.

Protestant denominations do not differ significantly in the importance that they ascribe to family, friends, or themselves.

Combining the Bible and church items into a single scale of religious importance, scored zero if neither is very important, one if either is very important, and two if both are very important, we find that Conservative and Afro-American Protestants score the same (mean = 1.03 on the importance scale) and Mainline Protestants significantly lower (mean = .51). Adjusting for denominational differences on the EVANGELICAL scale accounts for 69 percent of this difference (residual difference is just .16). It is hardly surprising that in Bible Christianity the Bible is critical to decision making. However, the puzzle remains about the influence of the Church. Most of the Conservative Protestants belong to churches that are "congregational" with a small "c," that is, the local congregation makes its own decisions, which are not subject to review by a hierarchy. As Paul Harrison argues in his classic *Authority in the Free Church Tradition* (1971), the central church organizations—like the Southern Baptist Convention—speak to the local churches but not for them. Nor do they give formal orders to the local congregations. However, it would appear that the Church still has considerable influence and that our Conservative Protestant respondents do not find any contradiction that the Church should be important within a religion tradition that in principle does not need churches. Indeed, one might be persuaded that the efficacy of local control increases the Church's influence relative to the distant echo of hierarchical pronouncements.

Another series of question asks how important to the respondent are a number of religious attitudes and behaviors. The one of interest in the present context is, *How important to you is it to follow the teaching of your church or synagogue?*

Forty-eight percent of the Conservative Protestants say that it is very important as opposed to 26 percent of the Mainline Protestants. In this respect at any rate, the Mainline seems more consistent with the Reformation heritage. (Again the Conservative Protestants are almost twice as likely as Catholics to insist on the importance of the Church.) Indeed the Conservative Protestants are more likely to consider following the teachings of the Church more important than following their own consciences—48 percent to 38 percent (as opposed to 26 percent and 28 percent for Mainline Protestants.[17]

Sociologists ought not be surprised by this phenomenon. The iron law of oligarchy suggests that means easily become ends in themselves. There is, we know, a historical tendency for sects to evolve into denominations and churches. The Reformation itself, in revolt against the Roman church, produced, in time, its own churches. The Reformation's aspiration to replace Church with Bible was only partially fulfilled. The apparent importance of churches to the rank and file of contemporary Bible Christians suggests that the influence of individual members and congregations over Church cycles back in the form of a strong influence of Church over individuals.

MORALITY, SCIENCE, AND LAW

The original Reformation set out to reform not only the Roman Church but also individual lives. It was important for the leaders of the Reform that their followers lead godly lives. The early settlers in New England were Puritans in more than name. Are the Conservative Protestants of today equally stern in their moral orientations?

Responses to four items in the religion modules provide possible answers for these questions:

- *Those who violate God's law must be punished.*
- *Right and wrong are not usually a simple matter of black and white, there are many shades of gray.*
- *Immoral actions by one person can corrupt society in general.*
- *Morality is a personal matter and society should not force everyone to follow one standard.*

Thirty-eight percent of the Conservative Protestants and 37 percent of Afro-American Protestants versus 18 percent of the Mainline Protestants agree strongly on the punishment of sinners.[18] In the matter of an immoral person corrupting society the proportions agreeing are 68 percent for the Conservative Protestants versus 47 percent and 48 percent for Afro-American and Mainline Protestants, respectively. The Conservatives have a far greater tendency to see moral issues as black and white—29 percent agree that they are *not* that way compared with 39 percent of Afro-Americans and 44 percent of Mainline Protestants. There are no differences across religions on the subject of morality being a personal matter. Mainline Protestants score about one-third of a point below Conservative Protestants on the moral ambiguity item; the EVANGELICAL scale accounts for 40 percent of that. Some of the Conservative Protestants' taste for moral absolutes grows out of their Reformation theology, but a significant residual remains.[19]

This code might explain why many Conservative Protestants were so eager to demolish former president Bill Clinton. He was a sinner who would corrupt society unless society proved its worthiness by punishing him. Taking the longer view, we also note that several of the great socioreligious movements of American history were driven by fervent religious enthusiasm—abolition, prohibition, civil rights.[20] Perhaps the contemporary antiabortion, antihomosexuality, antipornography crusades represent continuity in moral righteousness among the Conservative Protestants.

There are also four multiple choice responses in the 1991 ISSP questionnaire that touch on issue of morality and law.

- *Right and wrong should be based on God's law.*
- *Right and wrong should be decided by society.*
- *Right and wrong should be a matter of personal conscience.*
- *Books and films that attack religion should be prohibited by law.*

As one might expect Conservative Protestants endorse God's law as superior to society and personal conscience and also believe that the law should ban books that attack religion. Thus 44 percent strongly agree that right and wrong are determined by God (52 percent of Afro-American Protestants), twenty percentage points more than the Mainline Protestants, and 46 percent (53 percent of Afro-Americans) also strongly agree that the law should protect religion from attack again twenty percentage points more than the Mainliners. There are no differences across denominations in opinions about the importance of conscience, but only 32 percent of the Conservative Protestants and 36 percent of the Afro-Americans support society's right to decide right and wrong while 45 percent of Mainline Protestants support society's right to involve itself in determining what is right and wrong. Thus do the Conservative Protestants equip themselves with a theory of resistance or opposition to society's laws (legalized abortion, for example) in the name of God's law. The difference between Conservative and Mainline Protestants is statistically significant (it amounts to .63 standard deviations). As in so many of these issues, there is no difference between Conservative and Afro-American Protestants. A modified version of the EVANGELICAL scale accounts for 55 percent of that difference (leaving .28 unexplained).[21] Biblical Christians have thus substantial support from their core beliefs in appealing to God's law.

Conservative Christians are prepared to array themselves against the rest of society when it is an issue of God's law. This stand is obvious especially on the issue that caused the Conservatives to break with other Protestants—modernity as represented by Darwinian evolution. Society may praise science, but the word of science must be exposed to the judgment of God's law. Responses to four items from the 1988 religion module measure the Conservative Protestant attitude to science.

- *Science will solve our social problems like crime and mental illness.*
- *One trouble with science is that it makes our way of life change too fast.*
- *Scientists always seem to be prying into things that they really ought to stay out of.*
- *One of the bad effects of science is that it breaks down people's ideas of right and wrong.*

It is hardly unexpected that the Conservatives are skeptical about science. The surprise is the lack of disagreement across denominational lines regarding science's inability to solve social problems; only one-fifth of Protestants share that faith in science (Catholics and people with no religion have more faith in science; 27 percent of Catholics and 31 percent of people with no religion think science can solve social problems). However, 45 percent agree that science changes our way of life too fast and 43 percent that scientists pry into things they ought not. Afro-American Protestants are even more critical; 52 percent say science makes life change too fast and 54 percent agree scientist pry too much. Mainline Protestant give much more support to science—only 38 percent and 27 percent, respectively, agree with these negative statements. Most tellingly, substantial minorities of Conservative and Afro-American Protestants believe that science tends to break down ideas of right and wrong—41 percent and 48 percent—versus 28 percent for Mainliners. On a three-point scale of attitudes toward science, Conservative Protestants score one-quarter points lower than Afro-Americans and one-third of a point higher than Mainline Protestants. Adjusting for EVANGELICAL accounts for 62 percent of the difference between Conservative and Mainline Protestants. Thus Conservative Protestants have different attitudes on science from those of the Mainline Protestants mainly because of the core beliefs of their brand of Reformation religion—Bible, rebirth, and saving the unsaved.

The 1992, 1994, and 2000 ISSP environmental modules had a similar item: *We trust too much in science, and not enough in faith.* Only 20 percent of American adults disagree with this blunt critique of science, a finding that will offer very little consolation to scientists. Support of science however, is even weaker among Conservative Protestants. Only 13 percent of them reject the critique (and 15 percent of Afro-American Protestants) in comparison with 19 percent of Mainline Protestants. The significant differences among Protestant denominations come at the other end of the scale; 22 percent, 21 percent, and 11 percent of Conservative, Afro-American, and Mainline Protestants, respectively, strongly agree with the statement. In a multivariate analysis of this item, the observed difference between Conservative and Mainline Protestants is .68; it falls to .39 when we adjust for the literal interpretation of the Bible (the only element of the EVANGELICAL scale available in 1992, 1994, and 2000). In any competition between science and the Bible among Conservative Protestants the Bible easily wins. Therefore the Grand Canyon was created by Noah's flood.

There might be a temptation for some readers to say that the reason for this dislike of science is that the Conservative Protestants are uneducated. However, educational attainment does not affect these denominational differences.[22] Conservative Protestants take their stands not because they are uneducated but because they hold strong religious beliefs that take precedence over scientific facts. From a scientist's perspective this is an untenable view. But for many nonscientists, "the science is not in." Too many newspapers have reported contradictory findings about evolution and health for the nonprofessional to keep up. A study finds that the fat in milk increases the risk of a heart attack. A few years later another study finds that the calcium in milk can help ward off osteoporosis. Read the original studies, and it is easy to keep track. But watch the evening news and hear "University study shows milk causes heart attacks" and then "Women should drink more milk for their bones" and let the doubts creep in.

Another question in the 1993, 1994, and 2000 ISSP environmental modules enables us to ask about attitudes toward the core issue for Conservative Protestants—evolution: *Do you believe that human beings developed from earlier species of animals?*

Note that the ones who framed the question did not use the word "evolve"—not that such an evasion was likely to fool convinced Conservative Protestants. Half as many Conservatives as Mainline Protestants—25 percent versus 50 percent—agree that it was probably or definitely true. Afro-American Protestants are in between at 37 percent answering at least probably true. Three out of five of the Conservatives said it was definitely not true as opposed to one out of three of the Mainline Protestants.

Taking education into consideration changes the picture somewhat but does not wipe out Conservative Protestants' preference for the Bible over science. The proportion of them responding that it is definitely not true that humans developed from earlier species of animals is actually *higher* for high school graduates (64 percent) and people with some college (63 percent) than for dropouts (57 percent). It is the same for college graduates as for high school dropouts. Only among people with advanced degrees is "definitely not true" a minority response—and then just barely at 46 percent.

Figure 2.1 shows how biblical literalism deflects the influence of education on Conservative Protestants' views on evolution. For those who reject the literal interpretation of the Bible, some education mod-

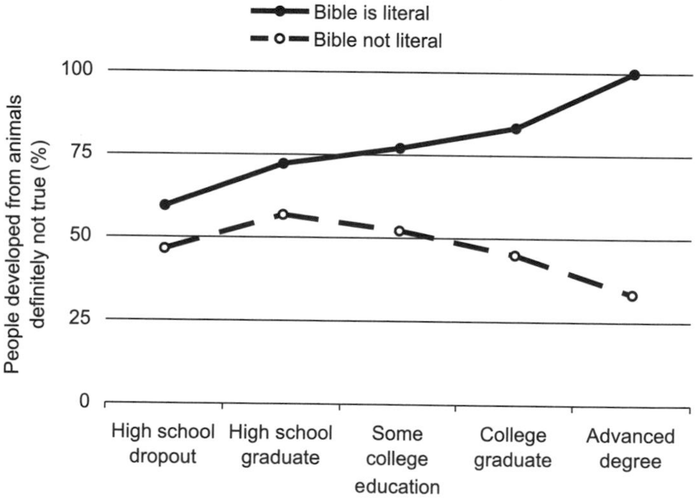

Figure 2.1 Evolution by education and attitude toward the Bible: Conservative Protestants. SOURCE: General Social Survey, 1993, 1994, and 2000.

estly raises the proportion saying that people definitely did not develop from other animals, but college and graduate education lowers it substantially. For those who read the Bible literally, though, more education means more dissent from science; each increase in education is accompanied by an increase in the percentage saying people did not develop from animals.

Higher education does not eradicate faith in biblical inerrancy.

CONCLUSION

We have tried in this chapter to navigate a torturous path through survey data to organize a sketch of Conservative Christianity as a religious system. We conclude that the Conservatives and Afro-American Protestants both embrace a systematic religious heritage, one that they can legitimately claim is an authentic updating of the Reformation. The central issue is the Bible as sole rule of faith. Once Mainline Protestantism began to equivocate about Genesis it compromised with modernity and lost its authenticity. Most elements of faith and practice that we have considered here point to differences between Bible religion, as espoused and practiced by the Conservative and Afro-American denominations, and the Bible-liturgical hybrid that is Mainline Protestantism. Over and over we found that a scale composed of the three solas accounted for between 60 and 99 percent of the differences between Conservative and Mainline Protestants.

Make no mistake about it, Conservative Christians and their Afro-American partners in faith are the real dissenters in America—some, no doubt, more than others. Dissent permeates their core beliefs, their worldviews, their morality, their relationships with God, and their devotions. It is not a fashionable dissent but rather a stern, consistent, and determined dissent.

As important, we think, as the distinction between Conservative and Mainline Protestantism, though, is the overwhelming similarity between the Conservative and Afro-American Protestants. When they differ it is almost always the Afro-Americans who take the more doctrinally conservative position. These Christian traditions share the Reformation's emphasis on Bible, rebirth, and reaching out to others. They share high levels of activity, and members of both report that their religion is very important to them. Afro-American

Protestants see God as a significantly more active presence in their spiritual life.

This strong similarity has intrinsic merit and interest. But our fascination with it comes from the question, What is conservative about Conservative Christians? Here we have two active groups that place God at the center of their thoughts and actions. But as we turn to politics we will see that their faith and spirit move them in opposite directions.

THREE

Conservative Christians in American Politics

INTRODUCTION

On election night 2004, the talking heads of network TV concluded that conservative religious voters put President Bush over the top. They based their instant analysis on one item—"moral values" topped homeland security, the war in Iraq, the jobless economy, and the worsening federal deficit as voters' number one concern in exit polling. Never mind that there was only a 2 percentage-point difference between "moral values" (22 percent) and "economy / jobs" (20 percent), the conventional wisdom seized on it. The election of 2004 was the values election and Mr. Bush won reelection because he was the better religious candidate. In response, Democrats have been eager to "get it" and craft new narratives to get their policy priorities before voters.

Conservative Christians are the center of attention when the discussion turns to values. But their voting priorities and internal divisions are widely and wildly misunderstood. For while Conservative Christians do indeed weigh issues like abortion and homosexuality when making a choice between political parties or candidates, they are also very sensitive to economic concerns. In fact, we will show convincing evidence in this chapter that economic interests sharply divide Conservative Christians—maybe even more than other Americans. Conservative Christians are the most economically divided of the major voting blocks in American politics.

Our findings challenge the premise of influential books such as Thomas Frank's *What Is the Matter with Kansas?* Frank asked why so many people in his native Kansas let their religious beliefs "get in the way" of their material interests when casting their votes. In enumerating the contradictions of Midwest politics, he argued that Kansans, especially poor and working-class Conservative Protestants and Catholics, hurt their communities and their families by voting for candidates who will take their money and give them nothing but holy talk. According to Frank, Republicans win Christians' votes by promising to suppress abortion and reinstitute prayer in school. Once in office they revert to economic priorities by cutting rich peoples' taxes and deregulating industry.

Frank's argument creates on a false dichotomy between values votes and interest votes. For the millions of affluent Conservative Protestants, values and class interests coalesce—who could tell if they cast their votes against abortion or for high-end tax cuts when they think that both are good ideas? Further down the economic ladder, though (and here is our main point), poor, struggling, and lower-middle-class Conservative Protestants are much less likely to vote Republican than are affluent Protestants of any denomination—conservative or otherwise. So-called values voting has not flattened the relationship between income and how people vote. Far from it. In recent elections, income influenced the propensity to vote Republican substantially more than it did back in 1972 or 1976. And, the growing importance of income differences in voting has been more pronounced—not less—among Conservative Protestants. Since the Reagan era began in 1980, income has influenced Conservative Protestants' votes even more than it affected other Americans' votes.[1]

The class gap in voting is the difference between the percentage of top-earners who vote Republican and the percentage of bottom-earners who vote Republican. Here we use $75,000 as the cut-off for top-earners and $30,000 as the cut-off for bottom-earners. Among Conservative Protestants, the class gap in voting was 6.5 percentage points before the Reagan era, 21 percentage points during the Reagan era, and 27 percentage points since.

To repeat, values and income *both* affect how Conservative Protestants and other Americans vote. Furthermore, both values and income matter more in the current era than they used to. Our full review of Conservative Protestants' voting patterns, party preferences, and political views shows, consistent with our theme throughout this book, that though Conservative Protestants are somewhat different from other Americans, they are far from extreme. Indeed in party preferences they are less partisan than most; a sizable minority think of themselves as politically independent and moderate.

In this chapter we also raise several other issues relevant to stereotypes about and critiques of Conservative Protestants. We look for evidence of greater racial prejudice and find none; we look for other kinds of intolerance and find some; and we assess the election night paradigm of red states and blue states and find that religious composition of states is a big part of that story.

Throughout the chapter we address two kinds of differences—those between Conservative Protestants and Americans with other religion or no religion and those that divide Conservative Protestants from one another. In doing so we keep the statistical analysis as simple as we can without being misleading; for example, we highlight patterns two and three variables at a time. However, all of our discussion and all the simple relationships we highlight emerge as statistically significant in comprehensive multivariate analyses of both voting and party identification. We attach our final models as an appendix so that specialists can refer to them. For readers who choose not to immerse themselves in technical details, note simply that we do not stress any relationship that is not robust enough to survive statistical cross-examination in a multivariate analysis.

VOTING BY RELIGION

Conservative Protestant voters chose Republicans over Democrats by a significant margin in recent presidential elections, Mainline Protestants split evenly between Republicans and Democrats, Catholics preferred Democrats over Republicans by ten percentage points, and the smaller groups—Afro-American Protestants, Jews, people of other religions, and those with no religion—had even stronger Democratic preferences. The largest voting margin was among Afro-American Protestants, who have voted for Democrats by nine-to-one margins or higher in presidential elections as far back as the 1960s.

As we discuss voting in this chapter we seek out broad, stable patterns that distinguish among religions. We focus more on the enduring features of religion's role in American politics and leave the ins and outs of particular elections to others. For that reason we combine elections into three political eras: pre-Reagan (the 1968–1976 elections), the Reagan era (1980–1988 elections), and the current era (1992–2004 elections).[2] The breakdown of the votes for Republicans, Democrats, and other candidates changes from one election to the next, of course, but how Conservative Protestants rank in comparison to other religions did not change from election to election within political era.[3]

The three biggest religious denominations—Conservative Protestants, Mainline Protestants, and Catholics—are, surprisingly, more politically similar than different (fig. 3.1). In the current era, Conservative Protestants are a modest 6.3 percentage points more Republican than Mainline Protestants—51.7 percent compared with 45.4 percent—and a more substantial 10.7 percent more Republican than Catholics (at 41.0 percent Republican in the current era). This evidence makes it hardly fair to say "evangelicals" are a distinctive political force. As a large group (they make up about 26 percent of voters), Conservative Protestants have clout. The similarity between their voting patterns and voting by Mainline Protestants, however, limits their unique electoral impact. To quantify the effect of Conservative Protestants on the Republican vote in an election, multiply the difference between their Republican vote and that of a relevant comparison group—Mainline Protestants in this case[4]—by their proportion of the electorate. That calculation yields an impact score of $(6.3 \times .26 =)$ 1.6 percentage points. Yes, as the 2000 election showed, even an edge that small can be decisive in a close race. But it hardly amounts to an overwhelming political base. Moreover, those 1.6 impact points are spread across all regions, not concentrated in the Southern states where the Conservative Christians supposedly contribute to the Republicans' red state advantage.

Clearly, claims that Conservative Protestants have hijacked the nation's politics are greatly exaggerated. They are only modestly different from Americans of other large religious groups. Whether you welcome or fear Protestant influence in social policy, an impact score of 1.6 points is a sobering calculation. As we shall show in a moment, the affluent have a far higher impact score because, though they are less numerous than Conservative Protestants, the affluent really are politically distinct.

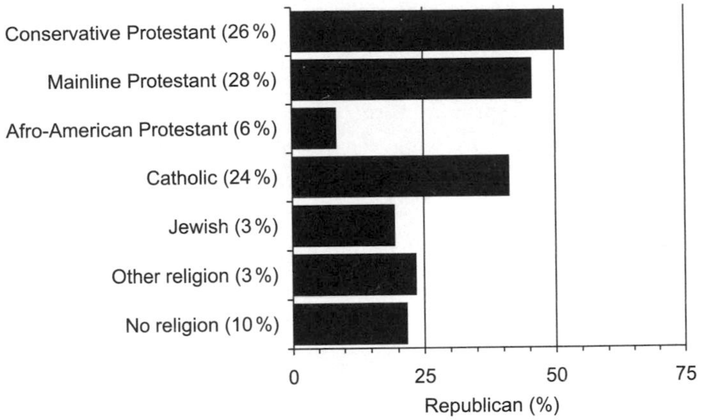

Figure 3.1 Republican votes by religion: 1992, 1996, and 2000 elections. Numbers in parentheses show each denomination's share of the electorate. SOURCE: General Social Survey, 1993– 2000.

Comparing the current era with the Reagan era, we see modest changes. Reagan was so popular, all three big denominations were more likely to vote Republican in the 1980s than in the current era. Conservative Protestants dropped from 61.4 percent Republican in the Reagan era to 51.7 in the current era. Mainline Protestants made a more substantial shift in the direction of the Democrats, dropping from 64.2 to 45.4 percent Republican. The biggest shift in political impact between the Reagan era and the current era involves people who prefer no religion. They generally lean toward the Democrats, and they became substantially more numerous in the 1990s (Hout and Fischer 2002a).[5]

Thus right off the bat we introduce important evidence that will surprise nonacademic readers: denominational differences are, for the most part, robust from election to election. This finding will not surprise academics familiar with the research in political sociology; Manza and Brooks said the same thing almost a decade ago in a major review of religious voting published in the *American Journal of Sociology* in 1997. Their analysis, like ours, identified stable denominational differences that changed little over time. Nonetheless journalists and deans ask us time and again to comment on what looks to them like a rising importance of religion in politics. We have to reject the premise of the question on the authority of Manza and Brooks and now on the basis of our update to their research. Religion burst out of seclusion to become a more legitimate topic of political conversation and public debate than it used to be. So we talk about it more. But its impact on elections is pretty much as it was in the past quarter-century and perhaps more.

The view of religion in the political arena has no doubt changed. After all, in the 1960 campaign, John F. Kennedy had to promise that his religion would not influence the decisions he would make if elected president, but John F. Kerry had to promise that his religion would influence him. But while talk has changed, voters by and large have not. Religion has been a source of what Brooks and Manza call "social cleavage" for decades. Reporters who ask us to comment on "trends" seem to have mistaken a trend in how they cover elections for a trend in how Americans actually vote.

THE PARTISAN PATTERN

In a late-October poll in 2004, the Gallup organization asked American adults if they thought President Bush was a "uniter" or a "divider." The nation split down the middle—48 percent said "uniter" and 48 percent said "divider" (with just 4 percent unable to choose). But the kicker was in the partisan breakdown on that question. While 87 percent of Republicans saw the president as a uniter; 81 percent of Democrats saw him as a divider. This is not an aberration; it reflects, perhaps more starkly than most statistics, the general partisan tenor in American politics.

Voters' perceptions of candidates have always followed party lines, but Americans' partisan leanings bear more weight now because the major parties are far more closely identified with liberal and conservative ideologies than they used to be. In the 1970s, 32 percent of Democrats described themselves as liberal, but 25 percent said conservative.[6] Republicans were, as expected, more conservative at that time: 18 percent said they were liberal, and 47 percent said conservative. In 2004, 41 percent of Democrats were liberal, and 66 percent of Republicans were conservative. Counter-types were rare to extremely rare: 20 percent of Democrats were conservative and a mere 7 percent

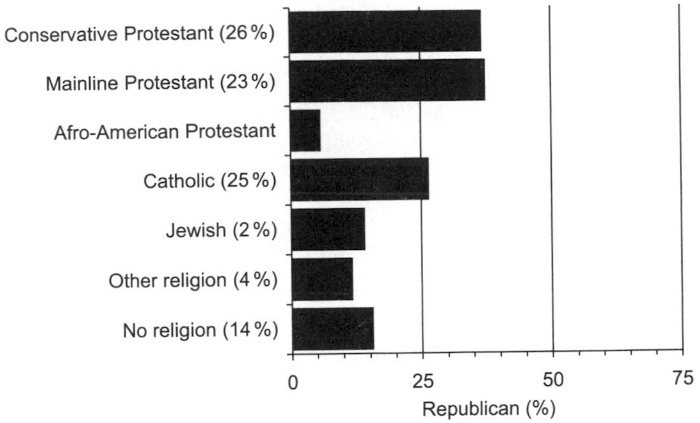

Figure 3.2 Republican identification by religion, 2000–2004. Numbers in parentheses show each denomination's share of the population. SOURCE: General Social Surveys, 2000–2004.

of Republicans were liberal. This greater correspondence between political worldviews and party identification makes presidential politics more contentious and more predictable.[7] Every partisan factor counts more now than it did before conservative Democrats became rare and liberal Republicans became all but extinct.

Despite the dramatic shifts within parties, the distribution of Americans across the liberal-conservative spectrum has not changed since the Reagan era (there was a significant conservative shift between 1972 and 1982).

Conservative Protestants have become slightly more politically conservative over the eras, going from 38 percent conservative prior to the Reagan era to 41 percent conservative in the Reagan era, and 46 percent conservative in the current era.

The distribution of religious denominations into political parties in recent years (see fig. 3.2) closely resembles the electoral split except that more people identify as "independent" in their party identification than vote for independent or third-party candidates.[8] Conservative Protestants (36 percent) and Mainline Protestants (37 percent) are significantly more Republican than Catholics (26 percent). Smaller denominations and people with no religion are about

15 percent Republican, except Afro-American Protestants who are just 6 percent Republican.

Conservative Protestants once identified significantly more strongly with Democrats and less so with Republicans. Tracing the trend over time (fig. 3.3) reveals that while their drift away from the Democratic Party has been on a steady pace since 1972, their Republican conversions occurred exclusively during the Reagan years. Before 1982 and since 1988, Conservative Protestants who have quit identifying as Democrats have switched to politically independent.

Political independence among Conservative Protestants challenges the images of religiously inspired culture wars and partisan polarization that feature so prominently in popular discussions of contemporary politics. But our findings confirm those of other academic researchers who continue to point out the glaring gap between religious and political conservatism.[9] Conservative Protestants are somewhat more politically conservative than other Americans, but, first, only a minority of Conservative Protestants identifies as politically con-

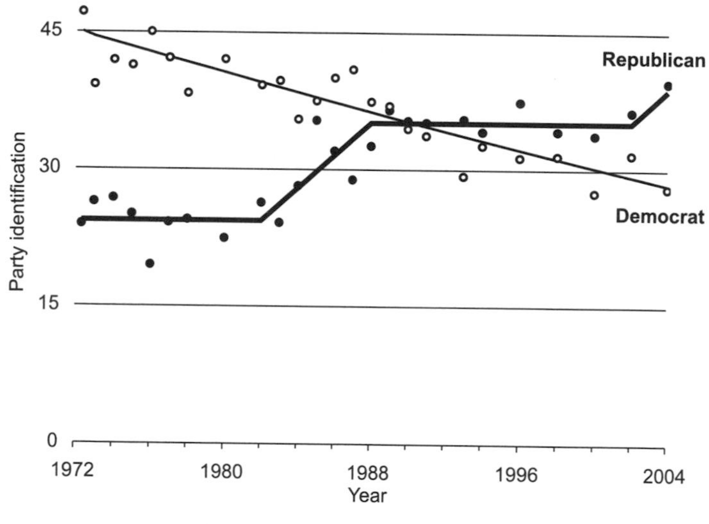

Figure 3.3 Party identification by year: Conservative Protestant voters, 1972–2004. Dots show the observed percentages; the lines show the results of a statistical model to smooth out sampling fluctuations in the observed data.

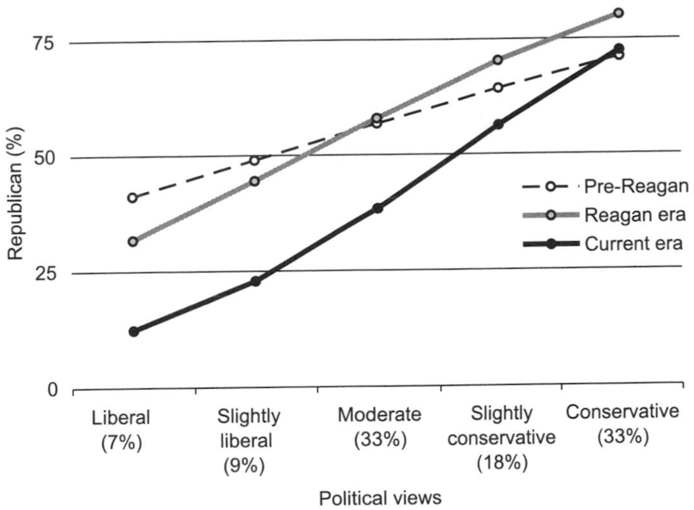

Figure 3.4 Republican votes by political views and political era: Conservative Protestant voters, 1972–2000 elections. We used a statistical model to smooth out sampling fluctuations in the observed data. Numbers in parentheses are the percentages holding each political view in the current era.

servative, and second, differences between Conservative Protestants and Mainline Protestants are marginal. First, 47 percent of Conservative Protestants call themselves politically conservative, 36 percent are politically moderate, and 17 percent are politically liberal. Second, among other religious groups the percentage conservative ranges from 38 percent of Mainline Protestants to 34 percent of Catholics, 28 percent of Afro-American Protestants, 23 percent of Jews, and 21 percent of people with no religion. These are differences of degree that have consequences for voting patterns and other socially important outcomes, but they are hardly the paroxysms of political polarization one might hear about on cable TV.

Differences over political worldviews nonetheless divide religious conservatives just as they divide the rest of the population. And divisions cut deeper now than in the 1970s (see fig. 3.4). Conservative Protestants who are politically liberal supported Clinton and Gore more than they supported Reagan's opponents (Carter and Mondale);

politically conservative Conservative Protestants shifted strongly to Reagan and have maintained that allegiance since. The record shows that a thirteen-point gap between the voting patterns of politically conservative and politically liberal Conservative Protestants in the 1970s grew to a 31-point gap in the 1980s, and a yawning 50-point gap beginning in the current political era. The partisan pattern reinforces the gaps in presidential votes in any particular election. The 47 percent of them who are politically conservative are strong Republicans; the 16 percent who are politically liberal are just as loyal to the Democrats. On balance the conservative leanings give Republicans an advantage, but it is clearly an error to equate religious and political conservatism. As with any group large enough to encompass one-fourth of the adult population, Conservative Protestants are quite varied, and overall their political views overlap with those of many others, especially other Christians.

Typically discussion of how religious conservatism intersects with political conservatism and political polarization turns quickly to the wedge issues that animate the supposed culture clash. But our multivariate analysis of the differences that divide Conservative Protestants and that set them apart from other religious groups shows that family income and economic issues are far more significant than moral values for the trends in both voting and party identification. We now turn to the key pieces of evidence of how income and economic issues affect Conservative Protestants' votes and party identification. Then we will compare these economic patterns with wedge issues like abortion, sex, and evolution.

CLASS, ECONOMICS, AND POLITICS

The key class and economic issues since the 1970s have been family finances, taxes (and public spending), and unions. Unemployment has been part of the debate some years and inflation others. The issue of federal regulations affecting bookkeeping, product safety, and pollution has motivated many managers and business owners. We address how they affect Conservative Protestants' voting and party identification first by looking to the bottom line—family finances—and then turning to how views on specific issues affect voting. We classified families and households according to whether their income (adjusted

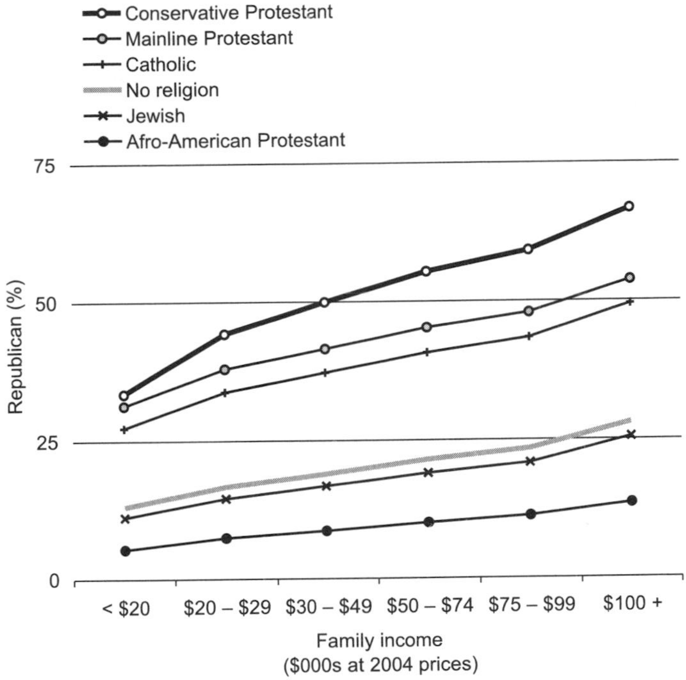

Figure 3.5 Republican votes by family income and political era: Conservative Protestant voters, 1972–2000 elections. We used a statistical model to smooth out sampling fluctuations in the observed data.

for inflation) fell into one of six income brackets: less than $20,000, $20,000–$29,999, $30,000–$49,999, $50,000–$74,999, $75,000–$99,999, and $100,000 or more.[10]

Family income affects voting in all denominations, and it affects the votes of Conservative Protestants almost 50 percent more than it does others' votes. Figure 3.5 shows the strong and evolving relationship between family income and vote for Conservative Protestants. Even in the 1970s, those in the top income bracket chose Republican candidates over their Democratic alternatives by a two-to-one margin. In the Reagan era the Republican edge in the top bracket rose to three-to-one, and it remained close to that through the current era. Meanwhile, the struggling one-fifth of voters whose incomes were less than $20,000 per year split their votes pretty close to one-to-one right up to the current era. But beginning with the 1992 election, they shifted slightly to the Democrats. The presidential candidacy of H. Ross Perot helped peel away some Republican support among lower-income Conservative Protestants, but, as we will see soon, they also changed their assessments of how to manage the economy and the federal budget.

The same pattern holds when we analyze party identification (not shown). Republican identification rises with rising income, and it does so more sharply in the current era than it did in the 1970s. Class gets less attention than other issues in American politics. Few candidates and few journalists raise class issues during campaigns, even though scholars have noted rising class cleavages over the past ten years.[11]

Each religious group exhibits a similar pattern of sharp economic differences. Working-class and low-income voters of all religions got it when Clinton said he stood for those Americans who "work hard and play by the rules" and when Gore asked if they wanted a president who represented "the people or the powerful?" The Republicans' real base is not the religious right but the affluent. Michael Moore filmed President Bush joking about "the haves and the have mores."[12] And the data back the president on this point. Fifteen percent of American voters have family incomes of more than $100,000 a year, while twice as many earn less than $30,000. The affluent group (a substantially smaller share of the electorate than the Conservative Protestants) voted Republican by an 14-point margin, while the low-income group favored Democrats by a 28-percent margin. The distinctive voting pattern of the affluent earns them a political impact score of 1.8 points (despite their relatively small size) and the low-income group has a political impact score of −2.8 (indicating their Democratic leanings). Thus the affluent contribute more political impact to the Republican cause than Conservative Protestants, despite the numerical advantage of the Conservative Protestants.

With red-state versus blue-state rhetoric competing with religious rhetoric for airtime, it is imperative to note that, in our multivariate analyses, neither region nor religion can override the class divide evident in these calculations. The net effect of family income—controlling for a wide variety of sociodemographic factors and several key political opinions, including abortion attitudes—is statistically significant. The importance of income is statistically and politically significant whether we look at adults in general or Conservative Protestants in particular (see appendix table).

We wondered whether it was fair to consider income differences in voting as evidence of class politics or just some odd, unanticipated connection that has little to do with class interests. After all, affluent people have different lifestyles and preferences than the middle class and the poor. So we investigated some issues that could connect the class gap in voting to a class-based political agenda.

Spending priorities help set a class-based political agenda. Democrats Clinton, Gore, and Kerry have proposed national health plans that would aid lower-middle-class and middle-class voters who lack health coverage; Republicans opposed those proposals. Democrats also tend to speak more about promoting racial equality; Republicans spearheaded efforts to erase affirmative action. On the other side, Republicans criticize unions and have restricted their role in workplaces across the county; Democrats usually oppose those efforts.

To see if they explain the statistical correlation between income and voting, we formed an index that gives each person a point for thinking that the government does not spend enough on improving the nation's health or the condition of blacks and a point for having a great deal of confidence in the people running labor unions.[13] Conservative Protestants were *more* likely to support increased spending for health and improving the condition of blacks in the recent years than in the 1970s. In the pre-Reagan era, 59 percent of Conservative Protestants thought that the government spent too little on health care; in the current era 70 percent think so. Support for increased spending to improve blacks' living conditions rose from 20 to 32 percent among Conservative Protestants. And differences among them predicted well which Conservative Protestants voted for Democrats and which voted for Republicans (fig. 3.6). The more of these liberal issues the person supported, the less likely she or he was to vote Republican. Together these three items explain about 40 percent of the baseline effect of family income on votes.[14]

Thus, not only can we say that class matters for how Americans vote, but also that much of that pattern refers to specific spending and organizational issues associated with class issues.

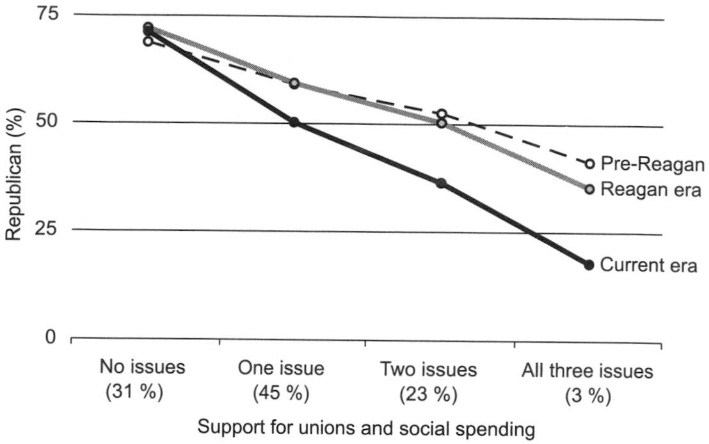

Figure 3.6 Republican votes by support for unions and social spending and political era: Conservative Protestant voters, 1972–2000 elections. We used a statistical model to smooth out sampling fluctuations in the observed data.

MORAL VALUES AS POLITICAL ISSUES

Abortion is the prototypical moral wedge issue. When the U.S. Supreme Court decided the *Roe v. Wade* case on 22 January 1973, public opinion was about as divided as it is today on whether abortion should be legal. But, unlike today, liberals were only slightly more likely than conservatives to support legal abortion in a wide variety of circumstances. We use six items—opinions about legal abortions for women whose health is threatened by the pregnancy, those who became pregnant due to rape, those who have reason to believe that their baby has birth defects, pregnant single women, pregnant poor women, and pregnant women who want no more children—to form a seven-point scale (ranging from 0 to 6). Responses grouped by religious denominations differed more sharply: Jews approved abortion under most conditions, people with no religion were next, followed by Mainline Protestants while Catholics and Conservative Protestants opposed abortion under so-called social reasons like wanting no more children, not wanting to marry the father, or being poor but supported abortion in cases of rape, birth defects, or threats to the pregnant woman's health (see Hout 1999). We will show more details in our "sexual revolution" discussion below (see chap. 8), but for present purposes we note this kind of "it depends" reasoning on abortion prevails today, especially among Conservative Protestants and Catholics. In part the drift to the right in American politics came about because abortion opponents who take moderate or liberal stances on most issues now call themselves conservative because their abortion views are in line with those of conservatives. The trend got reinforced when political liberals who once opposed abortion moved closer to a pro-choice stance.

Conservative Protestants' opposition to abortion explains part of their shift toward political conservatism and Republican voting. Prior to the Reagan era, just under 40 percent of Conservative Protestants voted for Democrats McGovern and Carter (more for Carter and he won), and that percentage varied in an irregular and statistically insignificant way across the spectrum of attitudes toward abortion. Little changed in the Reagan era (Conservative Protestants were slightly more likely to vote Republican). In the current era, however, abortion rose to political significance. Conservative Protestants who disapproved of abortion in all conditions (10 percent of Conservative Protestant voters) or felt it was okay if the woman's health was threatened (another 9 percent of Conservative Protestant voters) backed Bush, Dole, and Bush as much as they had supported Reagan. All other groups fell away from Republican support to the point that a minority voted Republican among the 40 percent of Conservative Protestants who support legal abortion under four, five, or all six conditions (see fig. 3.7).

Gay rights eclipsed abortion as a wedge issue in 2004. A court case touched off the debate, just as *Roe v. Wade* intensified the abortion debate. The Massachusetts Supreme Court on 18 November 2003 instructed the state legislature to figure out how to quit discriminating against gay couples in the state's marriage laws. This action mobilized friends and foes of gay marriage. In January 2004, President Bush called on the nation "to defend the sanctity of marriage" during his State of the Union address. Through the winter and spring, ballot initiatives defining marriage as exclusively between one man and one woman qualified in several states. In February, San Francisco issued marriage licenses to same-sex couples, and the mayor presided over same-sex wedding ceremonies on the steps of City Hall on Valentine's Day. On 17 May 2004 same-sex marriages became legal in Massachu-

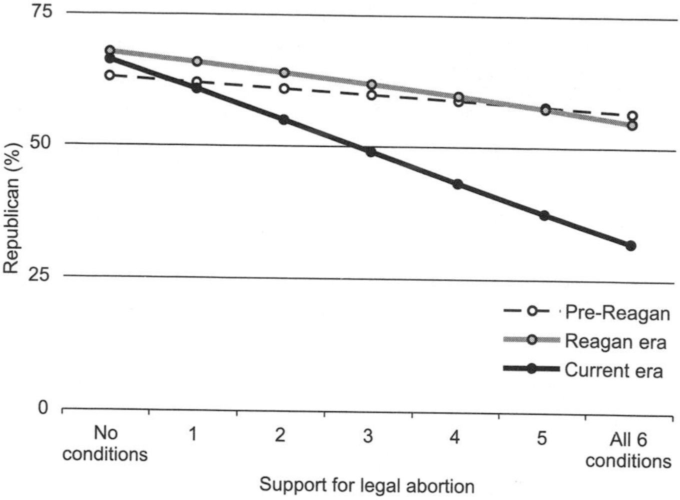

Figure 3.7 Republican votes by abortion attitude and political era: Conservative Protestant voters, 1972–2000 elections. We used a statistical model to smooth out sampling fluctuations in the observed data. Numbers in parentheses are the percentages supporting legal abortion that many times in the current era.

setts. On 12 August 2004, the California Supreme Court voided San Francisco's 4,000-plus same-sex marriages. On Election Day 2004, gay-marriage bans passed in all eleven states that voted on the subject.

Even before 2004, gay rights made liberal Democrats nervous. President Clinton faced a controversy over gays in the military in his first month in office then compromised with the "Don't ask; don't tell" policy. He later signed the "Marriage Protection Act" in 1996.

Our question is, does the Conservative Protestants' opposition to both abortion rights and gay rights explain their tendency to vote for Republicans? To answer that, we made a three-item scale using two of the abortion items—rape victim and single woman—and a question that asks if sex between partners of the same gender is wrong (with various qualifications) or "not wrong at all." We find no difference in voting between Conservative and Mainline Protestants who have the same views on abortion and gay sex. So this scale fully accounts for the difference between the two largest Protestant groups. Catholics, on the other hand, are significantly more likely to vote for Democrats than are Protestants with the same attitudes except among the most liberal group who approve of keeping abortion legal under both circumstances and say that gay sex is not wrong at all.[15]

The lesson to learn from these results is that the renewed emphasis on moral values is overblown two ways. First, values voting is not new. We see evidence of it in the 1988, 1992, and 1996 elections. The wedge was in before 2004. Second, although values help us comprehend Protestants' votes, they tell us much less about how others vote.

It is worth noting the sexual slant of values voting. Other moral issues, capital punishment for example, are curiously missing from presidential debates. About one voter in four opposes the death penalty for convicted murderers. Yet, as of this writing, neither party stands in opposition to it. Perhaps candidates are silent because Democratic candidates get the overwhelming majority—74 percent—of the death penalty opponents' votes without actually taking that stand.

BELIEFS, PRACTICE, AND VOTES

To summarize our analysis to this point, note that religion is a robust and persistent factor in American presidential politics. The basic outline of partisan denominational cleavage was obvious in the 1970s and changed very little since then. Manza and Brooks (1997) began their analysis with the 1960 election and found that the current regime applied in the 1964 and 1968 elections as well.[16] We have not seen the 2004 results yet but have little reason—based on these forty years of stable cleavage—to expect dramatic change. The Mainline Protestants have moved a few percentage points in the direction of the Democrats, and Conservative Protestants have moved the same amount to the Republican side. Catholics and non-Christians have remained in their positions—Catholics a few percentage points on the Democratic side of the electorate with Jews, members of Afro-American Protestant churches, and people with no religion further over on the Democrats' side. Differences on the abortion issue and attitudes on homosexuality account for the trends among the Conservative and Mainline Protestants and for the difference between Conservative and Mainline Protestants in any given election. That is, Protestants in the two largest groups of denominations who have the same views on abortion and homosexuality vote the same. None of the issues we have considered to this point fully account for why those two kinds of Protestants vote differently than people from other religions. Nor can those issues explain the strong Democratic leanings of members of Afro-American Protestant churches. Rooted in history and culture, the differences among Catholics, Jews, and people with no religion—and between each of them and Protestants—cannot be reduced to a single issue or bundle of issues.

In chapter 2 we found that peoples' perspective on the Bible helped explain the differences among religions. But the Bible is a weak political factor. We learn more about the differences among Protestants by focusing directly on abortion, gay sex, and capital punishment. Afro-American Protestants actually reverse the pattern we see among Conservative and Mainline Protestants, that is, those who take the Bible literally are more likely to vote for Democrats than those who deny the Bible's divine inspiration. Similarly, Catholics who take the Bible literally turn out to be the strongest Democrats among Catholics.

Church attendance emerged as a political predictor in the current era. Frequent attenders of all denominations are more inclined to support Republicans than their co-religionists who attend less often.[17] But while this factor is useful for understanding peoples' voting preferences, it does nothing to explain the greater affinity of Conservative Protestants for Republican candidates. At each frequency of attendance the Catholics are significantly more Democratic than the Conservative Protestants; Mainline Protestants are in between.

ADDITIONAL WEDGE ISSUES: EVOLUTION, PRAYER IN SCHOOLS, AND ASSISTED SUICIDE

The conservative social agenda that is identified with Conservative Christianity includes at least three other potential wedge issues: evolution (especially how it is taught in schools), prayers in school, and assisted suicide. Stem cell research emerged late in the 2004 election campaign, but we do not have a measure of that. We examined the two we do have measures of and found that they do little to help us understand either voting dynamics or religious voting cleavages.

Views of evolution are closely tied to the literal interpretation of the Bible, as we discussed in chapter 2. In the fundamentalist form of Conservative Protestantism, accepting evolution contradicts Genesis and Jesus Christ's testimony to the veracity of scripture. So some Protestants are especially enjoined to oppose the teaching of evolution in the public schools and to support political candidates who will support them in that effort. In the first part of the twentieth century it was Populists and Democrats who spoke out against evolution in the schools. William Jennings Bryan, three-time Democratic nominee for president, aided the prosecutor at the Scopes "Monkey Trial" in 1925. But opposition to evolution became a Republican issue when school board candidates started to campaign on forcing schools to teach creationism alongside evolution in science classes.

Conservative and Mainline Protestants who agree on evolution vote the same. Just over half of the Conservative Protestants (53 percent) and Mainline Protestants (51 percent) who believe in evolution voted for Republicans in the current political era. But evolution is irrelevant to how Catholics and Afro-American Protestants vote. Evolution turns out to be most divisive among people with no religion; 38 percent of secular voters who believe in evolution voted for Republicans in the current era compared to just 13 percent of secular voters who say it is definitely false.

Mandatory readings of Bible verses and recitation of the Lord's Prayer in public schools were banned by the Supreme Court in the *Engel v. Vitale* decision on 25 June 1962. Many accounts of the rise of the Christian right date its political relevance to that day and that case. And we have no doubt that many religious people feel strongly about the issue—69 percent of Americans who describe themselves as strongly attached to their religion disapprove of the ban (compared to 57 percent of those not strongly attached to their religion and 31 percent of adults with no religion). To our surprise, attitude toward prayer in school has only weakly affected presidential voting—and only among people who are not Conservative Protestants. Even though Conservative Protestants are the Supreme Court's harshest critics (75 percent of Conservative Protestant voters disapprove of the ban), the political gap between Conservative Protestants who approve and disapprove of banning school prayer is only 1 percentage point (and statistically insignificant). Disapproving of the school prayer ban does push Catholics and Mainline Protestants toward the Republicans; 11 points among voters in Mainline denominations and 10 among Catholics. Even these differences disappear when we control for other relevant variables.

Physician-assisted suicide is legal in only one state—Oregon—but other states considered making it legal in the 1990s. California and Washington voters rejected statewide ballot initiatives in 1990 and 1991. Maine voters narrowly defeated one in 2000. Court cases—prosecutions of people who assist in suicides, most notably Dr. Jack Kevorkian as well as test cases on various states' statutes—keep the issue before the public eye. The major parties and major party candidates, on the other hand, have never endorsed the idea. This issue may or may not be the next wedge issue. Has it affected recent elections?

The GSS asks two excellent questions about ending the life of terminally ill people: *When a person has a disease that cannot be cured, do you think doctors should be allowed by law to end the patient's life by some painless means if the patient and his family request it?* And *Do you think a person has the right to end his or her own life if this person has an incurable disease?* Both questions have "yes" and "no" as the possible answers. A majority of Americans object to ending life before its time, but they are more likely to accept the idea of physicians letting patients die (46 percent over the whole history of the GSS) than with suicide among the terminally ill (33 percent). But opinions have changed; a majority now approves of both—34 percent approved both in 1974–1980, 46 percent in 1982–1991, and 57 percent in 1993–2002. In the most recent period, the religions differ sharply on the issue—35 percent of Afro-American Protestants approve both, 43 percent of Conservative Protestants, 57 percent of Catholics, 64 percent of Mainline Protestants, 81 percent of people with no religion, and 83 percent of Jews approve of both. With the very notable exception of members of Afro-American denominations, the rank of religions on end-of-life issues corresponds to their rank on preferring Democratic candidates. And within denominations, people who think doctors should be allowed to let incurable patients die and that those patients have a right to end their own lives were significantly more likely to vote for Clinton or Gore than for their Republican opponents. The partisan difference between those saying "no" to both and "yes" to both was 16 points among Conservative Protestants, 1 point among Protestants in Afro-American denominations, 18 points among Mainline Protestants, 12 points among Catholics, −6 points among Jews, and 6 points among people with no religion. A multivariate model, though, shows that differences on this issue are correlated with liberal-conservative views in general and abortion and gay sex in particular. Among people who agree on abortion and gay sex, attitudes about ending the lives of terminal patients do not affect voting.

In sum, how to teach evolution in schools, prayer in schools, and choosing to end a life divide religions in the United States. But they do not directly affect presidential politics or advance our understanding of the source of religious differences in how people vote.

MASKED RACISM?

The red states glowing for Republicans on election night in 2000 and again in 2004 included all the states that had slavery in the nineteenth century and institutionalized racial segregation prior to 1964. Ever since Kevin Phillips crafted Nixon's "Southern strategy" for the 1968 election, liberals have suspected a connection between racism and voting for Republicans. The overwhelming Democratic vote by African Americans gives credence to the suspicions. Conservative opposition to many programs that African Americans advocate also raises the prospect of racism.

Political scientists have debated the impact of some voters' racism on presidential politics repeatedly over the past twenty years. We could not settle the larger debate here. We only raise it because it relates to religious cleavages. The visibility of Conservative Protestants in red-state politics makes it relevant to those who can comprehend religious motivations.

By 1990 the segregationist attitudes were largely discredited and abandoned. Overwhelming majorities of Americans espoused the principles of equal opportunity regardless of race. Once controversial questions of equal access to public facilities, jobs, and schools were, by 1990, almost universally endorsed (Schuman et al. 1997). Neighborhood segregation remained a subject of controversy, though. As did affirmative action—the policy of reversing preferences to help blacks catch up with whites. Two GSS items on neighborhoods showed serious dissensus in the 1990s:

> 54. *Here are some opinions other people have expressed in connection with black-white relations. Which statement on the card comes closest to how your yourself feel?* [Statements on the card: agree strongly, agree slightly, disagree slightly, disagree strongly]
>
> ■ *A. Blacks should not push themselves where they're not wanted.*

- *B. White people have a right to keep blacks out of their neighborhoods if they want to, and blacks should respect that right.*

And this item and its follow-up probes opinions on the frankest rendering of the affirmative action question:

- *58. Some people say that because of past discrimination, blacks should be given preference in hiring and promotion. Others say that such preference in hiring and promotion of blacks is wrong because it discriminates against whites. What about your opinion—are you for or against preferential hiring and promotion for blacks?*
- *Do you {favor / oppose} preferences in hiring and promotion strongly or not strongly?*
- *79. Now look at Card 16. Some people think that (blacks/African-Americans) have been discriminated against for so long that the government has a special obligation to help improve their living standards. Others believe that the government should not be giving special treatment to (blacks/African-Americans). Where would you place yourself on this scale, or haven't you made up your mind on this?*

CARD 16				
I strongly agree the government is obligated to help blacks		I agree with both answers		I strongly agree that government shouldn't give special treatment
1	2	3	4	5

Item 54b was discontinued after 1996, so we concentrate on the others. The "push" (54a) and the "preference" (58/58a/79) items refer to different issues, so we analyze them separately.[18]

Just over one-third of Conservative Protestants voted for Democrats in the 1990s regardless of their views about blacks "pushing." Their votes do not reflect their views of race relations in this sense or in the sense evoked by the rights whites may or may not have. The push item does come closer to the view of a majority of Conservative Protestants than it comes to views prevalent in other religions; among Conservative Protestants, 19 percent agreed strongly with "push" and 29 percent agreed slightly with it (compared to 13 percent and 17 percent among Mainline Protestants). But their votes are not cover for these views as Republican votes are as prevalent among Conservative Protestants who disagree as among those who agree that blacks should not push.

Racial segregation attitudes influence the votes of Mainline Protestants and people with no religion—but not Catholics or Jews. Mainline Protestants who strongly disagree with the push item and the white rights item are 10 percentage points more likely to vote for Democrats than other Mainline Protestants are (both statistically significant differences). Among people with no religion the tendency to vote Democratic rises as disagreement rises.

Affirmative action is very unpopular among non-blacks in the United States. On item 58, 62 percent strongly oppose preferences; on item 79, 32 percent strongly agree that the government should not give special treatment. Not surprisingly the minority who favor preferences and/or help vote Democrat in overwhelming numbers and those who oppose them favor Republicans. Within religions, the association is as strong as it is overall. Item 79—the one that uses the word "help"—affects Conservative Protestants less than it affects other religions. Democratic votes rise from 25 percent among those who oppose special treatment to 50 percent among those who think the government needs to help. The other three religious traditions all show a sharper increase as support for government aid rises. Democratic voting rises from 35 to 70 percent among Catholics as their attitude moves from no special treatment to help; among people with no religion the increase is 51 percentage points from 36 to 87 percent Democrat.

Are the Conservative Protestants racist? The evidence here acquits them of the charge. Grant the following:

- Most Conservative Protestants are politically conservative.
- They prefer volunteerism to government action.
- Their theology guides them to a harsh view of the material world.
- They tend to emphasize self-reliance and facing the consequences of bad choices over aid of any kind.
- Their churches are strict with them, and they prefer strictness in social policy.

So most of them do not like affirmative action or the word "preferences." And they vote for candidates who share those views and outlooks. That is true—truer actually—of all groups. Americans who have no religious preference are more liberal on average, less strict, and more inclined to want to right historical wrongs through government intervention. And they are even more likely to vote for candidates who share their views and outlooks. That is why professional pollsters who advise candidates hope most people agree that their clients "share our values." These concerns sound to us like genuine commitments and principles, not euphemisms for disparaged racist views. In conjunction with the lack of any association among Conservative Protestants between our other racism measures and voting, we think it is time to close the case on the evangelical racism claim. There is only weak evidence to support the charge.

A THREAT TO CIVIL LIBERTIES?

Another concern that liberals often use to disparage Conservative Protestants is the alleged threat they pose to civil liberties, especially free speech. A worldview hinged on absolute truth invites repression of false teaching. And most Americans are sensitive to that. In 1998, 49 percent of American adults agreed that religious people are often too intolerant (including 74 percent of those with no religious preference). So in this last empirical section we move from voting to civil liberties.

At the height of the McCarthy era, the great sociologist Samuel A. Stouffer developed a civil liberties battery that when applied to a national sample of American adults dispelled the myth of popular support for Senator McCarthy's brand of repression. *Communism, Conformity, and Civil Liberties* (1955) became a classic of what we would now call "public sociology." Although it is remembered for delivering the news that most Americans were willing to risk giving an audience to enemies in order to protect the Constitution, a minority was ready to back suppression of unpopular ideas.

The GSS has replicated Stouffer's items and added some new ones since its inception in 1972. The first item is very relevant to our study:

There are always some people whose ideas are considered bad or dangerous by other people. For instance, somebody who is against all churches and religion.

- *If such a person wanted to make a speech in your {city / town / community} against churches and religion, should he be allowed to speak or not?*
- *Should such a person be allowed to teach in a college or university or not?*
- *If some people in your community suggested that a book he wrote against churches and religion should be taken out of your public library, would you favor removing this book or not?*

For context we also consider two other items in this battery in which the scenarios involve blacks and homosexuals:

- *Or consider somebody who believes that blacks are genetically inferior. [questions about speech, teaching, and library book]*
- *And what about a man who admits he is a homosexual?* [questions about speech, teaching, and library book]

Protestants in Conservative and Afro-American denominations would protect the civil liberties and academic freedom of atheists, racists, and homosexuals less than people of other religions or no religion would. Conservative Protestants are the only group for which a majority would ban unpopular speakers, teachers, and authors of all three types we consider here. Afro-American Protestants are less tolerant of atheists and racists, but a slight majority of them would not ban gay speakers, teachers, or authors.

Let us go back to the premise of the question. "There are always some people whose ideas are considered bad or dangerous by other people." By the year 2000, many Americans did not consider gays or atheists bad or dangerous. And though racism declined, it did not go away altogether. So some people presumably agree to let a gay man, atheist, or racist speak, not to defend the First Amendment, but to give a platform to *their* beliefs. So we restrict attention to people with firm beliefs in God when looking at civil liberties for atheists, people who think homosexuality is always wrong when we look at the questions involving homosexuality, and people who support affirmative action when we look at the racist questions.

The majority of Americans think that atheists, gays, and racists all have the right to speak, circulate their books in the public library, and teach in colleges and universities. Even among Americans who disagree strongly with the point of view or behavior in question, the majority approves of protecting civil liberties. The margin of protection is modest. The biggest assurance comes with the 76 percent of people who have strong faith in God saying that the atheist should be allowed to give a speech. In general, gays and atheists are better protected than racists.

Conservative Protestants are significantly less likely to support civil liberties than other Americans are on all nine questions. The differences range from 9 to 17 percentage points. Among Conservative Protestants who disagree with the point of view or behavior, 65 percent would allow a speech by an atheist or gay man; only 46 percent would allow a speech by the racist. Fifty-eight percent would not remove an atheist's book from the library, 50 percent would not remove a gay man's book, but only 48 percent would protect the racist's book. Teaching is the least protected activity. Nonetheless, 45 percent of Conservative Protestants who disagree would allow the atheist to teach, 56 percent would allow the gay man to teach, and only 40 percent would allow the racist to do so.

Conservative Protestants' commitment to civil liberties comes up short compared to other Americans. The religious differences are quantitative, though, and modest. They amount to between 9 and 17 percentage points. No group is willing to protect civil liberties as an absolute imperative. Racist teachers would be dismissed by a majority of Americans who support affirmative action. The United States has a civil liberties problem; it is just a bigger problem among Conservative Protestants.

POLITICAL GEOGRAPHY

The electoral college builds state politics into presidential politics. But recent focus on the so-called red states that tend to vote Republican and blue states that tend to vote Democratic suggests a cultural difference that is not reflected in the usual variables of political analysis. Here our emphasis on religion and income can potentially solve the red state–blue state riddle. Or it could compound it. What if

Conservative Protestants tend to vote Republican not because of their religion but because they are residents of red states?

The social science approach to the question is the kind of statistical horse race we run throughout this book. (1) Classify states as solid Republican (red), solid Democrat (blue), and battleground (white).[19] (2) See how well we can predict votes with just these distinctions. (3) See if any differences between red and blue states remain after we adjust statistically for the effects of religious denomination, attendance at religious services, family income, and relevant socio-demographic factors like gender, race, age, marital status, and city-suburb-rural differences.

In the 1992–2000 elections, red-state residents were 4 percent more Republican and blue-state residents were 8 percent more Democratic than residents of battleground states. Adjusting for religion, income, and sociodemographic factors reduces those differences to 3 percent and 4 percent, respectively. More important, the large and significant differences in vote by denomination, attendance, and income are the same with and without the type-of-state variables. In sum, the evidence is clear that the religious and income patterns we describe here are not artifacts of some red-state / blue-state phenomenon. Furthermore our model accounts for 40 percent of the recent red-state / blue-state divide. We can account for the rest of the red-state / blue-state differences by adding attitudes toward legal abortion to the equation.[20]

CONCLUSION

Conservative Protestants' moral values matter for politics in the first decade of the twenty-first century. And they matter modestly more in the current era than they did before. Nearly every political observer would agree with us on that. What we add to the conversation is the observation that almost anything that affected voting behavior in the past matters more for presidential politics in the current era than it did prior to the Reagan era. These are partisan times. Elections are close. All the cleavages are mobilized. Any one of them could make the difference in a tight election. The increased salience of religion and moral values parallels the growing class divide in voting, the gender gap, and the difference between central cities and their suburbs.

Voters weigh their values and their economic interests in choosing a candidate. The modest shift in America's religious cleavage did not blunt the economic cleavage at all. The impact of family income on voting increased more than the differences among religions did from the 1970s to 2000. Values voting is not a form of false consciousness; voters do not forget their material interests when they vote their values or vice versa. The strongest evidence on that point is the contrast between Conservative Protestants from affluent and poor families. Over 80 percent of affluent Conservative Protestants voted Republican in the 1992, 1996, and 2000 elections; slightly less than half of poor Conservative Protestants did. All groups defined by their religious affiliation (or lack thereof) follow their pocketbooks these days, but the economic cleavage was deepest for Conservative Protestants—the group most identified with values voting.

Yet religion and not economics emerged in high relief on election night 2004. The sense that President Bush won reelection because he was better on religion has not gone away either. Religion mattered but not much more than before and probably less than economic issues did. We suspect that religion remains the story of 2004 because it suits both the interests that want to further the influence of their brand of religion on important decisions like Supreme Court nominations and those who want to raise money to stop them. Tales of triumph bolster religious activists' claims for election spoils. As early as November 2004, evangelical spokesmen chastised Senator Arlen Specter (R, Pa.) for voicing his doubts that judicial nominees who opposed *Roe v. Wade* could get through the Judiciary Committee he headed. They wanted him removed from that leadership role if he was going to give up before any fights began. Tales of threats help liberals, too. If they can puff up the otherness of the opposition, they can rally their base. And by exaggerating how strange the religious right is, demagogues can assure themselves that they will run afoul of very few real people. If you insult a real opponent you have to face his answer; if you insult a mythical opponent you get the floor all to yourself. Is that fairness for the values voter? Probably not.

Real religious cleavages exist; it is not all hype. Where do they come from and how do they persist? Differences among Conservative and Mainline Protestants reflect their differences on abortion and homosexuality. Protestants who agree on these issues, regardless of denomination, vote alike. Turning to the differences between Protestant denominations and other religious groups in the United States, we can find no single issue or cluster of issues that explains those differences. History and culture meld into politics in mysterious ways. One way is outsider status. Afro-American Protestants, Catholics, Jews, people of small minority religions, and people who prefer no religion all feel an outsider status that finds validation in the politics of Democrats. Even when they have similar opinions on social issues and the same family income, Catholics and non-Christians are less likely than Protestants to vote Republican.

Conservative Protestants feel embattled, too, as Christian Smith pointed out in *American Evangelicalism: Embattled and Thriving* (1998). But Conservative Protestants' embattlement is not an outsider's sympathy for other outsiders. It has an unmistakable entitlement. The Conservative Protestant leadership talks like people who feel they are outside by mistake. They are certain of their place at the heart of America just as they are certain of their faith in God. Their original name for their political movement—moral majority—captures this sensibility. From the point of view of Conservative Protestant leadership their movement differs from what is going on with outsider groups because the others are neither as American nor as close to God. To evangelical leaders, Conservative Protestants deserve more say, and the others can wait to speak.

One of us recently had an experience that illustrates the mentality in a small but telling way. The Commonwealth Club of California put together a panel on "fundamentalism" for broadcast in December 2004. The planners wanted spokespeople for the atheist, the Jewish, and the evangelical Protestant points of view. They also recruited an academic who could chip in some survey data from time to time to be an arbiter of disputes that turned on social science issues.[21] When the host recognized Greg Koukl, the person representing the evangelical view, as the first panelist to speak, he said, "I guess I am the token Christian here tonight." Christians outnumber atheists and Jews in the United States and Mr. Koukl genuinely felt that one of each, even in the confines of the panel format, slighted his Conservative Christian constituency.

The sure and absolute faith of Conservative Protestants makes them this way. In *Christian America?* Smith (2000, 200) reports that 77 percent of Conservative Protestants and 87 percent of self-identified evangelicals think of the United States as a nation founded on Christian principles, and a majority agrees that "Christian morality should be the law of the land even though all Americans are not Christians." Only one-fourth of other Americans, including Mainline Protestants, agree with that statement.

Moral values got the headlines in 2004. But the religious cleavage is less about the relevance of values than about which values ought to be relevant. Conservative Protestants, like any large aggregation of Americans, are a mixed lot thrown together by one common factor—their religious affiliation, in this case. But that common factor makes them more similar than a random assortment of Americans would be. And the things they have in common have made them closer to Republicans than to Democrats in recent years.

But Conservative Protestants have important differences. Above all, they are more deeply divided on class and class issues than any other similarly large group in American society. In the 1990s, Bill Clinton got more votes from Conservative Protestants with below-average incomes than either George H. W. Bush or Bob Dole did. To repeat Clinton's success in future elections, Democrats need to appeal to the economic needs of those Conservative Protestants who share the values announced by their leaders but who vote their families' interests on election day.

FOUR

The Politics of Conservative Christianity in Black and White

INTRODUCTION

The basic theme of this book is that the correlations between religious conservatism and political and social attitudes are not necessarily overwhelming. Bible Christians are indeed more likely than other Protestants, for example, to oppose abortion under every circumstance, to believe that homosexuality is always wrong, and to advocate restrictions on pornography. They are also more likely to vote Republican. However, not all Conservative Christians are consistently pro-life; in fact, the majority of them are not. And, while the majority still believe that homosexuality is always wrong, the proportion with that conviction declined rapidly in the 1990s. Finally, the additional vote of Conservative Protestants for Republican candidates, over and above that of Mainline American Protestants, is meager—about seven percentage points. Despite the depiction of Conservative Protestants by the media, by frightened liberals, and by the conservative leadership as if they were a massive and disciplined religio-political voting block, they are not. Indeed, we have argued, this image is a stereotype based on overgeneralization and prejudice. It is also a dangerous image because it marginalizes a major segment of American society because of inadequate information, bad information, or often no information at all. There may be a link between Conservative Christian religious convictions and political behavior but it is modest, even by social science standards.

Any attempt to forge a link of logical or doctrinal consistency between conservative religious belief and conservative politics falters when one considers African American Conservative Christians. In general, as we have reported, the doctrinal and ethical perspectives of African Americans in Afro-American Protestant denominations are, if anything, more conservative than those of whites in other Conservative Protestant denominations. Yet religiously committed African Americans, especially those in the Afro-American Protestant denominations, are the most politically liberal of any major group in American society. Whatever their feelings about abortion or evolution or homosexuality, they still vote in overwhelming numbers for Democratic candidates. Thus, while 52 percent of lower-income, white, Conservative Protestants voted Democratic in the 1990s, 90 percent of lower-income Afro-American Protestants did. In the 2004 election those numbers were 22 percent and 96 percent, respectively.[1] Race, therefore, interacts with and ultimately reshapes the link between Conservative Protestantism and conservative politics.

This fact is so patent in contemporary politics that partisans and commentators alike tend to dismiss it as beside the point. We bring it up because of the questions it raises about the confluence of race, religion, and politics in American society. One of us was on the cable newsshow *Hardball* with a prominent Southern Baptist leader. He said rather proudly, we thought, that the evangelical vote had turned heavily Republican in the 2000 presidential election. We replied with the quote from our *New York Times* article that the vote was only marginally higher than for Mainline Protestants. He said that was because we were counting African American voters.[2] We had a chance to interject that his statement was inaccurate before the ineffable Chris Matthews steered us to other matters.

If there had been more time, we might have said that his statement wasn't true and that even if it were, so what? Is not a black evangelical every bit as much an evangelical as a white evangelical? Are they not a quarter of all Conservative Protestants? How do American political commentators overlook the racial difference among Conservative Christians? Is it ignored because it is so obvious? Is it discounted because African Americans are at the center of it? Is our analysis complete if we do not to wonder how very similar strains of traditional Bible Christianity can produce such different outcomes? Does not the diversity of outcomes suggest an intellectual puzzle that must be solved? Do African Americans who are religiously conservative lean Democratic because they are black while white religious conservatives lean in the opposite direction because they are white? If race is what really matters, is the conventional wisdom about Conservative Christian politics confounded?

A lot of questions spring from one overlooked fact. A generation ago white Conservative Protestants were New Deal Democrats. Is there anything "natural" or logical about the apparent link—however weak it may be—between conservative religion and conservative politics? Or does it result from the strife introduced into American society by the civil rights movement, the resulting play of the race card by Richard Nixon, and subsequent attack on big government of the Reagan era and the ongoing struggle between religion and "secular humanism?" Did religious convictions become a surrogate for changing political attitudes?

To put the matter differently, did not Afro-American Protestants drift into the Democratic party after 1934 because that's where their social class and racial position in American society indicated they belonged? Did white Conservative Protestants drift into the Republican Party after 1968 because their failing social and racial position indicated that they belonged there? Did both groups bring into their new political home many of the political styles they once had in common, especially in the South? Was (and is) the "big government" mantra a code word, not necessarily for racism, but for racial conflict—or perhaps more precisely for the wins and the losses both groups experienced in the later years of the twentieth century? Is the politically conservative propensity of white Conservative Protestants at least in part a protest against their perceived loss of political power, a protest only marginally linked to their religious convictions? Is it also a protest against what they perceive to be an attack on all religious faith by "modernists" or "secularists" who are allies of big government?

These questions are important and we must ask them, even if answers are not easy to find. History is a rough and somewhat contradictory guide. Religion inspired abolitionists, black and white. From the Emancipation to the 1920s, African Americans supported the "party of Lincoln." But Franklin D. Roosevelt sought black support, north and south. Truman integrated the armed forces, and the Kennedys aggressively went at segregation when the Supreme Court called for "all deliberate speed." Does the hue and cry about "evangelicals" and "fundamentalists" in fact provide a religious cover for a more basic experience of gain and loss? Might both blacks and whites bring their religious stories along with them as they change political places so that the same stories will correlate with opposed political reactions? Operationally might belief in the word-for-word literal inerrancy of the Bible intensify white Conservative Protestants' propensity to vote Republican and black Conservative Protestants' propensity to vote Democratic? If this should be the case then "evangelical"—in the strictest sense of the word—means *Republican* in some circumstances and *Democratic* in other circumstances.

RACE "DIRECTS" RELIGIOUS IMPACT

Literal interpretation of the Bible and frequent religious practice push African Americans toward the Democrats and whites toward the Republicans (see table 4.1).[3] Literalism intensifies the diametrically opposed political orientations in the two groups; it pulls them further apart politically. Belief in the "fundamental" common doctrine that identifies each as "evangelical" in fact moves them in opposite political directions. To put the matter differently, the Gospel does correlate with political orientation; the direction of the correlation depends on believers' social contexts, which in this case means their differing racial ancestries.

Religious practice also affects the direction of partisanship. African Americans who attend services and/or read scripture more often are more inclined to vote for Democrats; whites move in the Republican direction as they increase their attendance and scripture reading. The strongest Democrats in this tabulation are the African Americans in Afro-American denominations who read their Bible daily, followed closely by those who attend church weekly. The strongest Republicans are the whites in Conservative Protestant denominations who read their Bibles daily and attend services weekly.

We note also that the correlations represented in table 4.1 are very robust. They exist even when our statistical adjustments hold constant the possibly confounding effects of gender, region, marital status, education, income and liberal/conservative political orientation.

Table 4.1 reveals similar tendencies outside the Afro-American and Conservative Protestant denominations, especially among the white

Table 4.1 Votes for Democrats in the 1992–2000 presidential elections by race and denomination

	African American		White	
Item	Afro-American Protestant (%)	Other religion (%)	Conservative Protestant (%)	Mainline Protestant (%)
Bible is:				
Word of God	96	92	34	40
Inspired word	94	89	37	47
Book of fables	86	—[a]	54	61
Attend services				
Weekly	95	91	28	40
2–3 times per month	95	90	43	43
Once a month	93	98	41	50
Less often	91	90	48	51
Never	—[a]	—[a]	48	57
Read the Bible in past year				
Daily	100	82	27	42
Weekly	95	—[a]	34	35
Less often	95	—[a]	52	53
Not at all	—[a]	—[a]	47	56

[a]Too few cases for reliable calculation

SOURCE: General Social Surveys, 1993–2004.

Mainline Protestants. But the effects of attendance and frequent Bible study turn out to be significantly weaker for Mainline than Conservative Protestants when tested in the multivariate context.

How can the same religious doctrine produce in people who are similar in all other matters such different political behavior? Conservative Christianity in both its American forms constitutes a single powerful religious story—God is on the side of His people as they struggle for freedom. In their own way the Conservative Protestants and the Afro-American Protestants identify with that story and bestow their allegiance of party loyalty to the party that best reflects that collective self-image. Is that dubious? Hardly. Religious stories are multilayered and polysemous. They are not completely malleable, not inkblots into which any meaning can be projected. But they do admit of different interpretations depending on the context in which they are being told. The Exodus story in which Moses led the chosen people out of Egypt can be applied by any group that feels that it is going forth on some sacred mission.

God communicates absolute religious truth to those on the mission and watches over them as they struggle for freedom, whether the exodus on which they are marching is liberation from racism or liberation from secular humanism. Since this story is there for Christians to make their own, it is adaptable to whatever struggle for freedom a given Christian people might experience. One might perhaps argue that biblical literalism provides rich resources for any populist Christian movement since it provides motivation and validation of one's particular populist cause. "Mine eyes have seen the glory of the coming of the Lord . . . His truth is marching on." One names the truth, and there is the Lord marching with "us" against "them." Conservative Christianity, once mobilized, is likely to be militant politically for whatever godly cause—abolition, prohibition, civil rights, the right to life. The directionality of the militant march depends on whom the cause defines as the opponent. Race, as such, is not so much the issue in contemporary Christian militancy in the United States as it is occasion of the difference between the two Christian militant marches—one towards a time when we shall overcome and the other towards a restoration of God's place in public life.

POINTING FINGERS

Liberals who decry the militant political stands of Conservative Protestants should beware of trying to have it both ways when they turn around to praise the militant political stands of Afro-American Protestants—and perhaps sing black freedom songs. Logically they should oppose the political effects of militant literalism wherever it appears—or accept it as an inevitable populist political story in this country. Republicans, it must be remembered, supported prohibition and Democrats (in the north) opposed it.

Therefore we suggest as the conclusion to this chapter that Conservative Christianity can promote a political agenda. American political history teaches us, though, that the direction it leads men and women cannot be determined in advance. Evangelical militancy is not new, and while it is distasteful when it marches in the opposite direction of our own cause, it can be also be embraced (at risk of inconsistency) to support the "onward, Christian soldiers" march of one's own cause.

While some disregard history to demonize Conservative Christianity's involvement in politics that promote a conservative social agenda, we remind them that religious zeal in the pursuit of political objectives has not been the monopoly of one particular political camp. In the present era the same religious principles that lead whites to the right lead blacks to the left.

FIVE

Freedom, Inequality, and Conservative Christianity

Congress shall make no law respecting an establishment of religion or prohibiting the free exercise thereof.
—*Bill of Rights, Article 1*

INTRODUCTION

The First Amendment to the U.S. Constitution guarantees two kinds of religious freedom—the freedom to practice one's own religion and the freedom from having to practice other peoples' religions. Congress cannot interfere with citizens' religious practices or impose practices on them. There is a symmetry and tension between the freedom to do a thing and the freedom from being forced to do it that animates a lot of discussions about Conservative Christianity. Christians take pains to express their religion in public, and their critics take equal pains to avoid participating in those expressions. It works the other way, too. Secularists and modernists read the establishment clause as a ban on all religion in public, and Conservative Christians hear that as a ban on their right to free exercise. The First Amendment rights that foster American religious freedom can, if people press their claims to those rights to the maximum, divide the nation too.

Activists can get pretty loud on these subjects. And both sides tend to look for opportunities to assert their rights in order to rally support to their side of the issue. So in 2000, Alabama Chief Justice Roy Moore installed a 2.6 ton granite monument to the Ten Commandments at the Alabama high courthouse knowing that federal courts would force him to remove them; they did in November 2003. But Judge Moore scored his points; a CNN-*USA Today* poll found that 77 percent of American adults disapproved of the federal court ruling. On the other side, Michael Newdow sued to stop his daughter's California school from opening the school day with "willing students" reciting the Pledge of Allegiance. A California judge ruled the practice unconstitutional, and the Ninth Circuit Court of Appeals upheld that ruling. The Supreme Court dismissed the case for lack of standing without deciding the First Amendment issue.[1]

Lost amidst the duels over liberty are concerns regarding equality. Do Christians have any brief for equality? The words after "under God" in the Pledge of Allegiance tout "liberty and justice for all." Does justice demand equality? Jesus exhibited a bias toward the poor but is quoted at least as often for saying "the poor you shall always have with you" as for admonishing his followers to feed and clothe "the least of my brothers."

Before this discussion raises any concerns about who is a hypocrite and who has their priorities out of line, let us note that religions have more standing for their claims to religious liberty than for economic justice issues. Their own liberty if not their existence depends on how the religious liberty debates are resolved. Their image of a just society is also important but not as central. And those who would speak up for a religious perspective on social justice cannot stake out the kind of privileged place in the debates about justice that they can in the debates about liberty.

In this chapter we explore the hot issues of freedom and equality. What we find conforms to many other findings in this book. Conservative Christians differ by degrees. But they are far from being extremists.

THE QUALITY OF OUR FREEDOM

The 2000 GSS included an extensive module on freedom. Several items are relevant for what they reveal about how American religious traditions view liberty today. The first two ask how much:

- *How much freedom do you think Americans have today? Would you say they have complete freedom, a great deal of freedom, a moderate degree of freedom, not much freedom, or no freedom at all?*
- *And about you yourself? Would you say right now that you have complete freedom, a great deal of freedom, a moderate degree of freedom, not much freedom, or no freedom at all?*

Seven of ten American adults are very pleased with freedom for their fellow Americans and for themselves; 10 percent see "complete freedom" and 60 percent see "a great deal." The other 30 percent say Americans in general and they personally have "a moderate degree" or less.

Conservative and Afro-American Protestants are significantly less sanguine about freedom in America than Mainline Protestants, Catholics, and Jews are (see fig. 5.1). Over one-third of Conservative and Afro-American Protestants think that there is moderate freedom at best; only one-quarter of the other Christians and Jews share their negative assessment. Concerns are even higher for people who prefer other religions or none at all; 40 percent of them see a moderate degree or less. The fact that the greatest concerns arise among people outside the Judeo-Christian majority is itself a cause for concern. So too is the correspondence between answers to the first question, about Americans in general, and the second, about the respondent personally. Conservative Protestants, Jews, and secularists are the only groups that see more threat to the freedoms of Americans in general that threats to their own freedom.

People who feel their personal liberty threatened tend not to vote. Respondents who answered the freedom questions were also asked how they voted in 1996. Turnout in that election was 70 percent among those who felt complete freedom or a great deal but less than 50 percent for those who felt only moderate freedom or less.[2] Among voters, President Clinton won 60 percent among those with a sense of complete freedom, but just 39 percent among those who felt they do not have much freedom. Perot did best in that discontented "not much freedom" category—winning 22 percent of their votes. Another question asked about changes in freedom. Clinton won 61 percent among voters who felt they had more freedom than "in the past" but lost with just 37 percent among voters who felt they had less freedom. Perot got 22 percent among voters who felt they had less freedom. These results are robust; we see the same pattern when we add these two freedom measures to the multivariate voting model we used in chapter 3.

The same module includes several questions about the freedom to do some things and the freedom to avoid doing others. None are specifically about religious freedom, but that actually helps us uncover general philosophical differences by removing religious peoples' self-interest in religious freedom from the deliberation.

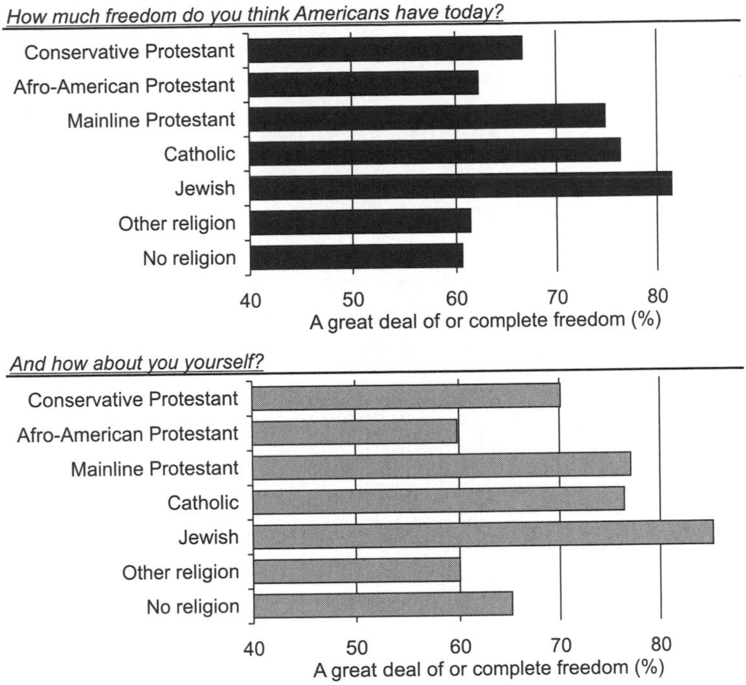

Figure 5.1 Assessments of freedom by religion. SOURCE: General Social Survey, 2000.

I'm going to read you several statements about freedom.
Each one may say something true and important about freedom, but I'd like to know how important each statement is to you. Is it one of the most important things about freedom, extremely important, very important, somewhat important, or not too important?

- *A. Freedom is being left alone to do what I want.*
- *B. Freedom is having a government that doesn't spy on me or interfere in my life.*
- *C. True freedom is feeling an inner spiritual peace.*
- *D. Freedom is having the right to participate in politics and elections.*
- *E. Freedom is having the power to choose and do what I want in life.*
- *F. Freedom is being able to express unpopular ideas without fearing for my safety.*

The answers to these items tend to affirm the question's premise that "each one may say something true and important about freedom," that is, all the answers are skewed toward "one of the most important" and "extremely important." But there is some interesting variation. Most of the items focus on individual freedoms. Pairing D and F, though, gives us a chance to see the "freedom to" and "freedom from" tension in action. In particular, Conservative Protestants are the only group to score below average on both the freedom to participate in politics and the freedom to express unpopular ideas (see fig. 5.2, which arrays both items by religion). They are not the lowest on either, just the only denomination to score below average on both. Surprisingly, Afro-Americans score lowest on political participation—surprising because the right to political participation was so central to the civil rights movement. Mainline Protestants are the denomination least interested in the freedom to express unpopular ideas without fear. Catholics and, by a wide margin, Jews think both political participation and the expression of unpopular ideas among the most important aspects of freedom.[3] People with other religions or no religion are not distinct on political participation but place more than average importance on the freedom to express unpopular ideas—a telling ranking considering that their religious views are likely to be unpopular with most Americans.

Libertarians often allay worries about rising inequality with arguments to the effect that, in a free society, people ought to get to keep the money they earn. The freedom module approached it with this item: *In a free society, it is all right if a few people accumulate a lot of wealth and property while many others live in poverty.* This proved to be a difficult item; 20 percent of American adults could not decide if they agreed or disagreed with it; that is high for a survey of this kind. Responses differed significantly by religion, but the association was weak. Forty percent of Conservative Protestants disagreed with that item, identical to the fraction of Mainline Protestants and virtually the same as Catholics (41 percent) and people with no religion (42 percent). Jews were significantly less likely to disagree (33 percent), and Afro-American Protestants (59 percent) and people with other religions (51 percent) were significantly more likely to agree. Jews look less distinctive if we focus, instead, on the agreements. But the main point is that religion does little to guide Americans through

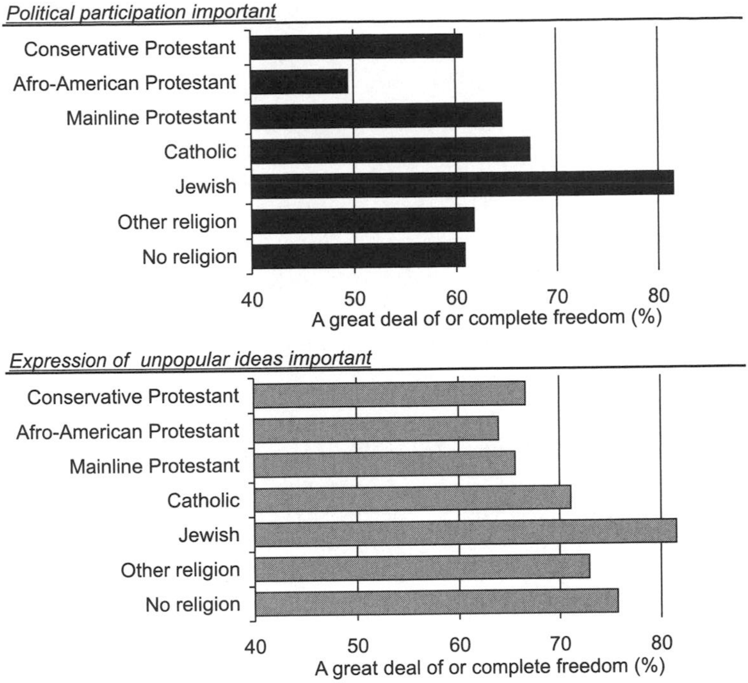

Figure 5.2 Importance of different kinds of freedom by religion. SOURCE: General Social Survey, 2000.

the dilemma of economic freedom. We will return to the topic of inequality later in this chapter.[4]

The freedom module also asked for a summary judgment about satisfaction with American democracy: *On the whole, are you very satisfied, fairly satisfied, not very satisfied, or not at all satisfied with the way democracy works in the United States.* Four of five Americans were satisfied, at least to some extent, with American democracy in the spring of 2000. Dissatisfaction, where it existed, differed sharply by religion. One in four Conservative Protestants were dissatisfied; we would have expected one in five if they were right on the national average. People with no religion share the same level of concern (slightly higher at 27 percent). Mainline Protestants (16 percent dissatisfied), Catholics (also 16 percent), and Jews (just 7 percent) are the most satisfied with how American democracy works. Afro-American Protestants are, somewhat surprisingly, only average in their level of dissatisfaction with American democracy (19 percent).

NATIONAL PRIDE

When chants of "USA, USA, USA" ring through the stands at the Olympics and other international events, millions of Americans get goose bumps while Europeans cringe. Some Americans share the European reaction. The cringing has less to do with sports than with international affairs. The United States has the power to go it alone in world events and it makes some people—abroad and at home—nervous. In the context of the 2003 invasion of Iraq, in particular, European critics from public officials to editorial writers to public intellectuals thought they saw a link between American religiosity and U.S. foreign policy. They fear a connection between religiosity and nationalism as the road to fascism.[5] Are Conservative Protestants more nationalistic than other Americans?

The 1995 national identity module of the ISSP, included in the 1996 GSS, offers us a few questions to use in assessing this hypothesis.

How much do you agree or disagree with the following statements?

- *A. I would rather be a citizen of America than of any other country in the world.*
- *C. The world would be a better place if people from other countries were more like the Americans.*
- *D. Generally speaking, America is a better country than most other countries.*
- *How proud are you of America in each of the following?*
- *B. Its political influence in the world.*
- *C. America's economic achievements.*
- *E. Its scientific and technological achievements.*
- *G. Its achievements in the arts and literature.*
- *H. America's armed forces.*
- *I. Its history.*

Now we would like to ask a few questions about relations between America and other countries. How much do you agree or disagree with the following statements?

- *D. America should follow its own interests, even if this leads to conflicts with other nations.*

Conservative Protestants have more national pride than other Americans and feel more strongly than people of other religions that the rest of the world ought to imitate the United States (see table 5.1). Almost half strongly agree that they would rather be citizens of the United States than of any other country in the world compared with roughly 40 percent of Americans in other Christian religions and 35 percent of secular Americans. Only 16 percent of Conservative Protestants—compared with a quarter or more of other Christians and 35 percent of people with no religion—disagree that the world would be better off if it was more like America.

While there is no harm in rooting for sports teams or even touting one's standard of living or achievements in culture or science, other countries could have cause to worry if the source of pride falls closer to the militaristic and historical roots associated with rampant nationalism. And that, for the most part, is where the distinctive pride of Conservative Protestants lies. While their attitudes toward America's place in the worlds of politics and the arts and sciences are indistinguishable from those of Mainline Protestants,[6] they are significantly

Table 5.1 National pride and nationalism by religion

	Religion				
	Protestant				
Question / Answer	Conservative (%)	Afro-Amer. (%)	Mainline (%)	Catholic (%)	No religion (%)
"America is a better country than most"					
Agree (%)*	46	39	37	40	35
"World better if people more like Americans"					
Disagree (%)*	16	24	28	27	35
Very proud of:					
Political influence in the world	24	16	24	24	14
Economic achievements	30	17	30	33	24
Achievements in arts and literature	27	31	27	37	26
Scientific and technical achievements	52	30	52	53	47
Armed forces*	57	36	52	50	39
History*	55	36	52	53	38
Spending on the military					
Too little (%)*	28	16	17	13	10
America should follow its own interests					
Agree (%)*	51	54	39	44	40

SOURCE: General Social Survey, 1996.

* Conservative Protestants significantly different from at least one other denomination ($p < .05$).

more likely than others to express pride in the armed forces. Conservative Protestants back that up by calling for an increase in military spending that others see no need for. And as we described in chapter 3, people who support more military spending vote Republican. Finally, on the one item that asks about foreign policy directly, Conservative Protestants and Afro-American Protestants are significantly more likely than Mainline Protestants to agree that the United States ought to pursue its own interests even if doing so leads to conflicts with other nations. In every respect, people with no religion express less pride and more opposition to these nationalist items.

THE LIMITS OF STATE AND MARKET

Freedom and nationalism can foster inequality. But equal treatment is a key element of America's fundamental freedoms. Inequality, in that sense, presents Americans with a dilemma. They tolerate some inequality, at least unequal economic outcomes, as a necessary consequence of the freedom to pursue economic opportunities. But how much inequality is too much? More crucially, do they agree on how much inequality to tolerate and does their religious commitment help them in that assessment? Does religion hasten or impede consensus on how America's riches ought to be distributed?

The study of inequality and how people view it have been recurring themes in the ISSP. The 1999 inequality module (part of the 2000 GSS) is typical of those efforts. We focus on a few key questions from it. First the assessment (which was asked in 1987 and 1996 too):

Do you agree or disagree:

- *A. Differences in income in America are too large.*
- *B. It is the responsibility of the government to reduce the differences in income between people with high incomes and those with low incomes.*

Americans noticed the rise in inequality. The fraction agreeing strongly that the income differences are too big more than doubled—from 16 percent to 33 percent between 1987 and 1996—then dropped back to 25 percent in 2000. Differences among religions were not statistically significant, which is, in fact, sociologically significant. Stereotypes would characterize Afro-American Protestants, Jews, and secularists as egalitarians and other Protestants and Catholics as nonegalitarians. But all of America's religions divide equally into egalitarians and nonegalitarians.

Religious differences kick in when the question shifts to government action to reduce the gap between rich and poor. In 2000, 28 percent of Conservative and Mainline Protestants agreed the government should do something compared with 36 percent of Catholics, Jews, and the secular, 44 percent of those with other religions, and 53 percent of Afro-American Protestants. Furthermore, the finding is quite robust. Conservative and Mainline Protestants are significantly less likely to agree to government efforts to close the gap between rich and poor incomes even after we statistically adjust for family income and personal political views, when we further adjust for the extent to which they think the income gap is too large (i.e., item A in this pair), and even when we control for the full battery of sociodemographic variables.[7] The differences appear to have little actual religious content because literal interpretation of the Bible and church attendance have no effect on whether one thinks the government has a responsibility to reduce economic inequality. Nor is it about taxes. An item that asks about personal taxes (too much tax, the right amount, too little, or no tax at all) has no effect either. People who support the principle of progressive taxation also support government taking action to reduce income differences, but the difference between Conservative Protestants and Catholics actually increases after adjusting for supporting progressive taxation. That is because Conservative Protestants support progressive taxation as much as Catholics do (and significantly more than Mainline Protestants do).

If religious views, general liberal-conservative orientation, and taxes cannot explain the robust religious differences, what can? Perhaps a preference for the government taking egalitarian action is one of the irreducible Catholic-Protestant differences over whether social problems have communal or individual solutions (see Greeley 2000, chap. 4).[8] Before pursuing this explanation further, it is important to note that Conservative and Mainline Protestants see eye-to-eye on this issue. It is really a Protestant-Catholic divide this time, not a distinction between Conservative and Mainline Protestants that is at issue.

We have relatively few measures to use in attacking this problem. The social networks measures that Greeley (2000) used were not repeated in 2000. One possibility is to work with other policy preferences. The idea of a living wage, making sure that workers are paid enough to support families, has been associated with Catholic thought since the nineteenth century.[9] The 2000 inequality module asks two relevant questions:

In deciding how much people ought to earn, how important should each of these things be, in your opinion:

- *D. What is needed to support a family?*
- *E. Whether the person has children to support?*

We combine these two items into a nine-point scale. Another item in that battery—*F: How well he or she does the job*—works as a reverse measure, emphasizing the Protestant work ethic. Two other items approach the issue of social justice by focusing on the consequences of income disparities:

Is it just or unjust—right or wrong—that people with higher incomes can

- *A. . . . buy better health care than people with lower incomes?*
- *B. . . . buy better education for their children than people with lower incomes?*

We combine them into a second nine-point scale. Finally, we consider this question about rich and poor countries:

Turning to international differences, do you agree or disagree:

- *B. People in wealthy countries should make an additional tax contribution to help people in poor countries.*

The idea here is that those with a communal bias typical of Catholic social justice might be more inclined than others to endorse an internationalist approach to global inequalities.

We consider three models to explain differences in answering the question about the government's responsibility to reduce the gap between rich and poor. The first one measures the gross differences among Conservative Protestants, Mainline Protestants, and Catholics.[10] The second model adds the most relevant personal characteristics, given the topic the dependent variable raises: family income, personal political liberalism-conservatism, and one's view of how big the income differences between rich and poor are.

Table 5.2 Differences among Christian denominations in attitudes as to the government's responsibility to reduce income inequality

Religion	No controls	Income, perception income gaps are a problem, and political views	All controls
Conservative Protestant	−.45	−.45	−.48
	(.16)	(.16)	(.17)
Afro-American Protestant	.44	−.01	.01
	(.29)	(.30)	(.31)
Mainline Protestant	−.65	−.66	−.57
	(.17)	(.17)	(.18)
Catholic	—	—	—

NOTES: Numbers are ordered logistic regression coefficients; numbers in parentheses are robust standard errors. All models also include dummy variables for Jewish, other religion, and no religion. The additional controls in the "all controls" model are education, gender, Latino ancestry, region, and suburban residence. $N = 1{,}004$.

While living wage, justice perception, international redistribution, and attitudes regarding progressive taxation all affect egalitarian attitudes, they only explain a small part of the Protestant-Catholic difference. Together these factors account for one-sixth of the difference between Conservative Protestants and Catholics and one-fourth of the difference between Mainline Protestants and Catholics. With better measures of communalism, we might do better, but at this point we have exhausted the data resources.

What would a government do if it had a mandate to reduce income differences? History and comparative analysis show that industrial management works. In the 1950s and 1960s inequality in the United States fell to historically low levels, largely through the institutionalized collective bargaining of the time (Fischer et al. 1996). And today the countries like Germany, the Netherlands, and the Scandinavian countries that have industrial management systems in place have lower inequality. But scandals involving pensions and rackets, first in the United Mine Workers and then in the Teamsters, eroded Americans' confidence in unions. More recently the savings and loan bailout in the 1980s and the Wall Street frauds of recent years eroded confidence in business (Paxton 2005). These trends do not differ by religion.

If the parties to wage-setting cannot regulate themselves to hold down inequality, then the government's only recourse, if it is to reduce inequality, is to tax affluent people to supplement the incomes of those who are struggling. That policy, known as progressive taxation, was put in place for the first time in the United States in 1913 after passage of the Sixteenth Amendment to the U.S. Constitution. Support for progressive taxation has come into question in recent years. Even though candidates who run on "flat tax" platforms do not do very well, the general "starve the beast" approach to taxation that conservatives tend to take challenges the redistributive efforts of progressive taxation. And the combination of welfare "reform" in 1996 and tax cuts in the George W. Bush era raise the specter of regressive taxation.

Are Conservative Christians a prime constituency for ending the era of progressive taxation? From the 1996 ISSP module on the role of government we have two items that suggest not.

> *Generally, how would you describe taxes in America today?*
> *We mean all taxes together, including social security, income tax, sales tax, and all the rest.*
>
> - *A. First, for those with high incomes, are taxes . . .*
> - *B. Next, for those with middle incomes, are taxes . . .*
> - *C. Lastly, for those with low incomes, are taxes . . .*
> - [answers: much too high, too high, about right, too low, much too low]
> - *Do you think that people with high incomes should pay a larger share of their income in taxes than those with low incomes, the same share, or a smaller share. . .*

We combined parts A and C of the first question to classify people as "progressive" (i.e., rich peoples' taxes are too low and poor peoples' taxes are too high), "anti-tax" (i.e., rich and poor peoples' taxes are too high), "satisfied" (i.e., rich and poor peoples' taxes are about right), regressive (i.e., rich peoples' taxes are too high and poor peoples' taxes are too low) and "mixed" (i.e., all other combinations). Table 5.3 shows the results.

The religious differences are statistically significant but small. Even more important for understanding what is (and is not) conservative about Conservative Protestants is that they are more progressive (30 percent) than Catholics (23 percent). Thus the premise adopted

Table 5.3 Attitude toward taxes by religion

	Religion			
	Protestant			
View of taxes	Conservative (%)	Afro-Amer. (%)	Mainline (%)	Catholic (%)
Progressive	30	30	28	23
Antitax	25	37	26	28
Satisfied	9	7	10	16
Regressive	36	25	37	33
Total	100	100	100	100
N	309	67	276	267

SOURCE: General Social Survey, 1996.

by many who approach the religious factor in American politics is wrong. As our data show, the Conservative Protestants are conservative on religious issues but not on the equality issues we discuss in this chapter.

EGALITARIAN VIEWS AND THE VOTE

Egalitarians of all religions strongly support the Democrats; people who want to keep government away from the income distribution support Republicans. And this is one of the strongest statistical relationships we will see in this book.

Over three-fourths of strong egalitarians voted for Clinton in 1996 while two-thirds of strong laissez-faire types voted for Dole. This result is very robust; it holds up in our full voting model. It does not

Table 5.4 Presidential vote by egalitarianism

	Government's responsibility to reduce income differences			
Vote in 1996	Agree strongly (%)	Agree (%)	Disagree (%)	Disagree strongly (%)
Clinton	79	70	50	25
Dole	7	14	35	59
Perot	12	14	15	13
Other	2	1	1	2
Total	100	100	100	100
N	121	311	387	264

SOURCE: General Social Survey, 2000.

explain any of the pattern of voting by religion. It does, however, account for 72 percent of the effect of family income on vote.

CONCLUSION

Conservative Protestants are conspicuously patriotic. Their members are prominent in the military and at public events that have a patriotic flavor. They express more pride, especially in the military, than other Americans do.

Conservative Protestants approach American inequalities pretty much how other Americans do.[11] Majorities of both Conservative and Mainline Protestants assert that reducing the income gap between rich and poor is not an appropriate government role. Like most Americans, Conservative Protestants vote for Democrats if they want more equality and for Republicans if inequality is not an issue.

Across the board, religious differences in both nationalist and egalitarian values are modest differences of degree. And Conservative Protestants are neither extreme in their views of the U.S. place in the world nor ignorant of differences between rich and poor at home. They are nationalistically inclined more than other groups, to a degree and significantly more militaristic.

Most important, though, is the way that the differences that exist in the economic worldviews of Conservative Protestants affect their politics. We already saw an income divide that makes working-class and struggling Conservative Protestants far closer to the Democrats than to the Republicans while affluent Conservative Protestants join other affluent Americans in forming the current Republican base. Here we see an ideological cleavage that not only corresponds exactly to the material divide but also amplifies it. The political gap between egalitarian and libertarian is wider even than the political gap between those who would gain from redistribution and those who would pay for it.

SIX

A Social Portrait of Conservative Christians

INTRODUCTION

Stereotypes about Conservative Protestants abound. Religious issues aside, they are pigeonholed as Southern, uneducated gun owners who live in trailers parks or at least far from town. In a word, "rubes." Some send-ups caricature them as abstemious teetotalers; others put a beer bottle in their hands. While there are hints of these kinds of geographical, educational, and lifestyle differences in the data, the similarities between Conservative Protestants and other Americans swamp their differences. Yes, they are more prevalent in the South. Yes, they have slightly less education and money. Yes, they live life somewhat differently than others might. But all these characteristics are shades of difference—matters of degree, not kind.[1] Indeed, our research identifies only one truly distinctive religious tradition—the Afro-American Protestant one.

In this chapter we will draw a social portrait of Conservative Protestants and other religious traditions from data on where each lives, the race and ethnicity of members, marriage and family patterns, education, socioeconomic status, and key habits and activities. All of our calculations come from the General Social Surveys conducted between 1996 and 2004.[2] Most percentages are based on the whole English-speaking adult population. Calculations involving education and socioeconomic status restrict attention to adults twenty-five years old and over whose main activity was something other than "attending school." We will see that the Conservative Protestants are everywhere—though they are more Southern than other groups. They are whiter because segregation split them from the Afro-American Protestant churches with whom they share most religious precepts and practices. They are also slightly more likely to be married, less educated, and less affluent than many other groups. Most behavioral differences between Conservative Protestants and others reflect these differences of geography, education, and income.

GEOGRAPHY

A slim majority—51 percent—of Conservative Protestants and a bigger majority—57 percent—of Afro-American Protestants live in Southern states. One in five Catholics (21 percent), one in five Jews (also 21 percent), and one in four people with no religious preference (25 percent) live in Southern states; Catholics and Jews concentrate in the Northeast (33 and 43 percent, respectively) while people with no religion are spread pretty evenly across the nation (their 23 percent in the Pacific region is significantly above the overall Pacific share of 14 percent). The overall association between religion and region is moderately strong as gauged by κ, our preferred measure of qualitative association (see our methodological appendix for a discussion of this measure of strength of association); κ for religion by region is .60.[3] Figure 6.1 displays the differences on this and other aspects of geography.

The political geography of red and blue states conforms to many expectations but unveils a few surprises as well. The first surprise is that the majority of American adults live in blue states. Kerry did not win because his majority in these states was much narrower than Bush's edge in the red states. And the president won more electoral college votes in the battleground states than the Democratic challenger did.

Conservative Protestants and Mainline Protestants alike settle away from the major metropolitan areas. Half are in the urban areas of places too small to rank in the top one hundred metropolitan areas. In contrast, nearly half of the Protestants who belong to Afro-American denominations are in the central cities of the top one hundred metropolitan areas.

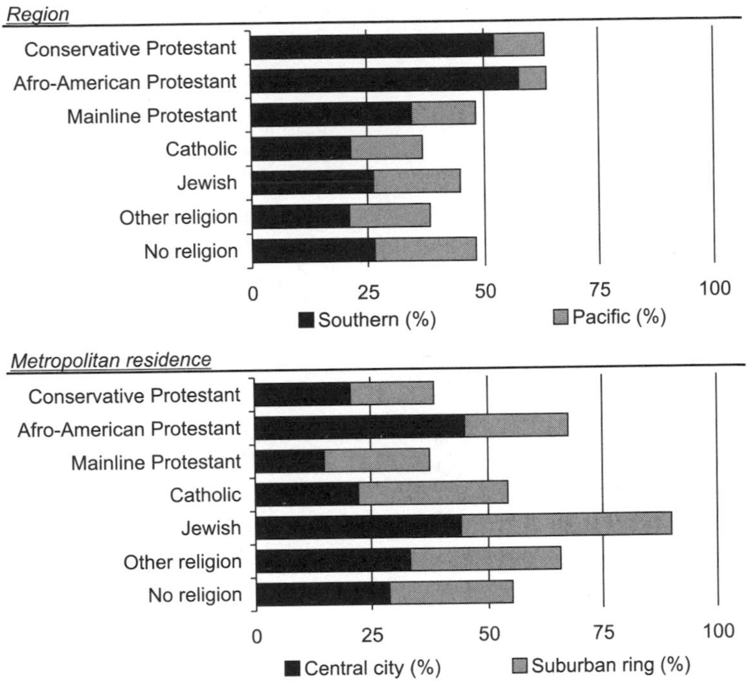

Figure 6.1 Region and metropolitan residence by religion. SOURCE: General Social Surveys, 2000–2004.

ANCESTRY

Whites predominate in both the Conservative and Mainline Protestant churches—89 percent of Conservatives are white and 92 percent of Mainline Protestants are. Afro-Americans predominate in the traditionally black churches—95 percent. Jews are 97 percent white. The Latino immigration has diversified the ancestry profile of Catholics, and the pattern of falling away from religion affects each ancestry group and diversifying the "no religion" category. The κ of 1.16 indicates an even stronger association than we find for the geography variables. The details are in table 6.1.

Immigrants are reshaping the American religious landscape. Many come from Catholic countries, and they are definitely affecting Catholicism the most. Only 4 percent of Conservative Protestants, are

Table 6.1 Race, immigrant status, and ethnicity by religion

	Religion						
	Protestant						
Variable / category	Con-servative (%)	Afro-Amer. (%)	Mainline (%)	Catholic (%)	Jewish (%)	No religion (%)	
*Racial Ancestry**							
White	79	5	89	73	97	77	
African American	14	93	6	3	1	10	
Latino	5	1	2	19	2	8	
Other	2	0	2	4	0	5	
Total	100	100	100	100	100	100	
N	2,886	714	2,625	2,762	223	1,573	
						κ	1.32
*Immigrant generation**							
Foreign-born	5	4	5	16	15	10	
Foreign-born parent	3	2	4	8	14	5	
Generation 3	14	5	21	37	52	23	
Generation 4+	78	90	69	39	19	62	
Total	100	100	100	100	100	100	
N	2,882	711	2,624	2,756	223	1,569	
						κ	1.02
*Ethnicity**							
German	18	0	24	15	3	15	
Irish / Scotish	11	0	11	15	1	10	
English	18	1	25	5	2	16	
Italian	2	0	2	12	0	5	
Other European	11	1	16	19	92	16	
Native American	7	1	3	1	0	4	
Latin American	5	1	2	19	1	8	
African	14	93	6	3	0	10	
Asian	1	0	2	4	0	4	
"American"	2	0	2	2	0	1	
Uncodeable	12	1	7	4	0	10	
Total	100	100	100	100	100	100	
N	2,886	714	2,625	2,762	223	1,573	
						κ	1.09

* Differences among religions statistically significant ($p < .05$).

immigrants and another 4 percent are the children of immigrants. Furthermore, the Conservative Protestants are overwhelmingly from the groups that came to the United States first—English, Irish, German, and African. The white Conservative Protestants are also the adults most likely to give a response that the GSS cannot code; 15 percent of them name no country or part of the world or cannot choose a single one out of their complicated ethnic background.

Although 95 percent of all Afro-American Protestants are African American, a sizable minority of African Americans—45 percent in recent years—belong to other denominations. Table 6.2 shows the distribution of African American across denominations along with several variables that differ significantly across denominations. The Afro-American denominations attract a significantly larger proportion of African American women (59 percent) than men (53 percent). The other denominations are equally attractive to men and women;

Table 6.2 Denominational differences among African Americans

	Religion						
	Protestant						
Variable / category	Conser-vative	Afro-American	Main-line	Catholic	Other religion	No religion	Total
	African Americans 18 Years and Older						
Total (%)	11	57	11	8	3	10	100
Women (%)	12	59	11	7	2	7	100
Men (%)	10	53	10	9	4	13	100
Southern (%)	46	57	54	39	33	39	51
65 years and older (%)	10	14	11	9	5	3	11
Foreign-born (%)	11	3	9	23	24	7	7
	African Americans 25 Years and Older						
College graduates (%)	9	8	15	14	13	9	10
Family income ($000s)							
Women	$18	$21	$20	$22	$17	$17	$19
Men	$25	$30	$30	$27	$31	$29	$26
Marital status							
Married once	25	36	26	29	19	17	26
Remarried	8	8	8	5	9	5	8
Widowed	13	6	13	12	7	6	11
Divorced /separated	26	22	32	20	39	21	26
Never married	28	28	21	34	27	52	30
Total	100	100	100	100	100	100	100

NOTES: Differences among denominations are all statistically significant (.05 level). The total number of cases is 2,012; number of cases 25 and over is 1,797.

the other element of difference in black men's and women's religious preferences stems from men's greater aversion to organized religions altogether, that is, their preference for no religion (11 percent for men and 7 percent for women).

African Americans in Afro-American denominations are more Southern, senior, and native than other African Americans, especially when contrasted with Catholic blacks and those who have other religions and no religious preference. They also have less education and income. African Americans in the Mainline Protestant denominations and those who are Catholic or prefer other religions are better educated and have higher annual incomes. The income differences are particularly large among the men. Some of Afro-American Protestants' economic disadvantages can be ascribed to other factors that affect income—education, age, region, and marital status (especially among women). But large residual differences persist even after we adjust the income data for a long list of relevant factors. Our data do not allow us to say whether religion is a consequence or mere correlate of income.

FAMILY

Family values and an emphasis on marriage give the current fascination with Conservative Protestants its political edge. But Conservative Protestants are not distinct in marital status. They rank third—behind Jews and Catholics—in the prevalence of stable marriages. Protestants in Afro-American denominations are the most likely to divorce (leaving out those who never married); Conservative Protestants nearly as likely. That shows up here in the high percentages currently remarried and currently divorced or separated. African Americans in general are significantly less likely to marry than others as reflected in the 31 percent of Afro-American Protestants who are unmarried. The high percentage of never married respondents among adults with no religion reflects the youth of this group. The association between religion and marital status is statistically significant, but the κ of .61 indicates that the overall association is weaker than the associations involving religion and ethnicity. Details are in table 6.3.

In the middle of the twentieth century, Conservative Protestants had about one child more than other Protestants. That difference

Table 6.3 Family status by religion

Variable / category	Protestant: Conservative (%)	Protestant: Afro-Amer. (%)	Protestant: Mainline (%)	Catholic (%)	Jewish (%)	No religion (%)	
*Marital status**							
Married once	39	23	39	42	44	26	
Remarried	15	8	13	9	11	10	
Widowed	11	13	13	8	8	4	
Divorced / separated	19	24	19	16	15	21	
Never married	16	31	17	25	22	39	
Total	100	100	100	100	100	100	
N	3,847	1,332	3,990	3,852	321	1,932	
						κ	.64
*Children Ever Born**							
None	23	18	25	30	34	45	
1 or 2	44	41	45	40	45	38	
3 or 4	26	27	25	22	18	14	
5 or more	7	15	5	8	3	3	
Total	100	100	100	100	100	100	
Mean	2.01	2.44	1.83	1.85	1.51	1.21	
Standard deviation	1.67	2.03	1.51	1.77	1.37	1.42	
N	3,841	1,327	3,981	3,839	319	1,925	
						κ	.71
*Family of Origin**							
Both parents	69	49	74	74	82	63	
Mother only	12	26	11	12	9	17	
Other	19	25	14	14	10	21	
Total	100	100	100	100	100	100	
N	3,847	1,333	3,991	3,851	321	1,931	
						κ	.32
*Siblings**							
None	4	3	6	5	6	5	
1 or 2	35	20	44	35	60	44	
3 or 4	30	26	27	29	26	29	
5 or more	30	51	23	31	9	22	
Total	100	100	100	100	100	100	
Mean	3.92	5.40	3.27	3.88	2.47	3.31	
Standard deviation	3.26	3.87	2.90	3.18	2.59	3.10	
N	3,835	1,326	3,974	3,841	320	1,926	
						κ	.62

*Differences among religions statistically significant ($p < .05$).

disappeared in the mid-1980s. The data in table 6.2 mixes cohorts that were and were not different in their fertility so Conservative women's fertility appears to be slightly higher than that of Mainline women. Indeed, the larger differences involving numbers of siblings—Conservative Protestants had more siblings than Catholics had—show the legacy of high former fertility better. Family disruption held Conservative women's fertility below its full potential as we see when we compare Conservative Protestants' family types with others' family types.

EDUCATION

Conservative Protestants are less educated than most Americans. Seventeen percent of them have graduated from college (5 percent going on to earn advanced degrees) compared to 64 percent of Jews (30 percent with advanced degrees), 31 percent of adults with no religion, 30 percent of Mainline Protestants, and 26 percent of Catholics. The Conservative Protestants also have weaker vocabularies, falling more than half a word below the national average.[4] Much of the difference is due to education, but a significant residual of −.16 remains after controlling for differences among denominations in education and immigration. Jews do best on the vocabulary quiz, although half of their gross advantage is best ascribed to their education and long residence in the United States. Education data are in table 6.4.

We might expect Conservative Protestant women to be stay-at-home mothers. One-fourth of them are, a rate typical of Mainline and Afro-American Protestants and Catholics. The women with no religious preference are the distinct ones; a statistically significant 17 percent of them are stay-at-home mothers (see table 6.4 for this and other socioeconomic indicators).

Conservative Protestants are slightly but significantly less likely to be professionals and more likely to be blue-collar than other Christians. Jews' professional employment far outpaces that of other groups. The occupational distributions of women and men from all groups differ more in the less-prestigious occupations than in the professions and management.

Conservative Protestants' family incomes lag behind those of people with no religion, Mainline Protestants, Catholics, and Jews by amounts ranging from a low of $8,100 to a high of $21,000. Almost

Table 6.4. Socioeconomic indicators by religion: persons twenty-five years old or older

	Religion					
	Protestant					
Variable / category	Conser-vative (%)	Afro-Amer. (%)	Mainline (%)	Catholic (%)	Jewish (%)	No religion (%)
*Education**						
Incomplete secondary	19	27	12	15	5	13
Complete secondary	47	44	39	39	15	36
Some college	17	17	19	20	17	20
Bachelors degree	12	8	20	18	34	20
Advanced degree	5	3	10	8	30	11
Total	100	100	100	100	100	100
N	3,523	1,211	3,745	3,451	303	1,616
						κ .81
*Labor Force Participation: Men**						
At work or looking	79	73	75	81	76	87
Retired	18	20	23	15	20	10
Other	3	7	2	4	3	4
						κ .46
*Labor Force Participation: Women**						
At work or looking	60	63	58	64	66	76
Retired	15	13	20	13	15	7
Other	25	25	22	23	19	17
						κ .37
*Occupation: Men**						
Professional	18	15	25	21	46	25
Managerial	12	6	19	15	16	11
Other white-collar	20	22	20	22	25	19
Blue-collar / service	50	57	36	41	12	44
						κ .67
*Occupation: Women**						
Professional	18	22	28	26	40	29
Managerial	18	11	17	19	22	21
Other white-collar	45	48	38	43	31	30
Blue-collar / service	19	19	16	12	8	19
						κ .44
Family income: Men						
All*	$35,200	$25,200	$39,900	$39,600	$59,000	$37,200
Married*	$43,000	$38,100	$51,300	$51,000	$75,300	$49,800

(continued)

Table 6.4 (*continued*)

	Religion					
	Protestant					
Variable / category	Conservative (%)	Afro-Amer. (%)	Mainline (%)	Catholic (%)	Jewish (%)	No religion (%)
Family income: Women						
All*	$27,300	$18,200	$33,700	$34,500	$48,800	$29,800
Married*	$42,700	$38,500	$51,900	$53,800	$65,900	$49,400
*Dwelling type**						
House: single-family	65	51	67	60	48	52
House: multifamily	9	18	11	15	17	15
Trailer	10	4	7	5	1	7
Apartments and other	16	27	16	20	34	25
					κ	.82

* Differences among religions statistically significant ($p < .05$).

half of the difference can be attributed to education, geography, and immigration, but there remains a substantial income gap ascribable to religious denomination. Though large enough to be statistically significant, the gaps are far smaller than the caricatures imply. Some of the differences—and all the gender difference—stem from differences in marital status; together education, immigration, and marital status account for 59 percent of the gross differences.

Despite the income gaps, Conservative Protestants tend to live in single-family houses. Although they do have a slightly higher trailer-park residency, per the stereotypes, that seems to be a substitute for living in condos or apartments, not single-family houses. Jews and Afro-American Protestants—the groups at the high and low extremes of the income distribution—are the groups most likely to live in apartments and condos.

LIFESTYLE: ALCOHOL, TOBACCO, FIREARMS, AND ENTERTAINMENT

About a third of Conservative Protestants smoke, a proportion different only from that of Afro-American Protestants (40 percent) among all the denominational groups. However, they are much less likely than mainline Protestants to report that they drink—50 percent versus 79 percent.[5] The correlation is .27, which is reduced to .19 when their biblical faith is taken into account. Faith in biblical literalism is part of the abstemiousness of Conservative Protestants but only part of it. However, if they are less likely to drink than the Mainline Protestants, Conservative Protestants are as likely to say that on occasion they have too much to drink—37 percent, more than any of the others, save for those with no religious affiliation. It is possible, of course, that coming from an abstemious religious culture, Conservative Protestants are likely to estimate "too much" as much less than Catholics, for example, are.

Between 1996 and 2002 the GSS included several questions about the cultural life and interests of Americans. One of the more surprising findings was that Conservative Protestants were marginally more likely to watch PBS news programs daily (19 percent) than other Americans (with the exception of those with no religion where the rate is also 19 percent). The difference is not statistically significant in comparison with Mainline Protestants but that one out of five Conservative Protestants are tuned into public broadcasting every day is a strong challenge to stereotypes and also suggests that they are not perhaps all that different from the rest of us.

They are less likely to enjoy operatic and classical music though 16 percent enjoy the former and 44 percent the later and more likely than others to enjoy bluegrass and country and western music more than anyone else—small wonder both are part of their heritage—and also like gospel music more than anyone but the African Americans. However, twenty-one percent dislike bluegrass.

They are also more likely to engage in fishing and hunting and watching car races than anyone else, though 68 percent of the men and 91 percent of the women have not attended any such races in the last year—which says nothing about how often they watch it on television. They are also marginally less likely than Mainline Protestants to attend sports contests.

Gun ownership is much more prevalent among Conservative and Mainline Protestants than we find for other groups. The margin is large; 56 percent of Conservative Protestant men have a gun at home compared with 17 percent of Jewish men and about 37 percent of Afro-American, Catholic, Jewish, and secular men. The differences are similar though the levels are lower among women. What fascinates us about the contrast between gun ownership and drinking and smoking is the silence of denominations on gun issues in contrast to their public stances on alcohol and tobacco. The religious differences on the items denominations speak to are smaller than on the item they have not taken a position on.

CONCLUSION

The portrait of the Conservative Christians that emerges from this chapter hardly provides any support for the stereotypes. Conservative Protestants' tastes in entertainment and recreation are somewhat different, though hardly odd. While they like country music and own guns, they also like PBS. If one finds the temptation irresistible to picture all "Jesus people" as religious fanatics, one should picture a fifth of them glued to PBS stations every evening. They smoke as much and drink less than others, though they are about as likely as any one else to drink too much.

In this chapter we have discovered that many of the broad stereotypes about Conservative Protestants have, at most, limited basis in fact. American religious denominations are all national, not regional, in scope and draw from all social and economic classes. Similarities overshadow the differences. The geographical and socioeconomic differences are differences of degree, not kind. No group is geographically or social isolated from the others. Nor are Conservative Protestants socially disenfranchised by their lack of education or money.

The most distinct denominations are the Afro-American Protestant ones. Their concentration in the South and in the nation's biggest cities echo racial segregation in general. Their low ranking on education, occupation, and income reflect the socioeconomic disadvantages all African Americans face to some extent. However, it bears notice that the Afro-American Protestants are a subculture even within the full African American population.

SEVEN

Conservative Christian Growth

Membership Begins at Home[1]

INTRODUCTION

More American Protestants today prefer the Conservative denominations than the Mainline ones. That is a relatively new development. One hundred years ago, the Mainline denominations held a two-to-one edge in membership. Throughout the twentieth century, the Conservative denominations increased their share of the Protestant population—at the Mainline denominations' expense. To quantify the growth of the Conservative Protestant population, we begin by tracking membership in the Conservative denominations. Because few reliable data sources classified Protestant denominations in any detail before 1972, we construct our time series out of people's religious origins.[2] Figure 7.1 outlines the trend. Except for a slight slowdown in the 1960s, the Conservative Protestant population has grown unabated.

The broad outline of this trend has been well known among religious scholars for over thirty years—at least since the publication of Dean M. Kelley's classic study *Why Conservative Churches Are Growing* in 1972. Most observers of this phenomenon—Jeffery Hadden, Richard John Neuhaus, James Davison Hunter, and Thomas Reeves—assume that the Conservative churches are growing because of conversions from the Mainline churches. The Conservatives, it is said, have a strong appeal for American Protestants because of their emphasis on traditional evangelical teachings. The Mainline clergy have sent their flocks elsewhere by some combination of liberal politics and "feel-good" religion. By their collective reckoning, the growth of the Conservative denominations represents a reaction against "excessive

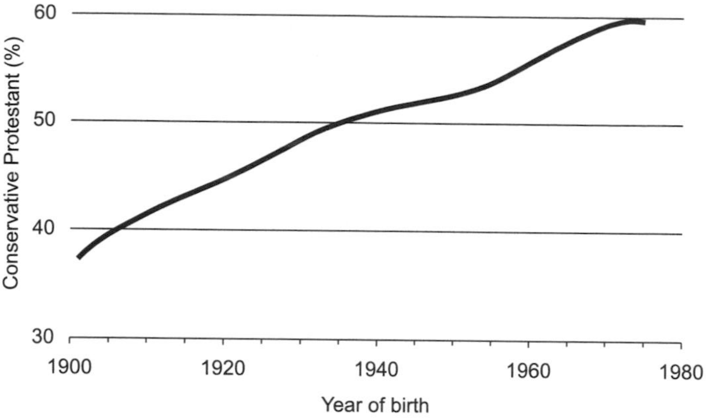

Figure 7.1 Conservative Protestants as a share of all Protestants by year. We used a statistical model to smooth out sampling fluctuations in the observed data.

liberalism" in which people raised in Mainline denominations register displeasure with the (supposed) liberal ethos of Mainline Protestantism by leaving to join denominations that emphasize the Conservative beliefs they share.

Our purpose in this chapter is to dispatch the "excessive liberalism" argument and to supplant it definitively with a demographic one.[3] First, note that figure 7.1 shows the trend in religious origins, not current denominations. By definition, conversions play no part in a trend involving religious origins. Furthermore, the timing is way off. The excessive liberalism of Mainline Protestantism, if it exists at all, is supposed to be a post-1960s phenomenon, but Conservative churches have been gaining for over seventy-five years. Thus, even if dissent over excessive liberalism motivated some conversions, it can be neither the first cause of Conservative growth nor the quantitatively most important one. Conversion data we present below finish off the excessive liberalism argument. Not only do the data contain no trace of evidence that conversions from Mainline to Conservative denominations might have increased in the late 1960s or through the 1970s, they definitively support the conclusion that conversions from Mainline to Conservative denominations held steady for at least seventy-five years. Nor is that steady rate very high; our best estimate is 13 percent. An explanation for the Conservative upsurge must be sought elsewhere in factors unrelated to the rumored but not realized epidemic of conversions.

Where should we look for a more effective explanation? First we need an explanation that encompasses origins as well as current affiliations. Nor can it rely very heavily on conversions whether before the 1960s or after. As one of us remarked in 1969, without realizing the implications of the observation, the surest source of new adult members for a denomination is in the pews already—among the children of the present members of that denomination. So we look to the children. For most of the twentieth century, women in Conservative Protestant denominations had more children than women in Mainline denominations did. The larger families gave Conservative denominations such a huge demographic advantage that it explains 70 percent of the Conservative upsurge. The remaining 30 percent came from a drop in conversions out of Conservative denominations into the Mainline.[4]

DETAILS OF THE DEMOGRAPHIC EXPLANATION

The discussion to this point has identified three of the five logically possible explanations why the Conservative denominations have increased their share of the Protestant population: 1) increased conversion from Mainline to Conservative denominations, 2) natural increase due to Conservative women's higher fertility, and 3) a decline in switching from Conservative to Mainline denominations. The other two potential explanations that exhaust the logical possibilities are: 4) more apostasy among people raised in Mainline denominations than for those raised Conservative and 5) greater inflow from outside Protestantism to the Conservative denominations.

Possible explanation 4 fails because apostasy is rising at the same rate for both kinds of Protestantism. Possible explanation 5 also fails; in this case it is because Mainline denominations actually have a slight advantage over Conservative ones among people not raised Protestant—6.3 percent of people not raised Protestant join Conservative Protestant churches in adulthood while 7.8 percent of them join Mainline Protestant denominations. One last detail about switching: in cohorts born since 1950, people leaving the Mainline denominations were more likely to become Catholics or to reject all religious affiliation (16 percent) than to join a Conservative Protestant denomination (11 percent).[5]

With three of four competitors eliminated, the demographic explanation holds considerable promise. The demographic explanation relies on the so-called "demographic imperative": in a population made up of two groups, the one with the higher net reproduction rate will increase its share of the total at the expense of the group with the lower net reproduction rate, all other things being equal. In rich countries like the United States, fertility determines the net reproduction rate. So in this country, a group with higher fertility will grow faster than one with lower fertility (all other things being equal). Thus the plausibility of the demographic explanation for denominational change rests on the answers to the following questions: 1) do women in Conservative denominations have higher fertility than other Protestant women? and 2) is the fertility difference big enough to result in a redistribution as dramatic as the evangelical upsurge within American Protestantism?

Figure 7.2 demonstrates that Conservative women's fertility has indeed been higher than Mainline women's fertility since the early

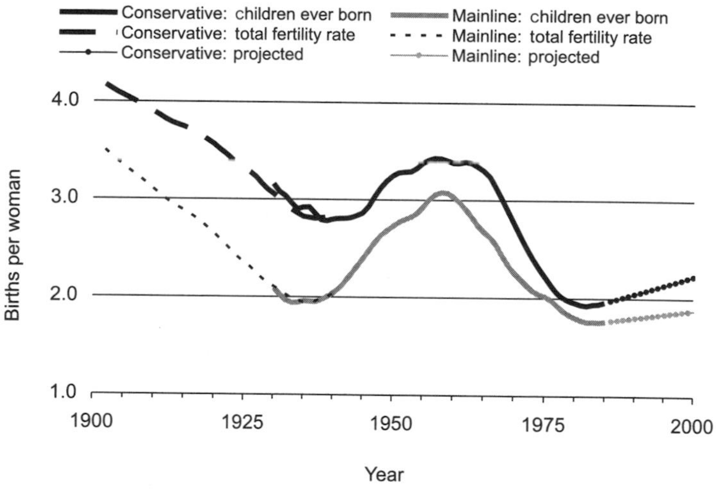

Figure 7.2 Fertility rates for Protestant women by denominational type. Children ever born data are GSS data–smoothed using locally estimated (loess) regression. The total fertility rate for each denomination was projected from vital statistics (Heuser 1974) using a model of denominational differences described by Hout et al. (2001).

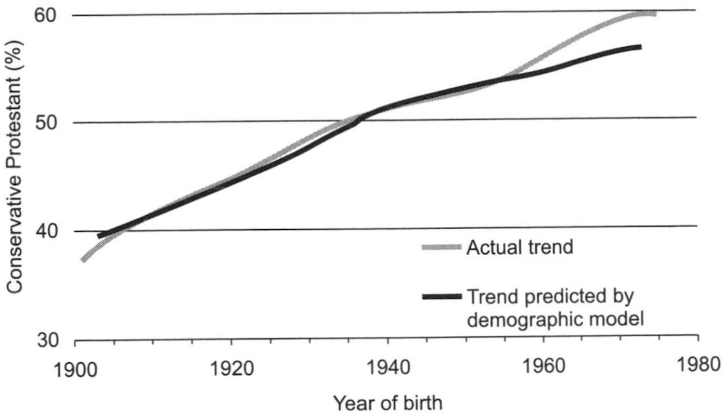

Figure 7.3 Percentage of Protestant adults who are in conservative denominations by birth cohort: actual trend and trend predicted by demographic model. We used a statistical model to smooth out sampling fluctuations in the actual trend.

days of twentieth century. The gap fell from early in the century when Conservative women had on average one more child than did Mainline women to .15 births in the late 1970s. Conservative and Mainline women are moving apart again, though slowly; recent cohorts will most likely finish childbearing with a Conservative advantage of about .3 births.[6] Small fluctuations within the overall pattern of convergence and divergence are also noteworthy. Mainline women's fertility increased more during the baby boom than Conservative women's did. The baby boom ended sooner for Mainline women, though—probably because Mainline women started using birth control pills earlier. At no point did Mainline women's fertility exceed that of Conservative women. So the first condition for the demographic explanation is satisfied—Conservative and Mainline women have different fertility rates.

Is the fertility difference big enough to account for the evangelical upsurge? To find out, we used standard demographic projection methods to predict Conservative versus Mainline breakdown of the Protestant population using the higher fertility of the Conservative women as the only factor that varied.

Figure 7.3 compares the projected percentage Conservative with the actual percentages. The similarity of the two implies that the Protestant population would look remarkably like it does today if nothing but fertility rates changed. Our demographic model accurately predicts the sharp upsurge of the Conservative population through the baby boom cohorts. Its only error is at the end; it predicts a slowdown in Conservative upsurge earlier than it occurred in recent cohorts. In real life, the Conservative denominations kept growing until very recently. Our model expected the slowdown to occur about ten–fifteen years sooner than it actually did. Overall, Conservatives' higher fertility accounts for 75 percent of the total change.

Declining conversions from Conservative to Mainline denominations account for the 25 percent of denominational change that demography cannot explain. This is the fifth logical possibility. It has two components. First, mixed marriages result in fewer conversions than they used to. There was a time, not so long ago, when a marriage involving one Conservative partner and one Mainline partner resulted in a shift of the Conservative partner to the Mainline. That is less prevalent for cohorts marrying since the late 1970s. Mixed marriages involving two Protestants of different kinds of denominations are more likely to stay mixed now than they used to be. For marriages between people raised in different Protestant traditions, 70 percent of those married before 1970 converted; that is down to 57 of those married since 1970.

The second key component of falling Conservative-to-Mainline conversion is a change among upwardly mobile Conservatives. The Conservative denominations are doing a better job of retaining the young people raised that way, but their greatest success is among the upwardly mobile. Early in the century upwardly mobile Baptists, Evangelicals, and Pentecostals announced their arrival in the middle class by joining the local Episcopal, Congregational, or Presbyterian church. This tendency dissipated in the 1970s and 1980s. Contemporary Conservatives announce their arrival in the establishment by starting a power brokers' prayer breakfast.

Table 7.1 quantifies the change. It simultaneously compares current versus childhood religion and their own education with that of their parents. Converts were raised in a Conservative denomination but now belong to a Mainline one. Upwardly mobile individuals have more education than their better-educated parent; immobile individuals have the same education as either of their parents. Conversions among the immobile show no significant trend up to and including the

Table 7.1 Conversions to Mainline Protestant denominations by cohort and intergenerational mobility: adults raised in conservative denominations

	Education	
Year of birth	More than parents (%)	Same as parents (%)
1900–1924	26	15
1925–1934	24	16
1935–1944	20	16
1945–1954	16	14
1955–1964	13	11
1965–1974	11	7

SOURCE: General Social Surveys, 1974–2002.

baby boom cohort of 1945–1954—it hovered around 15 percent—then dropped to 11 and 7 percent in the last two cohorts. The upwardly mobile once were far more likely to leave their Conservative upbringing behind as they moved up in society—26 percent of those born before 1925 converted. Status-climbing conversions of this sort declined steadily in each successive cohort to a low of just 11 percent of the Conservatives born since 1965. Speculating for just a moment, we see this development as reflective of two phenomena. First, we suspect that the status distinctions among denominations that once motivated at least some of the conversions we record (see Roof and McKinney [1987] for some data on their magnitude) have diminished. Second, though Conservative Protestants still worry that others look down on them, they are more defiant and less apologetic about their faith than they used to be (Smith 1998). Coupled with the fact that cohorts born since 1955 are more upwardly mobile than the ones that came before, this trend toward less conversion has boosted the proportion of American Protestants who are in Conservative denominations. Taken together, the various sources of decreased conversions from Conservative to Mainline denominations account for 25 percent of the gains by the Conservative denominations.

The various popular "culture wars" theories that have been used to explain the evangelical upsurge in contemporary American Protestantism are simply irrelevant. "Excess liberalism" is a myth. We need not invoke support of the Mainline denominations for homosexuality and abortion and modernist interpretations of the scriptures to account for the change. Nor do we need to cite antiabortion, antigay, or antievolution movements to explain Conservative success. Those factors all work through conversion from Mainline to Conservative denominations, and conversion is *not* increasing. The "excessive liberalism" argument proceeds from a false premise.

The Conservative Christian upsurge is a homegrown phenomenon. New adult members of Conservative congregations are coming from the Conservative Protestant homes they were raised in. Their parents were Conservative Protestant Protestants, and now that they have reached adulthood, they are, too. Mainline denominations do almost as well at socializing their youth. The advantage goes to the Conservative denominations because they start with more children; Conservative Protestant women have more children than other Protestant women do. The raw power of demography joins with the staying power of religious socialization to produce growth for Conservative denominations. Conservative Protestant parents increase their denominations' share of the American Protestant population by having more children.

The Mainline denominations are literally dying out. Slowly but surely they are not only becoming a declining share of the Protestant population but decreasing absolutely. They are not losing members to other congregations, to other kinds of Protestantism, or to no religion at rates out of line with other churches. Their losses are in the demography of their group. They are, quite simply, failing to reproduce themselves. Among Mainline Protestant adults born since 1950, 37 percent have no children and another 19 percent have just one—combined that makes 56 percent of recent cohorts having fewer than two children. Two children is an important demographic threshold because it takes an average of 2.1 children per couple to reproduce a population.[7] To stem their absolute decline, the Mainline Protestant denominations will need some childless couples to start having children or more couples with four, five, and six children each. As we saw in figure 7.2, Mainline Protestants are very near replacement level fertility at about 1.9 births per woman. So total disappearance is not in the foreseeable future. Indeed our model suggests that, barring a Conservative baby boom, the shift from mostly Mainline to mostly Conservative Protestantism is about over. Nonetheless fertility below replacement level implies a slow and steady decline for the Mainline.

It also implies ever-increasing difficulty in reversing the decline because below-replacement fertility leads inevitably to an "old" age distribution. We see that already in the GSS data gathered since 1996. A majority of Mainline Protestants—58 percent—are forty-five years old or over; very few, if any, of them will have any more children. Twelve percent of Mainline Protestants are over seventy-five years old. Only Jews—another group with below-replacement fertility—has a comparable age distribution. By contrast, the majority of Conservative Protestants—52 percent—and Catholics—56 percent—are of childbearing age; just 7 percent of these groups are seventy-five or older.

BEHIND THE DEMOGRAPHIC EXPLANATION

Why was the reproduction rate of the Conservatives higher than that of the Mainline for so many decades? Presumably the opposition of the Conservative denominational leadership to artificial birth control influenced the child bearing practices of Conservative women while birth control advocacy by Mainline clergy and laity encouraged Mainline women's use of contraceptives. Thus beneath the demographic explanation there is also a cultural one, though not the cultural explanation that most of the "culture wars" writers have advanced: It took most of the twentieth century for Conservative women to "catch up" with family planning practices that have become dominant in American society. Or to put the matter differently, the so-called decline of the Mainline may ultimately be attributable to its earlier approval of contraception, just as the decline of Christians in Lebanon as compared with Muslims seems to have the same explanation.

CONCLUSION: THE END OF THE UPSURGE?

Predicting the future is precarious at best, but our evidence suggests that the trends underlying the Conservative upsurge may be nearing their end. The demographic momentum, as it affects cohorts, is spent; our demographic model predicts an increase of less than 1 percent in the proportion of Protestants who belong to the Conservative denominations over the next decade. Unless the fertility gap reopens—either because Conservative Protestants increase their family size or Mainline Protestants further reduce theirs—the main source of the Conservative upsurge will not be a factor in the future.

The other key predictor—the falling rate of switching from Conservative to Mainline denominations—is reaching an end point of its own. Conservative-to-Mainline conversions fell from 21 percent to 9 percent in the last twenty years; it cannot continue to fall much longer simply because it cannot get less than zero.

The main source of change is stabilizing and the second source is approaching its logical limit. Exhaust both sources of change and change will stop unless and until a third source comes along.

A word of caution is in order. We have focused on cohorts because the key changes in behavior show themselves most clearly in the succession of cohorts. However, the cross section of Protestants in any particular year for the next half century or more will still include the people born during times of differential fertility. The demographic momentum of differential fertility will remain present in the cross section until the cohorts born in the late 1960s pass away—and they will not do that any time soon as they are just in their thirties as we write. The upshot is that the Protestant population will continue to shift in the Conservative direction for many years to come, even if no further changes in the underlying behaviors occur.

Our finding that demography explains three-fourths of the most important religious change affecting contemporary Protestantism provides good news for both the Mainline and the Conservative churches. The Mainline clergy were often cited for a supposed "excessive liberalism" that, many prominent writers claimed, pushed people away from the Mainline. The evidence exonerates them. Their denominations are not casualties on the cultural battleground. Their changing numbers reflect, more than anything else, the private fertility decisions of Mainline families. Meanwhile Conservative clergy and laity can feel gratified that their most recent growth has little or no ideological content; its source is the greater number of young people raised in their tradition and, in part, those young peoples' greater reluctance to leave it. Both sides, however, must give up certain attitudes—triumphalism among the Conservative clergy and guilt among the Mainline. It may be hard. Conventional wisdom changes slowly. But the ascendancy of Conservative Protestantism reflects their demographic edge and their attraction for the already converted. Their growth is not a referendum on the Mainline clergy.

EIGHT

Conservative Christians in the "Sexual Revolution"

INTRODUCTION

It is widely believed that in the last decades of the twentieth century a "sexual revolution" occurred. Like all metaphors this one can become a substitute for thought about social change rather than a hint of it. There certainly has been a change in sexual attitudes and behavior—mostly because the development of convenient forms of fertility control and the greater ease of divorce. It would appear (Smith 2003; Laumann et al. 2000) that changes in attitudes have been more striking than changes in behavior—perhaps because of the physical, physiological, and logistical constraints on behavior. However, not all attitudinal change is in a revolutionary direction. There is greater tolerance for cohabitation before marriage and for homosexual sex (especially in the last decade) but little evidence that people are having sex more often or enjoying it more. In fact, given the findings of Laumann et al. that the most satisfying sex takes place in committed relationships, there may be less satisfaction than there used to be.

The question, however, in this chapter is not whether there has been a sexual revolution and, if there has been, what are its components. Rather we must address two questions:

1. Are the sexual attitudes and behaviors of Conservative Protestants significantly different from those of other Americans, especially mainline Protestants? Have they retained the stern sexual ethic of their Puritan predecessors?
2. To what extent have the changes in the larger culture affected the sexual ethics and behavior of Conservative Protestants?

The answers to these questions are in brief that in some matters Conservative Protestants do have stricter ethical norms than do other Christians and that, also to some extent, they have been affected by the changes in the norms of the larger society but not as much as have other groups.

PREMARITAL SEX

It will be useful in this chapter to use charts that show the attitudes of four Christian denominations[1] across time from 1972 to 2002 and thus portray the relative position of the Conservative Protestants from the early years of the sexual revolution to the present. They indicate the changes that have occurred in that position.

- *There's been a lot of discussion about the way morals and attitudes about sex are changing in this country. If a man and a woman have sexual relations before marriage, do you think that it is always wrong, almost always wrong, wrong only sometimes or not wrong at all?*

Attitudes towards premarital sex are the touchstone of the sexual revolution, indeed they almost define it. Over the thirty-year period 48 percent of Conservative Protestants have believed on the average that premarital sex is always wrong, as opposed to 32 percent of Afro-American Protestants and 28 percent of Mainline Protestants.[2] The association between Conservative Christianity and opposition to premarital sex among white Protestants is reflected in a $\varkappa$ of .46; adjusting for belief in the word-for-word inerrancy of the Bible reduces that to .28.[3] Thus the religious conviction of the Conservative Protestants accounts for part—our best estimate is 38 percent—of their greater opposition to premarital sex (than we find among white Mainline Protestants).

Figure 8.1 illustrates the impact of the sexual revolution on beliefs about premarital sex for various Christian groups. At the top of the chart one notes that there has been only a small decline in disapproval of premarital sex (barely meeting the standards of statistical significance) among Conservative Protestants and a much larger decline among Mainline Protestants (five percentage points versus ten percentage points). Moreover 60 percent of those Conservative Protestants who believe in word-for-word inspiration reject premarital

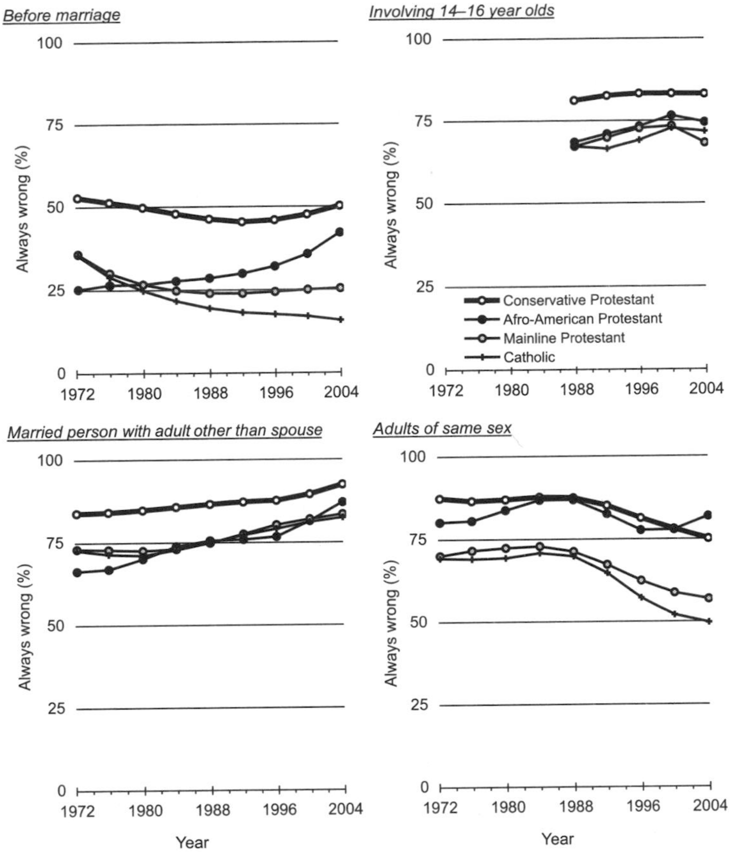

Figure 8.1 Attitudes toward sexual relations by year, denomination, and types of partners. Data-smoothed using locally estimated regression.

sex at every point in the three decades—so "Bible Christians"[4] seem immune to the influence of cultural change in attitudes towards premarital sex.

The notable upturn among Afro-American Protestants in the last part of the thirty-year period does indicate a statistically significant increase in opposition to premarital sex over time so that they are midway between the two Protestant denominational groups. The decline is sharpest among Catholics who believe that premarital sex is always wrong—from 32 percent to 17 percent.

Thus to the question whether Conservative Christians are Puritans one must respond that on the basis of their attitudes towards premarital sex, they may not be completely Puritan—40 percent of the Bible Christians do not think it is always wrong—but they are more Puritan than any other religious denomination. Moreover, regarding the second question, they remain more consistent across the thirty years than any other of the groups, especially if they believe in biblical literalism.

TEENAGE SEX

The next item (since 1990) on the list of reactions to sexual behavior asks about teenagers:

- *What if they are in their early teens, say 14 to 16 years old, do you think that sex relations before marriage are always wrong, almost always wrong, wrong only sometimes or not wrong at all.*

Eighty-three percent of the Conservative Protestants (90 percent of the Bible Christians), 72 percent of the Afro-American Protestants, and 71 percent of the Mainline Protestants believe that it is always wrong.[5] Thus a substantial proportion of Mainline Protestants and Afro-American Protestants do not totally reject adolescent sex. Sixteen percent of Afro-American Protestants think it is either sometimes wrong or not wrong at all, as do 10 percent of Mainline Protestants and 12 percent of Catholics. These are relatively low proportions yet indicate levels of tolerance for premarital sex that are somewhat surprising—or perhaps only an indication of awareness of how powerful sexual energies are in the middle teens. One might not approve, but one might understand on the basis of one's own memory of those years.

However, contrary to the expectations of a theory of sexual revolution, tolerance for premarital sex among teenagers has *declined* during the last decade and a half as the upper right portion of figure 8.1 illustrates. In all four denominational groupings the conviction that premarital sex is always wrong for early adolescents has increased and in a statistically significant manner, save among the Conservative Protestants where the 84 percent rejection rate is very high indeed. Afro-American Protestants have increased their rejection ten percentage points and Mainline Protestants seven percentage points.[6] Perhaps the national attention to the "problem" of teenage pregnancy has alerted older men and women to the "crisis" and thus prepared the way for the decline in such pregnancies in recent years. Perhaps parents are saying, "Not with my teenager." Patently the "sexual revolution" is not an equal opportunity event, not for teenagers anyway. If the Conservative Christians tend to be Puritans, then on the issue of teenage sex, others seem to some extent to be catching up with them.

EXTRAMARITAL SEX

The rest of the denominations also seem to be catching up with the Conservative Protestants on extramarital sex. The lower left panel of Figure 8.1 shows that all four denominations have increased their objection to extramarital sex in their response to this question: *What is your opinion about a married person having sexual relations with someone other than the marriage partner. It is it always wrong, almost always wrong, wrongly only sometimes, or not wrong at all?*

Over the last thirty years the average rejection rates have been 87 percent for Conservative Protestants, 74 percent for Afro-American Protestants, and 75 percent for Mainline Protestants (and Catholics). The correlation between Conservative Protestant and disapproval of extramarital sex (in comparison with Mainline Protestant) is .14. When belief in literal interpretation is added to the equation, the relationship diminishes to .09. Thus some of the difference between Conservative Protestants and Mainline Protestants on extramarital sex is that the former are more likely to believe in word-for-word literalism.

Over time, figure 8.1 shows, there has been a statistically significant *increase* in objection to extramarital sex for all four groups with the three who are not Conservative Protestants narrowing the gap with the Conservatives. Four-fifths of them reject extramarital sex, no matter how more tolerant they may have been in the early years of the survey—which was not all that tolerant. "Not with my teenager" was the response to teenage sex. "Not with my wife" (or husband) is a response to extramarital sex. It is reasonable to suspect that this increase in opposition to extramarital sex might be related to the AIDS epidemic.

Thus the Conservative Protestants are more Puritan than anyone else about extramarital sex and, perhaps in reaction to the problems in the "sexual revolution" other denominational groups are catching up with them.

HOMOSEXUAL SEX

The final question in the GSS battery of questions about sexual attitudes deals with homosexuality (see the lower right portion of fig. 8.1).

- *What about sexual relations between two adults of the same sex—do you think they are always wrong, almost always wrong, wrong only sometimes or not wrong at all?*

The issue of homosexuality has been an important agenda item for Conservative Protestant political activity. Hence one would expect them not only to continue to be stern in their judgments about such behavior but also to be immune to cultural pressures to modify their judgments. Indeed, of the four denominational groupings they are the most likely in a thirty-year average to say that it is always wrong—85 percent of Conservative Protestants (92 percent of their biblical literalists), 82 percent of Afro-American Protestants, and 69 percent of Mainline Protestants make such a judgment (and 65 percent of Catholics). The correlation that compares Conservatives and Mainline Protestants in their attitudes is .19, which declines to .12 when one considers that the Conservatives are more likely to be Bible Christians than the Mainliners.

However, in contrast to the findings of the last two sections, there is a statistically significant decline (fig. 8.1, *bottom right*) in opposition to homosexual sex in all four denominational groups beginning with 1990—nine percentage points for Conservative Protestants, eight percentage points for Afro-American Protestants, twelve percentage points for Mainline Protestants, and 19 percentage points for Catholics.[7] This change may well be the result of the fact that in the recent decade and a half many Americans have had to face the fact that people whom they love are gay and accordingly adjust their moral judgments. Moreover, the younger cohorts tend to differ sharply from their predecessors in tolerance of gays and lesbians.

Thus the Conservative Protestants are still the ones who are most likely to denounce homosexual sex but also are to some extent changing their minds along with others on the subject. If this change can fairly be called part of a "sexual revolution," Conservative Protestants show some signs of changing in the direction of the larger culture, though they have a long way to go to become as sympathetic to gays as Catholics are.

A hint of an explanation for the differences among the denominational groups may be found in a question asked in 1994 about the causes of homosexuality.

- *Do you think that being homosexual is something people choose to be or do you think that it is something they cannot change?*

Sixty-seven percent of Conservative Protestants think that homosexuality is something that people choose, as do 57 percent of the Afro-Americans, 47 percent of the Mainliners and 39 percent of Catholics.[8] One may well be inclined to judge the severity of an action in line with one's views about whether the orientation behind the action is a matter of free choice.

In summary of these last four sections, Conservative Protestants are unmoved on the issue of premarital sex, are similar to others in their increasing opposition to teenage sex, and are changing their mind slowly as others are in their rejection of homosexual sex.[9] They are, nonetheless, still the most conservative among the four denominations in these four areas of human behavior.

Respondents were also asked two questions about apparently controversial issues that focus on education—sex education in the schools and contraceptive information in the schools.

- *Would you be for or against sex education in public schools?*
- *Do you agree that methods of birth control should be made avail to teenagers between the age of 14 and 16 if their parents do not approve?*

Support for sex education in the schools is overwhelming—approximately three-fourths of the Conservative Protestants approve it as do seven-eighths of the Mainline Protestants (and four-fifths of Afro-American Protestants). Even 73 percent of the Bible Christians approve it.

Forty-eight percent of the Conservative Protestants approve of the availability of contraceptives in school, as do 60 percent of the Afro-American Protestants in comparison with 69 percent of the Mainline Protestants.[10] Forty-two percent of the Bible Christians inside the Conservatives agree with this choice. The difference between Conservatives and Mainliners in their reaction to this issue is measured by a correlation of .11, which is reduced to .06 when higher levels of belief in scriptural literalism is taken into account. As in all similar matters, belief in literalism explains much of the difference between the two groups but not all of it. In part, Conservatives are more negative on sexual matters in association with their literal interpretation of the Bible.

Both of these issues seemed to have been settled long ago. Over the history of the GSS there is no change in attitudes towards sex education or providing sex information to fourteen- and sixteen-year-olds against the wishes of their parents.

PORNOGRAPHY

Some Conservative groups such as the Mississippi-based Family Research Council have been vigorous in their attack on such magazines as *Playboy* and *Hustler*. Questions about the distribution of pornographic literature and a second about attending X-rated films provide an opportunity to examine these issues.

Which of these statements come closest to your feelings about pornography laws:

- *There should be laws against the distribution of pornography whatever the age.*
- *There should be laws against the distribution of pornography to those under eighteen.*
- *Three should be no laws forbidding the distribution of pornography.*

Have you seen an x-rated movie in the last year?

Only 4 percent of Americans agree that there should be no laws forbidding the distribution of pornography. The differences therefore are between those who want to forbid it completely and those who want to forbid it to minors.

Thirty-three percent of Conservative Protestants support a complete ban on pornography (and only 36 percent of the Bible Christians among them). Nineteen percent of the Afro-American Protestants agree with such a ban and 25 percent of the Mainline Protestants. Despite the Family Research Council, pornography does not seem to be an issue for the majority of Christians, though there is indeed a difference of .08 between the two white Protestant groups, which falls to .03 when one takes into account the larger proportion of the Conservative Protestants who believe in biblical inspiration. Again the issue of pornography appears as one already settled because there is no relationship between it and the time of the study. Nor is there any significant relationship with time for either of the white Protestant groups.

When the subject is pornography, therefore, the Conservative Protestants are more Conservative than Mainliners, but the majority of them are tolerant, perhaps more tolerant than might have been expected—and more tolerant than some of their leaders might like.

There is not much difference between the two major Protestant groups in viewing an X-rated film. Eighteen percent of the Conservative Protestants admit they have seen such a film versus 19 percent of the Mainline Protestants (compared with 26 percent of the Afro-American Protestants and 24 percent of the Catholics.) In each denominational group the proportion watching such a film has increased significantly by about four percentage points.

Thus, while pornographic literature and X-rated films are matters of considerable concern among some Conservative Protestants, they do not seem to create problems for large numbers of any denominational grouping.

ABORTION

Abortion has long been considered the central political issue of Conservative Protestants, joined more recently with the issue of homosexual unions. However, in analyzing the opinions of Conservative Protestants, one must remember that there are not two political opinions on abortion—pro-choice and pro-life, but three. The third is "It depends," and is larger than the other two put together.

Most abortion questions in political surveys require of respondents to be either pro-life or pro-choice. The National Opinion Research Center for almost forty years has proposed a battery of seven questions that enables respondents to choose ideologically inconsistent responses depending on the circumstances. Consistently through the years the majority of Americans have chosen in favor of legal abortion under some circumstances and opposed it under other circumstances. One cannot claim to be consistently pro-life if one is willing to permit legal abortions under any circumstances. Nor can one claim to be consistently pro-choice if one is willing to oppose legal abortion under other circumstances. The "wafflers" between choice and life may be morally inconsistent, they may be pragmatists, they may simply be American, but they are left out of most discussion on the subject.

Please tell me whether or not you think it should be possible for a pregnant woman to obtain a legal abortion

- *If there is a strong chance of serious defect in the baby?*
- *If she is married and does not want any more children?*
- *If a woman's own health is seriously endangered by the pregnancy?*
- *If a family has a very low income and cannot afford any more children?*
- *If she became pregnant as a result of rape?*
- *If she is single and does not want to marry the man?*
- *If the woman wants it for any reason?*

The battery was composed by our friend and colleague Alice Rossi in the middle 1960s and forms what sociologists call a Gutman scale—a steadily descending set of items that present different reasons for abortion, from abortion when a woman's health is in danger to abortion when a woman is single and does not want to marry the man.[11] In this analysis we will examine in detail the top and the bottom of the scale. Table 8.1 presents the most recent responses of the four groups to the six items on the scale.

One notes in the table that support for legal abortion among all groups increases as the seriousness of the circumstances increases and that no group is either consistently pro-choice or pro-life, not even the Mainline Protestants, a little less than half of whom do not support legal abortion even in the least dire of circumstances. These findings are moderately well known yet do not seem to enter the po-

Table 8.1 Support for legal abortion by circumstances of pregnancy and religion

	Those in favor of abortion in each circumstance			
Circumstance of pregnancy	Conservative Protestant (%)	Afro-Amer. Protestant (%)	Mainline Protestant (%)	Catholic (%)
Mother's health in danger	83	87	92	88
Risk of birth defect	66	72	83	74
Pregnant by rape	70	74	86	74
Too poor	28	40	45	37
Wants no more children	28	38	44	36
Unmarried	27	29	45	35

SOURCE: General Social Surveys, 2000–2004.

litical or media discussion of the issue because partisans are continually looking for ways to claim the majority on the abortion issue.

Large majorities of Americans favor legal abortion when there is a serious chance of a defect in the baby, if a woman's health is seriously endangered, and if she has become pregnant because of rape. Smaller majorities oppose it in the other circumstances. The question in this chapter is how consistently pro-life Conservative Protestants really are.

The answer is that most of them are not consistently pro-life. Eighty-three percent say that abortion should be legally possible if a woman's health is in danger, as compared to 87 percent of the Afro-American Protestants, 92 percent of the Mainline Protestants, and 88 percent of the Catholics. Among those Conservatives who believe in the literal interpretation of the Bible—whom we have been calling Bible Christians—tolerance for legal abortion if a woman's health is in danger falls to 78 percent. That is, four out of five of the most conservative of Conservative Protestants are pro-choice in the case of a threat to a woman's health.

In a comparison between mainline Protestants and Conservative Protestants in their attitudes toward abortion the gap is 9 percentage points, and it falls to 4 percentage-points when we take into account the differential understanding of Scripture as the word of God. Conservatives are more likely to believe in literal, word-for-word, interpretation of Scripture.

Attitudes towards abortion when a mother's health is in danger have changed somewhat with significant changes though in opposite directions (for all but the Catholics). In the left half of figure 8.2 we observe that in the three decades at the end of the twentieth century

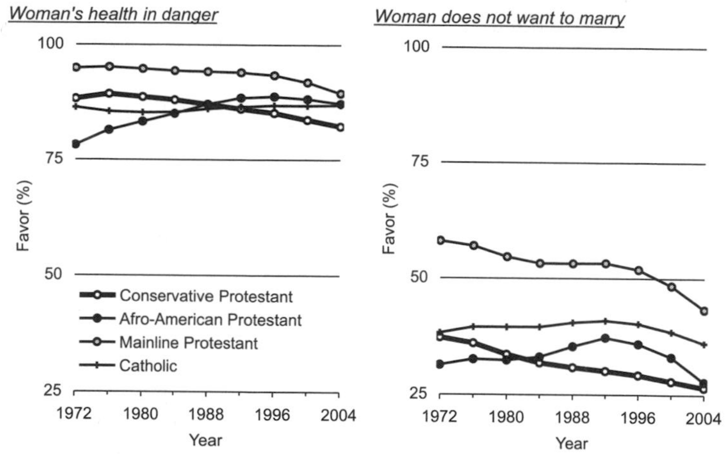

Figure 8.2 Attitudes about abortion by year, religion, and circumstances of pregnancy: Christian denominations. Data-smoothed using locally estimated regression.

there have been statistically significant changes in all the groups except the Catholics. Conservative Protestants have increased five percentage points in their opposition to abortion while Afro-American Protestants have increased their support by seven percentage points and Mainline Protestants have increased their opposition a couple of percentage points.

Thus Conservative Protestants are still the most likely of whites to oppose abortion for reason of threat to a mother's health, and that opposition has increased marginally through the decades. Thus, if abortion when a mother's health is in danger is part of the "sexual revolution," it has had the opposite effect on Conservative Protestants. Nonetheless four out of five of them are willing to tolerate it.

The gap between Conservative Protestants and Mainline Protestants widens when one descends to the bottom of the Rossi scale and considers attitudes toward abortion when a woman is single and does not want to marry the "man" (presumably the father of the child). Seventy-three percent of the Conservative Protestants (and 71 percent of the Afro-American Protestants) think such an abortion should not be legal as do 55 percent of mainline Protestants.[12] Eighty-two percent of the Bible Christians within the larger group of Conservative Protestants think that such an abortion ought to be illegal. Yet there is a substantial minority—about a quarter—of Conservatives who would defend a pro-choice position even in these circumstances. Thus Conservatives are more likely than Mainline Protestants to choose a pro-life stand on any abortion issue, but four out of five are pro-choice when a woman's health is in danger and only one in four are pro-choice in the case of a woman who does not want to marry. The Conservative Protestants are much less of a solid block of pro-life supporters than the media and even some academic experts portray them to be.

The left half of figure 8.2 shows that opposition to abortion by a single woman who does not want to marry has increased by ten percentage points for Conservative Protestants and by five percentage points among Mainline Protestants, both statistically significant changes that perhaps have resulted from the fervor of antiabortion propaganda during the decades since 1980. There is no change for either Afro-Americans or Catholics in that era.

The Bible Christians, then, are the closest to a solid pro-life block in the American population, and there is some fraying around the edge of even their consistency. Those who believe in the word-for-word inspiration of the Bible and reject abortion when a woman simply wants no more children represent 7 percent of the American population who stand for "family values" and 20 percent of the Conservative Protestants. These proportions have not changed since 1985. If the definition of the "family values" group changes to include only those who reject abortion even when a mother's health is at stake, the proportion of all Americans who are that consistently pro-life is 0.9 percent and of the Conservative Protestants 3 percent—numbers that also have not changed in recent decades. While even 1 percent of Americans is numerically a substantial segment of the population and a segment that did not increase in the last decades of the twentieth century or the first years of the twenty-first century, one can hardly hail it as a vast voting base, though political and religious leaders and the media and even some academics, each for their own reasons, have succeeded in creating the myth that it is.

These findings are not particularly original. Greeley reported a similar result in his essay on the Southern Baptists and Paul DiMaggio and his colleagues have uncovered similar findings in their work on polarization in America (or rather nonpolarization). Both sets of finding have been dismissed or ignored by the media, which delights in the myth of huge numbers of biblical Christians tramping to the polls in lockstep to cast their votes for moral values or family values.[13]

We are not critical of the Bible Christians for their crusade against abortion. In our free society it is their right to so crusade. Nor do we criticize their leaders for attempting to promote an image of a large and powerful mass movement. Rather we are impatient with those who accept that image without considering the evidence.[14] Why would someone in the media want to report that even Conservative Protestants, even the Biblical Christians among them, tend to be pragmatic on abortion and are neither overwhelmingly pro-choice or pro-life ideologues. Where's the glamour or the excitement in such a dull observation!

Despite the relatively marginal changes over time, we conclude this discussion of Conservative Christians and abortion with the observation that, while the Conservative Protestants are more likely to oppose abortion than are members of the other denominations and have not been affected by any "sexual revolution" propaganda in favor of abortion, they are nonetheless inclined in some circumstances to approve legal abortion. The battle over "abortion rights" has clearly not affected their case by case approach.

In summary of our discussion on attitudes toward legalized abortion, Conservative Protestants are still inclined to have traditional views on sexual matters and are able to resist the pressure of the larger culture over time to modify their views, save in displaying greater tolerance towards homosexual sex. However, half of them are tolerant about premarital sex and, like everyone else, the Conservative Protestants have increased their opposition to extramarital sex. Only a small group of them are consistently pro-life, and the majority are prepared to allow pragmatic exceptions when the mother's health is in serious danger, when there is a threat of a seriously defective child, or in cases of rape. Those who combine literalist faith in the Bible with consistent pro-life convictions are, for weal or woe, a relatively small minority of Conservative Protestants. Sex education in the schools, the availability of contraceptive information in the schools, and pornographic publications do not seem to be major issues for most of them.

None of these comments should hide the truth that Conservative Protestants are more conservative on sexual matters than those of other denominations, even perhaps more Puritanical. Neither should one with any regard for evidence write off Conservative Protestants as a hopelessly benighted band of zealots. Quite the contrary the zealots are a minority, as the tolerance for pro-choice decisions in certain cases vividly demonstrates. The proclivity of the media, the academy, religious leaders, and political operators to stereotype them is not only inconsistent with the data, it is also a socially destructive prejudice.

SEXUAL BEHAVIOR—THE PARTNERSHIP REVOLUTION

The National Opinion Research Center has asked since the late 1980s a battery of questions about sexual behavior. The data resulting from these questions constitute a base of more than 28,000 respondents. Some of them make it possible to explore the relationship between denominational background and sexual behavior and to investigate further the relationship between Conservative Christianity and the "sexual revolution." In the process of this investigation it will become necessary to ask whether the "revolution" has more to do with adolescent sex, marital infidelity, and homosexual sex than with the increasing tendency for Americans who are not married (widows and widowers, divorced, separated, and never married) to establish nonmarital sexual partnerships.

The following questions are pertinent for this exploration:

- *How many sexual partners have you have in the last twelve months?*
- *Was one of your partners your husband or wife or regular sexual partner?*
- *About how often did you have sex in the last twelve months?*[15]
- *Do you agree or disagree that it is alright for a couple to live together without intending to get married?*
- *It is a good idea for a couple who intend to get married to live together first.*
- *Have your sex partners in the last twelve months been exclusively male, both male and female, exclusively female?*
- *Now thinking about the time since your 18th birthday how many female sex partners have you had sex with?*
- *Now thinking about the time since your 18th birthday how many male sex partners have you had sex with?*
- *Did you live with your husband/wife before marriage?*
- *Do you have a main romantic involvement you think of as a steady, a lover, a partner or whatever? Do you live together?*

We must consider the pattern of responses in American society before examining the issues of whether Conservative Christians have created different patterns than other Americans and how these differences affect their attitudes on other sexual issues. The question about marital status was asked at the beginning of the interview so that it may not have occurred to some of the respondents that marital fidelity was an issue in the question about partners. Three percent of those who were married reported they had more than one sexual partner in the course of the year while 24 percent of those who were not married reported more than one partner. There does not, therefore, seem to be a lot of "sleeping around" in contemporary America. It does not follow, however, that those without spouses are celibate (though in fact 36 percent of them are). While 56 percent of the married respondents engaged in sexual relations at least once a week, so did 35 percent of those who are not married.

The explanation of this phenomenon is that a sizable proportion of those not married have "regular sexual partners." Seventy-nine percent of those who are unmarried and yet have engaged in sexual relations in the last year report that they have done so with "regular sexual partners"—83 percent of the widowed, 81 percent of the divorced, 88 percent of the separated, and 76 percent of the never married. Moreover about a third of these "partnerships" live together.

Is this propensity to form "regular" sexual partnerships, frequently involving cohabitation, something new in American society or is it rather something that has always existed and only now is being observed? It would appear that the increase began among those born in the 1940s and has sharply grown among more recent cohorts. Some confirmation for this conclusion can be found in the question of whether members of given cohorts lived together before their marriage. GSS family modules in 1988 and 1994 gathered information on living together under several circumstances. To turn that into data on trends, we broke it down by birth cohort. In figure 8.3 we observe a sharp rise in premarital cohabitation in the cohorts born in the 1940s and 1950s. Among stably married members of those cohorts, 10 percent of the 1940s cohort lived with their spouse before marriage compared with 33 percent of the 1950s cohort, 42 percent of the 1960s cohort, and 46 percent of those born since 1970. Cohabitation is even more common prior to remarriage. One-third of those remar-

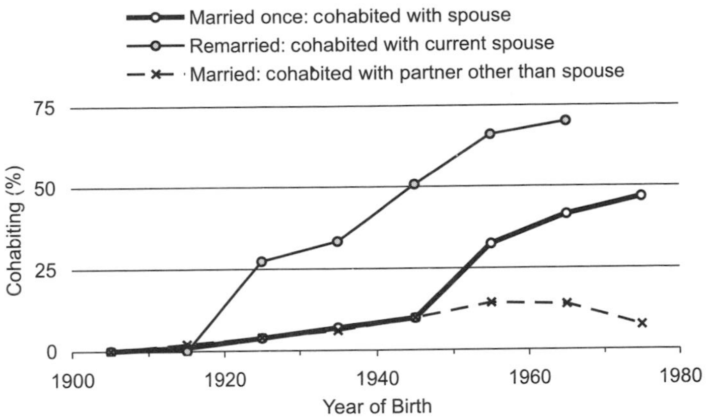

Figure 8.3 Cohabitation with spouse before marriage by birth cohort. SOURCE: General Social Surveys, 1988 and 1994.

ried from the 1920s and 1930s cohorts lived with their second spouse before marriage; that practice is now the norm as two-thirds of remarried respondents from the 1950s and 1960s cohorts lived together first. Consistent with other evidence that "sleeping around" is rare, less than 15 percent of any cohort has experience living with partners that they ultimately do not marry. Perhaps these cohorts introduced nonmarital cohabitation into American culture and it has now become more acceptable for all nonmarital groups.

Surely there is considerable tolerance for cohabitation—43 percent of respondents agree that cohabitation before marriage is a "good idea." Moreover, 42 percent agree that permanent cohabitation without intending to marry is all right—as do 65 percent of those who report a "regular sexual partnership." Thus those who, for one reason or another, have lost a spouse or who never had one and enter into a partnership, have little doubt that a permanent nonmarital relationship is acceptable. Women and men differ little on this issue; 64 percent of the women and 67 percent of the men agree that such partnerships are "alright." Thus the possibility of premarital cohabitation may have expanded the possibility—and perhaps the desirability—of nonmarital "regular" sexual relationships, even permanent ones.

This is behavior that traditional religious morality would have considered to be "living in sin." Clergy would have condemned it from their pulpits. Men and women would have been urged either to marry or to divorce and remarry. Now the judgment of the American people seems to be that it is "alright." One can understand that the need for intimacy, both emotional and physical, would have pushed the unattached in this direction. That the change has occurred, however, with little protest from the religious leaders who condemn permanent homosexual unions, premarital sex, pornography, and abortion and fiercely defend family values does seem a little strange.

So the question arises as to how Conservative Christians are reacting to this "partnership" revolution in which the unattached seek some kind of attachment—as an alternative to promiscuity. In this analysis we limit our analyses to whites in the Conservative and Mainline Protestant denominations.

We discover that 80 percent of both the Conservative Protestants and the Mainline Protestants who are not married report that they have had sexual relations in the last year (for the Bible Christians the rate is 76 percent). Moreover, there is no difference across denominational lines between the widowed, the divorced, and separated. However, the never-married Conservative Protestants are somewhat more likely than never-married Mainliners to have been celibate during the previous year (35 percent of the former and 27 percent of the latter). The majority of both groups, however, freely engage in premarital sex. One hears little protest from the clergy at the annual meetings of the Conservative denominations. Moreover four-fifths of the members of both denominational groups who have had nonmarital sex in the last year report that it was with a "regular" partner. It is logistically and emotionally much easier, one would assume, to have a "regular" partner than to engage in random sex, especially when one thinks that such a relationship is "alright." There is some disagreement across denominational lines among those with regular partners whether it is "alright" in the long run—62 percent of the Mainline Protestants think so as do 51 percent of the Conservative Protestants. Moreover, 37 percent of the Conservative Protestants with regular sexual partners live with their regular partner as do 26 percent of the Mainline Protestants. Bible Christians are in fact more likely than other Conservative Protestant (37 percent versus 26 percent) to cohabit with their regular sexual partner. Thus the Conservatives are if anything more likely to be affected by the partnership revolution than the Mainliners but with more than a third of their nonmarried population living in an arrangement once thought to be sinful, one again has to wonder why one hears so little about it. The behavior under consideration is the definition of fornication and, depending on the partners' marital histories, possibly adultery. The divines of Puritan New England might have put the guilty parties in the stocks. The Reformers would have denounced them in no uncertain terms. Yet those who in so many other ways carry the Reformation into contemporary life seem strangely unexcited about what's happening. Homosexuality is a threat to family values but regular sexual cohabitation outside of marriage apparently is not a threat against which society needs to be offering protection.

For an unattached person, does a regular sexual partner create happiness that is comparable to marital happiness? Apparently it does not. Forty-two percent of the married respondents say that they are "very happy" as opposed to 20 percent of the unattached, regardless if they have a regular partner. The proportions are similar for both men and women. The proportions are the same for both Conservative Protestants and Mainline Protestants. However, the presence of a "live-in" regular sexual partner does boost to 30 percent the proportion of Conservative Protestants who assert that they are "very happy"—an improvement over the situation where the regular partner and the respondent don't cohabit, though still ten percentage points lower than the happiness rate among married people.

Does the violation of Christian ethics that some would see in the "partnership revolution" lead Protestants to have less dedication to certain other sex-related issues? The evidence seems to indicate that it demolishes Conservative Protestant opposition towards premarital sex. Forty-eight percent of the married Conservatives believe that sex before marriage is always wrong while only 20 percent of the unmarried Conservative Protestants who have regular sex partners think so. The gap exists for Mainline Protestants, too, but there is much less opposition to begin with; 27 percent of married Mainline Protestants and 7 percent of unmarried ones with regular sex partners believe that sex before marriage is always wrong. However, there is little impact on the Conservatives' attitude towards extramarital sex with approximately four out of five in both groups believing that it is always wrong. Finally there is greater sympathy for homosexual sex among those with partners—69 percent of those in regular relationships believe it is always wrong as do 86 percent of those who are married. Partnerships lead to greater approval of premarital sex (in which many of the partners are in fact engaged) and of homosexual sex (though not majority support) than is present among those who are in marriages.

Finally there is little change in attitudes towards the admissibility of abortion when a woman's health is in danger. However those with regular partners are less likely (37 percent versus 27 percent) to approve of abortion for a single mother who wants no more children than those who are in married unions. Thus sexual partnership eats a little bit around the edge of the Conservative Christian sexual ethic but does not substantially weaken it. Many of those with regular sexual partners see no particular conflict, in other words, between their own sexual situation and the more general stands of their denominations. They can conclude that their own situation is "alright" and still campaign against homosexuality and easy abortions.

To conclude this section of the chapter, if the real sexual revolution in the United States is not the increase in premarital sex but rather the surge of nonmarital "regular" sexual partnerships, some of which involve cohabitation, then this sexual revolution has had a strong effect on Conservative Protestants and erodes somewhat, but only somewhat, the fabric of the Conservative Christian sexual ethic. Apparently a different set of absolutes governs such "regular" sexual unions than judges abortion and homosexuality. It is beyond the data available to us to attempt to suggest how the men and women engaged in these apparent contradictions resolve their consciences or how the leaders of the Conservatives reconcile their obligation (one would think) to condemn such fornication and adultery with their apparent silence on the subject.

BEHAVIOR: HOMOSEXUALITY AND PROMISCUITY

Two questions deal with possible homosexuality—the proportion of partners of the opposite sex you've had since you were eighteen and during the last year. Four percent of the Conservative Protestant women say that they had sex with at least one woman since they were eighteen as do 5 percent of the Mainline Protestants. However 95 percent of the former and 94 percent of the latter say they have had no such relationships. Ninety-six percent of Conservative Protestant males say they have had no sexual relationships with men in comparison with 94 percent of the Mainline Protestant men. These numbers are roughly comparable with the report of gay and lesbian behavior in the American population in the work of Laumann et al. (2000). Some 2 percent of Conservative Protestant men report a male sexual partner in the last year and 3 percent of the Mainline Protestants males. Two percent of Conservative Protestant and Mainline Protestant women admit a relationship with another woman. There are not enough cases to justify any further exploration of the nature, reasons, and consequences of such relationships.

Ninety-five percent of Conservative Protestant men have had only one sexual partner in the last year, compared to 96 percent for Mainline Protestant men. For women 98 percent of both the Conservative Protestants and Mainline Protestants have had no more than one sexual partner in the last year. These numbers are often ridiculed by some social scientists who point out the random sexual couplings at professional association meetings as evidence to the contrary. One has to reply that most Americans are not social scientists and do not attend conventions. Even if there are under estimations in these replies they suggest at a minimum that most Americans of either denominational group want to create the impression that, despite the enthusiasm for "affairs" in the women's magazines, such events are relatively infrequent. Moreover the rates for Jewish men are 95 percent and for Jewish women 98 percent and for those with no religion are 95 percent for men and 97 percent for women with no religion. During a given year, therefore, most married men and most women tend to be faithful, with only the most minute differences among the two white Protestant groups. A swinging society America is not.[16]

But what about the course of a lifetime? How much promiscuity occurs among Americans? Sixty-five percent of Mainline women report no more than three sexual partners in the course of a lifetime, 54 percent no more than two. Sixty-nine percent of the Conservative Protestant women say they have had no more than three sexual partners, 60 percent no more than two. By these standards white Protestant women are hardly promiscuous and in fact the Conservatives are somewhat more likely to have sexual partners than the Mainliners.

Forty percent of the Mainline men have had lifetime no more than three sexual partners and 30 percent no more than two. For Conservative men 46 percent have had no more than three partners and 38 percent more than two. Like Conservative Protestant women, Conservative Protestant men are somewhat more likely to have checkered sexual careers than Mainline Protestant men.

One hardly wants to argue that chastity is commonplace among white Protestants in this country, yet Americans are not the madly promiscuous men and women that some European intellectuals (not excluding certain observers in the Vatican) would like to imagine. On the contrary the norms would appear to lean in the direction of restraint and fidelity.

If Puritanism implies restraint and fidelity, then in this one respect of lifetime sexual activity at least, Mainline Protestants are more Puritanical than their Conservative brothers and sisters.

CONCLUSION

This chapter began as an exploration of the question of whether the Conservative Christian sexual ethic was stricter than that of other white Protestants and whether it has been affected by the sexual revolution. In fact, they are generally speaking more likely to be strict in their sexual attitudes and behavior than are the Mainline Protestants, somewhat more relaxed on premarital sex and abortion than the demands of their clergy would be willing to tolerate and also increasingly sympathetic to homosexuals. However, the real sexual revolution has been the increase in "regular" sexual partnerships among the nonmarried, sometimes with cohabitation, behavior by the standards of traditional Christian ethic—if not always of Christian behavior—which might well be called fornication or adultery. While Conservative Protestant widowed, separated, and divorced men and women are marginally less likely to enter such partnerships many of them are involved in such behavior, though apparently it does not appreciably narrow the gap between their own personal happiness and that of the married members of their denominations. These relationships tend to erode somewhat their commitment to the conservative ethic on other matters of sex and reproduction. Yet the erosion does not prevent those in the relationships from agreeing on issues of abortion and homosexuality with their clergy. "Family values" or "moral values" apparently means abortion and homosexuality and not regular nonmarital sexual partnerships. Moreover it is interesting and surprising that the sexual life stories of Conservative Protestants show more sexual partners than do the stories of mainline Protestants—exactly the opposite of what the Puritan/Reformation posture of their denominations might have lead us to expect.

It is not our intention here to suggest either hypocrisy or deliberate self-deception. If you want that, read Sinclair Lewis's *Elmer Gantry* (1927). We did not dig for inconsistencies. We simply found them in data on representative samples of American adults. The contradictions we found arise as part of the human condition. Unlike Lewis in another way, too, we are genuinely surprised by these findings. They show that in their own way Conservative Protestants are as inconsistent as are our fellow Catholics—whom we have often suspected of having a monopoly on religious inconsistency. As the evidence piles up we cannot escape the argument that the Conservative Protestants are a much more complicated group of humans than either pop psychology's attempts to explain them away or pundits' hand-wringing about moral values deciding an election would imply.

NINE

The Conservative Christian Family and the "Feminist Revolution"

INTRODUCTION

The battle cry of the politically involved Conservative Christians is "family values." As we observed in the last chapter the precise meaning of that shibboleth seems rather flexible. It applies to certain forms of abortion and to homosexuality but apparently not to a regular sexual partner and cohabitation. Equally important, if not more so, are the norms, roles, and mores that structure the daily lives of men and women. Traditional models of the proper roles of men and women in and out of family relationships have been recast by the women's movement. One supposition is that the "family values" cry of the Christian right is a call to resist those changes. Just as we asked in the last chapter to what extent the Conservative Christian sexual ethic would survive the sexual revolution, in this chapter was ask to what extent traditional convictions about family life have survived the feminist revolution—or more accurately, the technological and demographic changes that are articulated in the theories of the women's movement.

Others have been over this ground before. Linda Waite and Maggie Gallagher (2000) considered it in their *Case for Marriage* (also see Goldschieder and Waite 1991). The specific issues of family values, religion, and feminism are central to research articles by Duane Alwin (1986), John Barkowski (1997), and Clem Brooks (2002). Of these, Brooks's analysis is the most relevant for our purposes. Reviewing data collected between 1972 and 1996, he found a steady increase in the frequency with which people cited elements of "family decline" as the nation's "most important problem." He considered explicit mentions of "family decline" itself, of course, but included mentions of divorce, single-parent families, inadequate child rearing, and child poverty as well. The fraction of U.S. voters mentioning any of these aspects of family decline was tiny prior to 1984 when it was 2 percent.[1] From that low point it increased steadily to 9.4 percent in 1996. That may sound like family decline was still far from a burning issue. However, this is not a forced choice question. Respondents can (and do) say anything that is on their minds. The sheer variety of answers is impressive. Moreover, the increase was most intense for Conservative Protestants and frequent churchgoers, with an added boost among Conservative Protestants who attended church weekly. Brooks does not present the observed percentages, but the coefficients in his model 2 imply that over 40 percent of Conservative Protestants attending church weekly in the most recent year (1996) cited family decline as the nation's most important problem when less than 8 percent of their fellow Americans thought it was that important. Now Conservative Protestants who attend church weekly are but a small segment of the U.S. electorate, but their focus on the family is both impressive and distinctive.

Soft Patriarchs, New Men by W. Bradford Wilcox (2004) explores the link between religion and family from the family rather than a political perspective. In his comprehensive review of contemporary family ideologies and practices, he shows how Conservative and Mainline Protestant men differ when they approach families. He calls the conservatives "soft patriarchs" in deference to their aspirations to be traditional providers and beacons of virtue, but his main finding is that family trumps patriarchy in the modern Christian household. That means that Conservative Protestant fathers are more emotionally engaged with their wives and children than other men. He labels the Mainline men "new" because they truly value egalitarian family life and even though they fail to achieve it in absolute terms, they do a significantly greater share of household labor than other American men. Wilcox's research, and indeed most empirical work on religion and family, leads us to expect a quantitative rather than a qualitative difference between Conservative and Mainline Protestants' gender ideologies. The "quantitative, not qualitative differences" theme echoes the consistent findings of the preceding chapters of this book.

GENDER ROLES

From the very earliest years of the General Social Survey, the National Opinion Research Center has asked four questions that have constituted a feminism[2] scale that was designed in the late 1960s as a leading social indicator:

- *Do you agree or disagree with this statement? Women should take care of running their homes and leave running the country to the men.*
- *Do you approve of disapprove of a married woman earning money in business or industry if she has a husband capable of supporting her?*
- *If your party nominated a woman for President, would you vote for her if she were qualified for the job?*
- *Tell me if you agree or disagree with this statement.: Most men are better suited emotionally for politics than are most women.*

In table 9.1 we consider the average response of four Christian denominations to these four questions in 1996 and 1998 (the most recent years all four questions were asked).

The table demonstrates that contemporary Conservative Protestants are slightly more likely to manifest restraint on women's involvement beyond the home while Mainline Protestants and Catholics are more likely to support the moderate feminist positions encoded in the questions. Afro-American Protestants are moderate on three of the four items but actually more likely than Conservative Protestants to disapprove of married women working if their husbands are capable of supporting them. However, Conservative Protestants support the feminist position on each item by at least a two-thirds majority. This is the theme that often recurs in the present study—Conservative Protestants are different but not all that different.

These items were hardly avant-garde when they were introduced thirty years ago—surveys generally try to avoid shocking the people they interview—and by now they border on old-fashioned. As society has outpaced the constraints of these questions, feminists and other advocates have introduced new issues.[3] Obsolete or not, the questions do provide measures for social change across the three decades, as we see in figure 9.1.[4] Change is the dominant message in each figure, though the rate of increase on three of the four items slowed in the

Table 9.1 Attitudes about the role of women by religion

	Religion			
Item / Answer	Conservative Protestant (%)	Afro-Amer. Protestant (%)	Mainline Protestant (%)	Catholic (%)
"Women should take care of their homes . . ."[a]				
Disagree (%)	77	77	86	87
"Married woman earning money . . ."[a]				
Approve (%)	81	73	84	83
"Woman for president"[a]				
Would vote for her (%)	89	94	95	94
"Most men are better suited for politics"[b]				
Disagree	73	77	77	76

[a]SOURCE: General Social Surveys, 1996–1998.
[b]SOURCE: General Social Surveys, 2000–2004.
NOTE: Denominational differences significant (.05 level) for each item.

1990s. We should not ascribe the slowdown to its having maxed out, either, as the woman president item—highest from the start—is the one that continued upward until the series was discontinued.

The differences among items hint at the Conservative Protestants' somewhat different take on gender-role equity. On three of the four items—the three that mention politics—Catholics are the most liberal and Conservative Protestants the most conservative in each year. The frequency of feminist responses for both groups increased each year from 1974 to 1992 then leveled off. The average gap between them is 15 percentage points, and the trends neither converge nor diverge. Mainline Protestants are not statistically different from the Catholics (though slightly below) on each item. Afro-American Protestants closely resemble the Conservative Protestants on the first item (leave running the country up to the men), Mainline Protestants on the third item (vote for a woman), and split the difference on the fourth (men better suited).

These trends developed in a context in which women's public roles as elected officials, spokespersons for causes, and administrators in government, the nonprofit sector, and business all expanded exponentially. Opinions about women in public life may have pressured some institutions to open up while the trends gave other institutions the freedom to promote women without fear of public backlash. Yet in all these changes, Conservative Protestant women held back. They

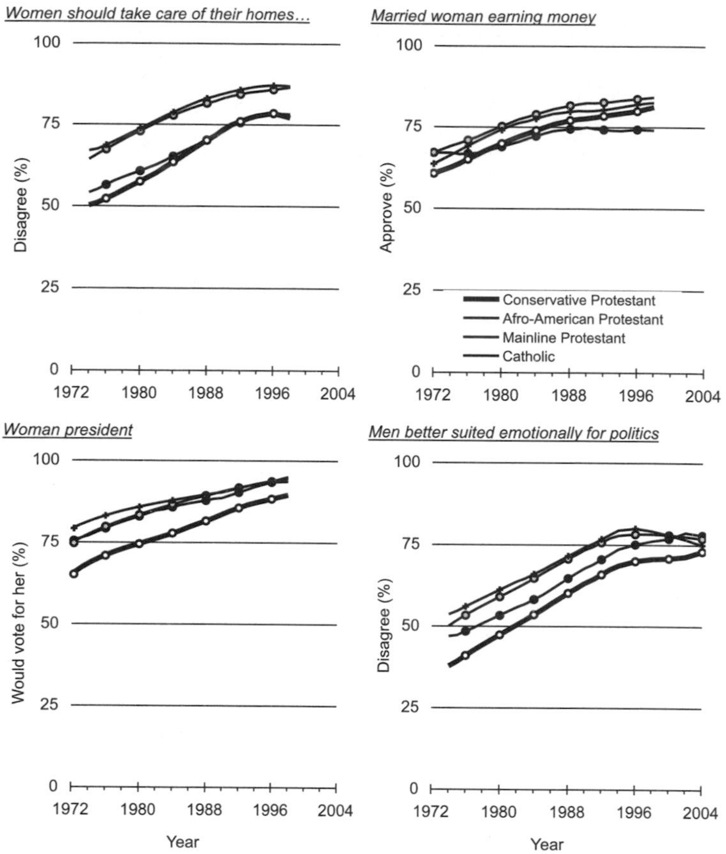

Figure 9.1 Feminism scale items by year and denomination. Data-smoothed using locally estimated regression.

did not go off in the opposite direction, they kept up, but they never caught up with Catholics or Mainline Protestants. On each of these three items about women in public life, Conservative Protestants' support looks like Catholic women's support did eight or ten years earlier.

The second question—should women be allowed to take paying jobs—differs from the other three in several ways. First, it makes no mention of public life. Second, religion did not affect answers to this question as much as the others, even in the early 1970s. Third, Afro-

American Protestants (the group with the highest married women's labor force participation rate in the first decade of the series) changed the least. Fourth, and most important for our purposes, the Conservative Protestants increased the most on this item so that the gap between them and Catholics and Mainline Protestants is not statistically (or substantively) significant after 1994.

The difference between the three public-sphere items and the private-sphere one suggests that a significant minority of Conservative Protestants dissent from women's growing public prominence. We would suspect partisanship if all prominent women were Democrats. But of course they are not. Secretary of State Condoleeza Rice and talk show host Ann Coulter arrived too late to affect these trends; the action here is in the 1970s and 1980s. That was when Margaret Thatcher was prime minister of the United Kingdom, the U.S. Senate had four Republican women, and Peggy Noonan wrote speeches for President Reagan. One can expect therefore as this analysis proceeds that the conservatives will lag behind the Mainline Protestants in their sympathy for the equality of women, but not far behind.

WIFE AND HUSBAND

In 1996 GSS asked three questions that presented paradigms for marital relationships:

- *A relationship where the man has the main responsibility for providing the household income and the woman has the main responsibility for taking care of the home and family.*

  OR
- *A relationship where the man and the woman equally share responsibility for providing the household income and taking care of the family.*

———

- *Relationship in which the man and the woman do most things in their social life together.*

  OR
- *Relationship where the man and the woman do separate things that interest them.*

———

- *A relationship where the man and the woman are emotionally dependent on one another.*
  OR
- *A relationship in which the man and the woman are emotionally independent.*

The first and third pairings tap the soft patriarchy that Wilcox (2004) identified. Both render the husband and wife dependent on one another. While a minority of Conservative Protestants chose the male breadwinner / female homemaker model, at 41 percent it is a much more popular option for those families than for others; 24 percent of Afro-American Protestants, 25 percent of Catholics, and 31 percent of Mainline Protestants chose the breadwinner / homemaker model. Likewise a bare majority (52 percent) of Conservative Protestants opted for emotional (inter)dependence over independence while minorities of other faiths made that choice; 45 percent of Afro-American Protestants, 41 percent of Mainline Protestants, and 44 percent of Catholics. Differences by denomination in the middle pairing are not statistically significant.

Combining the two items that do differ into a three-point scale we discover three things: (1) Women in all denominations opt out of the traditional model more that men do. (2) Conservative Protestants differ from other denominations more than the other denominations differ among themselves. (3) The EVANGELICAL scale accounts for only 28 percent of the Conservatives' traditionalism.

Does the traditional paradigm interfere with marital happiness for the Conservative Protestants? It would appear that it does not. Quite the contrary: 70 percent of the Conservative Protestants who accept emotional (inter)dependence say they are very happy as opposed to 57 percent of the conservatives who opt for the emotional independence. Fifty-eight percent of the Mainline Protestants report very happy marriages regardless of their paradigms; marital happiness does not vary by emotional model for the Afro-American Protestants or Catholics either. In an ordered logitistic regression analysis, both emotional (inter)dependence and Biblical literacy increase marital happiness for Conservative Protestants.[5] In some sense, Biblical Christianity seems to work when it underwrites the traditional martial paradigm in a community that stresses both.

In various times since the late 1980s the National Opinion Research Center has administered, as part of the General Social Survey, modules designed by the International Social Survey Program, three of which were about marriage and family life. Two of the items in the 2002 module are somewhat similar to the previous questions asked in the 1996 module.[6]

- *When you and your spouse make decisions about choosing weekend activities, who has the final say—mostly me, mostly my spouse, sometimes me, sometimes my spouse, we decide together.*
- *(Same wording) Buying major things for the house.*

Respondents tend to assert that these decisions are made together, regardless of gender. Forty-two percent of the men and 46 percent of the women claim joint decisions on weekends. And 49 percent and 53 percent say that the purchase of major things for the house are joint decisions.

The two variables correlate at .50 so it is not unreasonable to create a factor out of them. The emergent factor tilts in the direction of joint decisions. With the exception of Catholics, women are more likely to insist that the decisions are joint—with the Jewish women the most likely of all. Mainline Protestants are more likely, regardless of gender, to report joint decisions. Fifty-eight percent of the Mainline Protestant women report joint decisions as opposed to 51 percent of the Conservative Protestant women, but this seven-point difference is not statistically significant. Hence whatever paradigms might exist about marital life, they do not seem to create major differences between Conservative and Mainline Protestants about who makes important consumer decisions.

Matters are possibly different, however, when the issue is whether men should do more household work (see Barkowski 1997; Wilcox 2004). Sixty-three percent of male Conservative Protestants think that men should do housework as do women from the same denominational background. However, 74 percent of the Mainline Protestant women think the men should do more work. Thus there is a statistically significant difference between the women of the two denominations with the Mainline Protestants more likely to demand more work from their husbands. There are two possibilities: Conservative Protestant women are less likely to complain about the lack of housework help from their husbands or Mainline Protestants are more likely to complain.

Wilcox finds that housework—and denominational differences in how people think about it—is one of the hinges in the family values debates. Not only is Conservative Protestant theology and iconography deeply patriarchal, according to Wilcox, it is also very sentimental. In contrast to the fire and brimstone of the fundamentalist past, contemporary Conservative Protestantism goes for the soft focus. Emotions are very important (as we have just seen) and women act out their attachments to their families by keeping order at home. In that world, it is equally incumbent on the men to appreciate the work their wives do. Wilcox (2004, 142) points to Christian marriage counselor Gary Smalley who "advises husbands to 'verbalize' their 'thoughts of appreciation.'" Acting out traditional domesticity helps Conservative Christians feel their Christianity because it sets them off from the expectations of society in general and feminists in particular. Mainline Protestants and Catholics do not think about housework as part of Christian duty and so do not see their religious identities bound up in their daily drudgeries.

Wilcox's interpretations are large relative to the magnitude of the differences they are marshaled to explain (here and in his data that are drawn not only from the GSS but also from other national surveys like the National Survey of Families and Households).

However another question may provide some insight into the issue:

Which of the following best applies to the sharing of work between you and your household partner:

- *I do much more than my fair share of household work.*
- *I do a bit more than my fair share of the household work.*
- *I do roughly my fair share of the household work.*
- *I do a bit less than my fair share of household work.*
- *I do much less than my fair share of household work.*

Fifty-three percent of the Conservative Protestant men claim that they do at least their fair share of household work and 62 percent of the Conservative Protestant women argue that they do more than their fair share. Seventy percent of the Mainline men claim at least a fair share while fifty-three percent of Mainline women claim that they do more than their fair share. In both denominational groups men are more satisfied with themselves than women, and the difference between Conservative men and Mainline men is statistically significant.

There are many possible interpretations of the finding. Conservative men might simply be more modest in their claims, or they actually may do less of the housework than do Mainline men. The former reading of the data seems less probable because Conservative women are more likely to say that they do more than their fair share of work.

Another way to measure the impact of the traditional marriage paradigm is provided by responses to a variable we've appropriately labeled MRMOM: *It is not good if the man stays home and takes care of the children and the woman goes out to work.*

Thirty-five percent of Conservative Protestant men reject the Mr. Mom role as do 21 percent of the Mainline Protestant men, a difference that is statistically significant. Twenty-seven percent of the Conservative women and 22 percent of the Mainline women disapprove of Mr. Mom, and the difference is not significant. Two observations are in order—Conservative Protestant men are more likely to disapprove of behavior that is at odds with traditional family paradigms than are Mainline men. Nonetheless, 40 percent of them reject negative judgments about the Mr. Mom solution (the rest decline to either agree or disagree). If some of the Conservative Protestant denominations insist on the traditional paradigm, then that position is being eroded in the attitudes of their membership who are increasingly likely to support more "feminist" positions. On the other hand it would be wrong for those who see Conservative Protestants as enemies of the feminist revolution to write them off as unaffected by the changes it has created—or, more properly, the changes that are subsumed under the label "feminist revolution."

On one issue of considerable importance—the joint management of family funds (*How do you or your family organize the income that one or both of you receive?*) the Conservative Protestants have decisively chosen to share. Three-quarters answer that they pool the money and take out what they need—as do the Mainline Protestants. If the use of money is the most serious threat to a marriage—as the literature on the subject contends—then the joint administration of the funds ("we pool the money and each takes out what we need") is the most likely way to avoid conflicts over discrimination and one that strikes down the traditional assumption that the man as the head of the family should make the money decisions. The data on major purchases also confirm that married Conservative and Mainline Protestants are alike in spending money as couples rather than spending on one partner's say-so.

Responses to a series of questions in the 1996 family module round out our analysis:

Do you agree or disagree that

- *Divorce is usually the best solution when a couple can't seem to work out their marriage problems?*
- *When there are children in the family parents should stay together even if they don't get along?*
- *When there are no children, a married couple should stay together even if they don't get along?*
- *Working women should receive paid maternity leave when they have a baby?*
- *Families should receive financial benefit for child care when both parents work?*

Did you ever live with a partner you didn't marry?

Sometimes at work people find themselves the object of sexual advances, propositions or unwanted sexual discussions from the coworkers or supervisors. The contacts sometimes involve physical contacts and sometimes just involve sexual conversations. Has this ever happened to you?

Thirty-eight percent of the Conservative Protestants and 51 percent of the Mainline Protestants opt for the divorce solution. Thirteen percent of the Conservative Protestants and 20 percent of the Mainline Protestants contend that parents should stay together for the children, should there be any. The presumption in favor of the marriage that apparently existed in the middle years of the last century still finds some support among the Conservative Protestants, suggesting that the traditional paradigm still exercises some influence. Whatever the nature of the presumption there is no difference between the Conservative Protestants and the Mainline Protestants in the divorce rate—28 percent of both groups say they have been divorced.

However, Conservative Protestants are certainly on the liberal side of the maternity leave and child care issues. Eighty-one percent support maternity leave and 45 percent support child care programs. The comparable proportions of Mainline Protestants are 73 percent and 46 percent. One would have expected perhaps that the traditional marriage paradigm would have inoculated Conservative Protestants against such "liberal" innovations. However, once money becomes available for these programs, only the narrowly ideological would turn it down for the sake of principles.

Twenty-two percent of the Conservative Protestants lived with a partner before they were married, 17 percent of both groups with a partner they did not marry eventually—a practice that traditionally would have earned them the name of notorious and public fornicator. Moreover among the Conservative Protestants, living with someone they did not eventually marry makes them much more sympathetic to abortion on demand (a question used only in this module): *a pregnant woman should be able to obtain a legal abortion whatever if* for any reason *she does not want to have a baby.* Forty-nine percent of those who had cohabited agreed with this item as opposed to 26 percent of those who had not cohabited.[7] Finally, 36 percent of both denominations report sexual harassment experiences in the work place—a quarter of the men and two-fifths of the women.

In summary, the patterns that emerge so far in this analysis of the Conservative Protestant family turned up evidence of both continuity and change. The Conservatives still tend to lean more in the direction of the traditional marriage and family relations than anyone else. Yet they are by no means traditionalists. The forces that shaped the women's movement have affected them, too. They may derive a spark of oppositional identity when they defy the feminists in the sanctity of their own homes, but they also display commitment to joint decision making. Some Conservative Protestant women would like to see men helping more in the work of the home—which does not mean that the men will deliver it. In a pair of unanticipated findings we learned that Conservative Protestants of both genders support maternity leaves and do not disapprove of Mr. Mom situations.

If we had to boil the work in this section down to one finding it would be the happiness result: tradition makes Conservative Protestants happy in their marriages but does nothing for other Protestants or Catholics.

EXTENDED FAMILY

A question asked from the very beginning of the General Social Survey enables us to measure, however crudely, the existence of extended family networks as part of the Conservative Christian heritage: *How often do you spend a social evening with relatives?*

Thirty-nine percent of the Conservative Protestants report they spend evenings with relatives several times a week versus 31 percent of Mainline Protestants, 44 percent of Afro-American Protestants, and 37 percent of Catholics. While there may be many differences between Catholics and Conservative Protestants, they appear to be alike in acting on a commitment to family. Moreover, they are also more likely to believe that elderly people should live with their children—41 percent versus 37 percent for Mainline Protestants, 49 percent for Afro-Americans, and 48 percent for Catholics.

CONCLUSION

Conservative Protestants are not a socially isolated sect. Though they have some distinctive institutions including thriving specialized media that informs and entertains on radio and television and publishes fiction and nonfiction books, they are a fifth of American society spread (not quite uniformly) across the whole country. As such they are subject to the influences of the larger society just as they endeavor to move it. Conservative Protestant families feel the same economic pressures. They have welcomed the changes in employment possibilities and better fertility control that gave rise to "second-wave feminism"—the women's movement of the 1970s that demanded equal partnership in society. Are the Conservative Christians feminists? Surely some of them are. Use a broad enough net and you might conclude that many of them are.

They are not, in other words, totally different from the rest of America society in their family values, but not totally the same either. Wilcox's soft patriarch model is useful. Conservative Protestant men and women have given up the hard patriarchy of an older generation (though they still use—and advocate—corporal punishment for children) for a still-patriarchal family life that is softened by what Swidler (2002) aptly calls "talk of love." Soft patriarchy drops "what

I say goes" and adopts the organic solidarity of partnership. Spouses contribute in distinct ways but share goals and support each other in the struggle to see their joint project through to success and happiness. It is different than the family life found in other American homes, but neither as different as outsiders imagine nor as different as it could be.

TEN

Happiness and Lifestyle among Conservative Christians

INTRODUCTION

One of the more reliable generalizations in social science is that married and religious people are happier than people who have neither companionship nor faith (e.g., Biswas-Diener et al. 2004). That religion would be reliably linked to happiness may strike some as something of a puzzle. Religion, to the secular, is dour business built on a list of "Thou shalt nots" and pronounced by hectoring clerics. To them, happiness is freedom from constraint and discipline. Devout people seldom experience religion that way, and if they do, it is the choice they made from among many alternatives. A person, we submit, can believe in the literal, word-for-word inspiration of the Bible and still be a happy human person in a happy marriage (even if we believe that conviction is misguided or wrong).

The meaning and sense of belonging long associated with religious attachment (e.g., Greeley 1995; Wuthnow 1993; Smith 1998) seems a likely source of feelings of well-being, personal efficacy, and dare we say it, happiness. As a group that especially derives meaning and belonging from their religious attachment, the Conservative Protestants will not be exempt from this general tendency, their dyspeptic worldview (see chapter 2) notwithstanding. Our hypotheses:

1. People with a religious preference will be happier than people with none.
2. Among people with religious preferences, those who engage their religion more actively will be happier than those who do not.

2a. Members of liturgical denominations—Mainline Protestants and Catholics—will be happier the more they attend services.

2b. People who have a religion but do not participate in it will *not* be happier than people who have no religion.
2c. Members of Biblical denominations—Conservative Protestants and Afro-American Protestants—will be happier if they interpret the Bible literally as well as attend services.
3. People who are religiously active will be "inoculated" against shocks that the rest of society may suffer and against the general downward trend in the morale of American adults.

These hypotheses stem from the theory developed over many years, articulated most recently in *Religion as Poetry* (Greeley 1995). The key idea is that the religious stories engender a sense of transcendent reality that becomes, in turn, an important resource for identity and attachment in plural mass society. Overlaid upon these psychic resources are the positive feelings and associations that come from participation in practices that are, at once, local and world-historical. The first hypothesis refers to the mere fact of belonging. If we find that people with a religious affiliation are indeed happier than those who have none, we will have to discern whether the relationship reflects religious content or just something else that correlates with religion but is not substantively religion. Thus, the second hypothesis further specifies that attending religious services explains, for liturgical Christians, the association between affiliation and happiness. For Bible Christians we have the additional hypothesis that their happiness also depends on their primary source of religious meaning and belonging, the Bible in its literal truth. Finally, when we look at trend data, we hypothesize that church attendance can buffer the shock of September 11 and the overall trend toward slightly less happiness.

The happiness question is: *Taken altogether, how would you say things are these days—would you say that you are very happy, pretty happy, or not too happy?*

This simple item and similar single-item measures correlate well with more elaborate scales of morale and psychological functioning (Smith 1979).[1]

We begin with an analysis of data from the end of the twentieth century—1998 and 2000.[2] We pause for a moment over the 2002 data. Conducted in the immediate aftermath of the September 11 attack in March and April 2002, it shows Americans to be significantly less happy than in the "normal" times of the late 1990s and the first quarter of 2000. We will use the 2002 change to test hypothesis 3. Then we will turn to the longer time span.

THE MILLENNIUM

Approaching the millennium, almost one-third of American adults were very happy, one-ninth were not too happy, and the majority (57 percent) were in between ("pretty happy"). Religious people were slightly above the national norm in happiness and below the national norm in unhappiness (see table 10.1). People who had no religion were significantly less happy than average; only 23 percent were very happy, 64 percent were pretty happy, and 12 percent were not too happy.[3] The difference between the happiness of religious Americans and those who had no religion was statistically significant and accounted for three-fifths of the total association between religion and happiness. Only Afro-American Protestants are as unhappy as the people with no religion. Hypothesis 1 is confirmed.

Establishing a statistical relationship is just the first step in thinking about how religion might affect happiness; it does not establish religion as a cause. There is always the possibility that happy people are more likely to take up religion and that unhappy people lose their religion. This seems implausible on the face of it, but our survey data cannot resolve this issue of causal order. We can use our data to address the question of whether there are variables associated with having a religion that could be the underlying factor in happiness. For example, Waite and Gallagher (2000) argue that marriage makes people happy. Married people are also more likely to have a religion than single people are (Hout and Fischer 2002). So, arguably, the relationship we see in table 10.1 might just reflect differences related to marriage but correlated with religion. Similar arguments could be made about regional subcultures affecting both religious affiliation and happiness, or differences associated with living in suburbs rather than cities, being a woman or a man, having one racial or ethnic ancestry instead of another, et cetera. To test whether differences in happiness are somehow spurious due to the influence of these sociodemographic factors, we compare the gross effects of religion shown in table 10.1 with the results we obtain in a model that includes all of these variables along with religious preference. We find that the contrast between having a religion and not is robust; the coefficient for having

Table 10.1. Happiness by religion: 1998–2000

	Happiness			
Religion	Very happy	Pretty happy	Not too happy	Total
Conservative Protestant (%)	34	55	11	100
Afro-American Protestant (%)	24	58	18	100
Mainline Protestant (%)	36	55	9	100
Catholic (%)	32	57	11	100
Jewish (%)	29	58	13	100
Other (%)	32	55	14	100
No religion (%)	23	64	12	100
Total (%)	32	57	11	100

SOURCE: General Social Survey, 1998–2000.

no religion is −.54 with no controls and −.34 with (both significant at the .05 level). While Mainline and Conservative Protestants are significantly happier than Afro-American Protestants and Catholics, those differences are completely explained by the sociodemographic factors such as racial ancestry and marital status. After controls, Jews come out as less happy than would be expected of people with their sociodemographic profile.

The results are conclusive: religion is not a proxy for some other sociodemographic factor that is important for happiness. To make the substantive link between religion and happiness, though, requires evidence that a variable with religious content explains the distinction between people with and without a religion. Beliefs are not useful in this context because some religions dispute beliefs that are central to other ones. We need an aspect of religiosity that not only differentiates the religious from the nonreligious but that also does not divide the religious. Attendance at religious services is precisely that kind of general factor. Active participation in religious rituals exposes people to whatever benefits religion might confer, regardless of the practice or expression that the rituals themselves entail. Formally, we deduce that if the effect of religion on happiness is substantively religious, then we should see that people who attend frequently are happier than those who seldom participate in religious services and that people who never attend religious services are about as happy (or unhappy) as people who have no religion.

The GSS question on church attendance classifies people into nine categories of attendance (ranging from 0 for "never" to 8 for "more than once a week").[4] When we enter frequency of attendance into the equation predicting happiness, the differences between people with and without a religion reduces to statistical insignificance, as do the differences among the five denominations. The coefficient for having no religion is very close to zero (−.003 compared with its original value of −.54). We obtain this result whether we ignore the sociodemographic variables or include them in the model.

Frequent attendance increases happiness. The coefficient of .12 is not merely statistically significant; it represents real substantive impact. In percentage terms .12 translates to a two- to four-point increase in the expected percentage of very happy for each upward tick on the GSS scale of frequency of attendance.[5] For example, the percentage very happy among forty-five-year-old white Conservative Protestants who are otherwise average rises from 21 to 30 to 38 percent as attendance rises from never to once a month to every week. The greater happiness of an otherwise average person who attends religious services weekly compared with one who attends only once a month is the equivalent to (a) the difference between a white and an African American, (b) twice the difference between a suburban and a central city resident, and (c) twice the difference between a southerner and a northeasterner.[6] However it is only one-third the difference between a married and a single person.

These results go a long way toward confirming hypotheses 2 and 2a. That is, to this point we have shown evidence that, on average, people who attend religious services more often are happier *and* that people who have a religion but do *not* attend services are no happier than people who have no religion. Further testing—we leave out the technical details—reveals that the effect of attendance frequency does not vary among denominations.

With some trepidation that we may be starting on a path toward infinite regress, we now ask the same question about attendance that we asked about denomination. Could it be something nonreligious about attending religious services that is making people happy? One possibility is socializing. After all the religious content of religious services might have no effect on morale; it might be bound up in the chance to see other people. It seems reasonable to think, for example, that people who lack other opportunities to socialize might compensate by attending religious services, and that social element of attendance, not its religious content, is the source of happiness. The

GSS routinely asks people how often they spend a social evening with friends. If sociability, not religiosity, is the reason why attending services makes people happy, then adding frequency of social evenings with friends to the model should show that it—and not frequency of religious attendance—is the significant influence on happiness or that attendance only affects people who do not have social evenings with friends. Neither is the case. Social evenings with friends and attending religious services both increase happiness. More importantly, there is no statistical interaction between them, indicating that attendance increases the happiness of those who socialize frequently just as much as it affects those who never socialize. There is no evidence that church attendance increases happiness as a substitute for loneliness.

Finally we should have some positive evidence of the religious content of attendance as well as ruling out the competing hypotheses. For that we turn to the special subset of the 1998 GSS that ascertained peoples' religious beliefs and practices in some detail. Two important issues included a question about belief in God and a battery of questions about religious feelings. We discussed them in chapter 2 above.

We made a simple additive scale from the battery of religious feelings (normed to have a mean of zero).[7] Adding the question about God and the feeling scale to the model refines our sense that attendance at religious services has real religious content. First, the direct effect of attendance net of belief in God and religious feelings is only about half as large as its coefficient without controlling these intervening variables. Second, religious feelings increase happiness, but belief in God has no effect.[8] We interpret this pattern of effects (and noneffects) as evidence that religion fosters happiness not through socializing but through the emotional response to religious services. Belief is not enough to engender high morale on its own. But if attendance brings about a sense of closeness to God—"an aura of factuality" in Geertz's phrasing—then happiness follows.

Figure 10.1 summarizes our findings so far. Religious affiliation, mostly having a religious affiliation, or not, affects happiness indirectly through attendance at religious services. And attendance increases happiness mostly through the emotional attachment to God and denomination. Social life is an important contributor to happiness, but it is a complementary, not a competing, explanation.

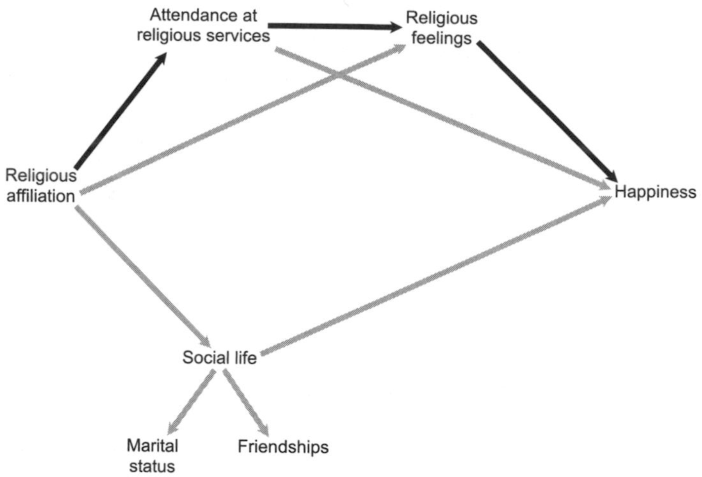

Figure 10.1 Path diagram showing how religious affiliation affects happiness through religious services, religious feelings, and social life.

We close this section with a test of hypothesis 2c proposed above that conforming to the Reformation constraint to interpret the Bible literally will make Conservative and Afro-American Protestants happier but have no effect on Mainline Protestants or Catholics. Table 10.2 reports the coefficients for our Bible scale (2 points for literal interpretation, 1 point for "inspired" interpretation, and no points for viewing the Bible as myth and fable) in multivariate models that include all the sociodemographic factors as controls. One version of this model includes just the sociodemographic variables; the other adds attendance frequency.

The results confirm hypothesis 2c for Conservative Protestants but not for Afro-American Protestants. Conservative Protestants who interpret the Bible literally are substantially happier than other Conservative Protestants and, though it is not obvious from the coefficients, they are also happier than people from other religions. The combination of interpreting the Bible literally and going to church weekly makes married Conservatives some of the happiest people in the United States. On the other hand, Conservatives who think that the Bible is inspired but not literal and attend just a few times a year are not as happy as Mainline Protestants and Catholics who agree

Table 10.2. Coefficients measuring the effect of biblical literalism on happiness by religion

Religion	No controls	Socio-demographic controls	Socio-demographic controls plus attendance at religious services
Conservative Protestant	.230	.278	.183
	(.055)	(.063)	(.063)
Afro-American Protestant	.275	.320	.232
	(.116)	(.131)	(.140)
Mainline Protestant	.041	.114	.012
	(.052)	(.059)	(.061)
Catholic	.046	.131	.082
	(.059)	(.060)	(.063)

NOTES: Numbers are logistic regression coefficients; numbers in parentheses are robust standard errors. The sociodemographic controls are gender, ancestry, region, suburban residence, marital status, year, income, and education.

that the Bible is inspired but not literal and attend the same amount. People who typify their denomination are the happiest ones.

The negative result for Afro-American Protestants and for African Americans in general is instructive. It reminds us that happiness is more than mood. And some of it is beyond an individual's power to control. The burden of oppression and discrimination continues to hold black people down. In each denomination African Americans are significantly less happy than others. Furthermore, while African Americans who have a religion are significantly happier than those who do not, the Bible and attendance at services are significantly less efficacious for African Americans than for other Americans.

SEPTEMBER 11 AND HAPPINESS

The al Qaeda attacks that felled the World Trade Center and damaged the Pentagon on September 11, 2001 shocked and stunned Americans. A residue of the response to the events of that day is evident in the 2002 GSS. Emergency workers and federal investigators were still recovering human remains from ground zero when the GSS was in the field. And Americans were not as happy as they were two years before.

Table 10.3. Happiness by religion and year: 2000–2002

	All		*No religion*		*Some religion*	
Happiness	2000 (%)	2002 (%)	2000 (%)	2002 (%)	2000 (%)	2002 (%)
Very happy	32	30	26	25	33	31
Pretty happy	58	57	64	58	57	57
Not too happy	10	12	10	18	11	12
Total	100	100	100	100	100	100
N	2,773	1,361	389	191	2,384	1,170

SOURCE: General Social Survey, 2000–2002.

The two-point increase in the unhappiness of the whole population was concentrated, it turns out, among the people with no religion. Exposed to the shock of September 11 without the meaning and belonging that others find in church, they became bluer. The fraction of people with no religion who were unhappy rose from 10 percent to 18 percent in two years—by our reckoning in a few hours of one day and lasted long enough to still register six or seven months later.

TRENDS SINCE THE 1970S

The 1990s were, by some measures, a decade of polarizing religion (e.g., Hout and Fischer 2002). Perhaps the relationship between religion and happiness is a recent development. Our theory says no. It is predicated on the long-term importance of religion for establishing meaning and belonging in peoples' lives. Thus it would be a complication for our theory if the effect of religion on happiness emerged recently. On the other hand, evidence of a persistent effect would strengthen our theory. We look at trends two ways: by denomination and by attendance.

Figure 10.2 shows the trends in feeling "very happy" for each religion except the residual "other religions" and for people with no religion. This figure contains all the pertinent information as there is no trend in unhappiness; 11 or 12 percent of American adults were "not too happy" each year from 1973 to 2000 and again in 2004. However there was an unmistakable erosion in the percentage "very happy" between the mid-1970s and the mid-1990s—from roughly 38 percent to 31 percent. Morale recovered a little from 1996 to 2000, dipped in 2002, and rebounded in 2004. Could the trend toward having no

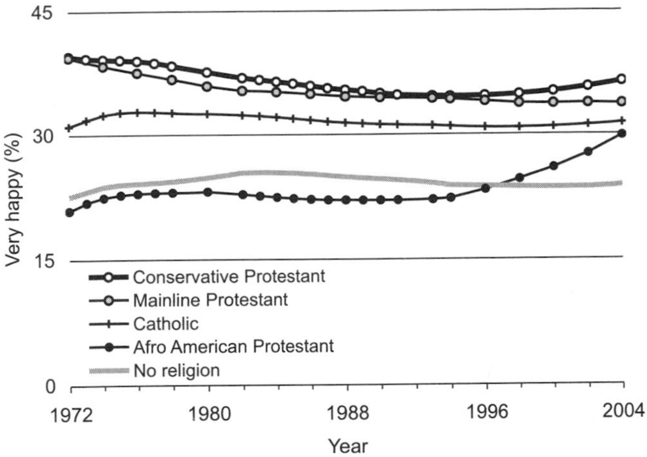

Figure 10.2 Happiness by year and religious preference. Data-smoothed using locally estimated regression.

religion (Hout and Fischer 2002) have contributed to the erosion of happiness? If there was no trend in happiness within denominations while the proportion in the least happy religious category—no religion—grew, then we could say that the changing religious combination explains the drop-off in happiness. If the trends within denominations echo the national trend, then the explanation must lie elsewhere.

The happiness of Protestants and Jews fell in concert with national trends. Catholics and people with no religion were about as happy in 2000 as they had been twenty-seven years earlier. These trends led to a modest convergence in the happiness of different religious groups. Denominational differences diminished, and religious people got ever so slightly closer to the level of happiness among nonreligious people.

Our main concern here is whether religious differences in happiness were peculiar to the end of the millennium. Clearly not. People with religious preferences have been happier than people without religion throughout the period. Among people with religions, the percentage very happy never fell below 30 percent; among people with no religion, the percentage very happy never got above 30 percent.[9] If the relationship between religion and happiness has changed at all, it

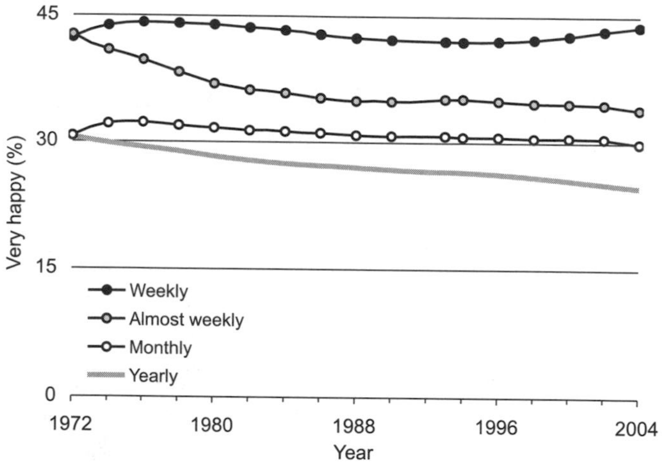

Figure 10.3 Happiness by year and attendance at religious services. Data-smoothed using locally estimated regression.

may have decreased somewhat. Conservative and mainline Protestants both became significantly less happy over time. Change over time is not statistically significant for any other religion category. With two of the three happiest groups decreasing while the others held steady, the association between religion and happiness decreased slightly.

Attendance at religious services accounts for the differences among denominations; our multivariate analysis of the happiness data shows no relationship between denomination and happiness when we include statistical controls for attendance. Among people who never (despite their nominal affiliation) attend religious services or do so only once or a few times a year, happiness fell from 30 percent to 25 percent for very happy between 1972 and 2004. People who attend services monthly changed little (a four percentage point decrease from 1974 to 1994 followed by a two-point increase in the late 1990s). Happiness plummeted between 1973 and 1990 among people who attend on an almost-weekly basis, but they changed little in the 1990s. The most religiously active people were, for the most part, unchanged; they actually became somewhat happier through the 1990s. These trends confirm hypothesis 3: frequent attendance at religious services offset the factors that made most Americans less happy over time; the drop-off in the nation's morale was concentrated among those with no religion and those who seldom or never attended religious services.

HAPPINESS CONCLUSIONS

Religion makes people happier. Theories of meaning and belonging in a pluralist society predict this result. The GSS data confirm four hypotheses derived from the theory. Initially we have replicated the well-known generalization that people who belong to a religion are happier than those who have no religion. In the entire thirty years of the GSS we found that religion increased happiness in each year. More importantly, the source of greater happiness is active participation in the religion of one's choice. People who frequently attend religious services are the ones who are happier; people who do not participate do not differ from the people who have no religion. Other kinds of social life improve happiness, too, but the effect of attendance is just as large for sociable people as it is for lonely people. Attendance appears to improve morale, in part, by engendering emotional feelings of closeness to God and church. Thus we conclude that religion per se is the causal factor in religious peoples' greater happiness; it cannot be sloughed off as a consequence of correlated but substantively irrelevant factors. Finally, adherence to the Bible principles in the Bible-oriented Conservative Protestant denominations also increases happiness.

Active and affective religiosity are the catalysts for happiness. Passive belief has no effect. Attendance accounts for the relationship between affiliation and attendance in the United States (and most other countries where there is a significant relationship between affiliation and happiness). Feeling close to God and finding strength and comfort in one's religion explains about half of the relationship between attendance and happiness. Altogether this pattern of effects and relationships adds support to the meaning and belonging perspective on religion.

ELEVEN

The Pentecostals

Ultimate Conservative Christians

INTRODUCTION

There are many different varieties of Conservative Christians, some of them often locked in combat with others. We have already mentioned the dispensationalists (chap. 2, n. 2). Unfortunately in the data available to us we are not able to compare them with other Conservative Christians. Perhaps the largest of the subgroups are the Pentecostals whose distinguishing characteristic is their emphasis on direct contact with the Holy Spirit and resulting glossolalia—speaking in tongues often in a state of trance or quasi trance. The Acts of the Apostles reports such phenomena on the first Pentecost in the history of the Christian Church on the Jewish feast of Pentecost fifty days after the Passover.[1] Contemporary glossolalia are usually wordless enthusiastic speech.

Pentecostal movements exist within many religious groups today. Six percent of all Americans report that they either are charismatics (the word that Pentecostals use to describe those who speak in tongues) or are associated with the Charismatic Movement—8 percent of the Conservative Protestants, 12 percent of the African Americans, 5 percent of Mainline Protestants, 5 percent of Catholics, 5 percent of those with no religion, and 4 percent of others. The more "fundamentalist" Protestants are sometimes uneasy with the enthusiasms of the Pentecostals and suggest that their claim of direct access to the Holy Spirit lessens the importance of the inerrant word of God found in the Bible. The proper role of the Holy Spirit, it would seem, is to inspire the proper reading of the Bible and not to generate incoherent speech which may distract from the Bible.

We can find no support for this charge in our data. Quite the contrary, Pentecostals are more likely to endorse the literal inerrancy of the Bible and read the Bible more often. Indeed, on most issues they are even more conservative than other Christians, though there are some interesting political exceptions to this generalization.

We will report on comparisons between Conservative Protestants in Pentecostal denominations—institutional Pentecostalism[2]—and members of all other Conservative Protestant denominations (both groups are white).[3] A little more than 9 percent of Conservative Protestants affiliate with the Pentecostal denominations. Members of these denominations are 2.5 percent of Americans. Seventy-three percent of the Pentecostals believe in the literal inerrant inspiration of the Bible as opposed to 53 percent of other Conservative Protestants. Twenty-three percent of the Pentecostals read the Bible more than once a day as opposed to 3 percent of the other Conservative Protestants. Forty-five percent of the former read the Bible at least once a day compared to 18 percent of the latter. Clearly the Pentecostals are the super-Conservatives.

Only 4 percent of the Conservative Protestants claim to be charismatic while 38 percent of the Pentecostals say that they are charismatics. Does the claim, which may well mean that they have actually spoken with tongues,[4] relate with more frequent reading of the Bible? Unfortunately that question cannot be answered because the three variables have never been asked in the same GSS questionnaire. However, the correlation between belief in an inerrant Bible and being a Pentecostal is reduced to statistical insignificance when the claim to a charisma is taken into account. It is precisely the experience of being a charismatic that seems to explain the higher levels of faith in biblical inerrancy among the Pentecostals. The latter seem to top the rest of the Conservative Protestants at their own game. The analytic question that we will try to explore in this chapter will be whether the charismatic experience itself or the greater belief in the Bible among the Pentecostals—or perhaps some combination thereof—will explain why the Pentecostals seem to be the super-Conservative Christians.

RELIGION

The Pentecostals also lead the other Conservative Protestants both in the experience of being born again and efforts to convince others to accept Jesus—85 percent (compared to 62 percent among other Conservative Protestants) on the born again experience and 91 percent (compared to 69 percent) in the effort to make converts. Since there are no cases in which Pentecostalism and charisma and born again or proselytizing were all asked, we cannot address the question of how important the charismatic experience might be in shaping responses to the items. However, the higher levels of faith in literal inerrancy do *not* account for the higher scores by Pentecostals on either rebirth or winning someone for Jesus. One can assume perhaps that it is the greater likelihood of an intense religious experience in the tongue-speaking events that accounts for the greater probability of the claim of rebirth.

Pentecostals also are more likely to agree with the Calvinist conviction that God shapes the course of our lives. Seventy-one percent of the Pentecostals agree that such is the case compared to 45 percent of the rest of the Conservative Protestants. However, neither faith in the Bible nor born again experience can account for any of the difference between the Pentecostals and the Conservative Protestants in their Calvinist conviction that God preordains the course of human life.

In line with the conviction of predestination perhaps is the greater likelihood of Pentecostals believing that the world and people are evil. Thirty-seven percent of the Pentecostals believe that the world is evil and 36 percent believe that human nature is corrupt while among the rest of the Conservative Protestants the percentages are 23 percent for both issues. Alas, only faith in the Bible can be entered into the regression equation which seeks to explain these differences and it has no impact. The greater pessimism about human life and the world is part of the Pentecostal worldview, but we are unable to account for it. The pessimism also involves a tilting away from an image of God as lover, friend, spouse, and mother among the Pentecostals which is even stronger than the tilt in that direction among the Conservative Protestants, but the difference is just barely statistically significant. In summary, the Pentecostal worldview tends to be grim, and the difference in this worldview in comparison with the worldview of the Conservative Protestants *cannot* be accounted for by their greater propensity to embrace the literal inerrancy of the Bible or any other measures available to us.

The Pentecostals are also more likely to believe in God, life after death, heaven, hell, and miracles than the other Conservative Protestants—93 percent to 82 percent in God, 96 percent to 83 percent, in life after death 79 percent to 71 percent, in heaven, 90 percent to 74 percent in hell, and 81 percent to 63 percent in miracles. When these variables are combine into a BELIEF factor, the correlation between that factor and Pentecostalism is .11. If the EVANGELICAL factor (Bible, reborn, convert for Jesus) is taken into account the correlation diminishes into insignificance. Just as EVANGELICAL increases the belief scores of the Conservative Protestants over mainline Protestants, so it also increases the belief scores of the Pentecostals over that of other Conservative Protestants. Once more the former emerge as super-Conservatives.

Their religious practice seems almost to make them hyperconservatives. Thirty-six percent of them attend church services more than once a week (16 percent for the rest of the Conservative Protestants) and 60 percent at least once a week (43 percent for Conservative Protestants). Forty-two percent pray several times a day and 78 percent at least once a day (31 percent and 65 percent for other Conservative Protestants. Thirty-six percent participate in religiously related activities compared to 8 percent of the rest of Conservative Protestants. Pentecostal church groups, in other words, display very high levels of religious involvement. They almost define the meaning of the word "sect" in classical sociological writings.

The correlation between Pentecostalism and engagement in religiously related activities is .14. It is cut in half when one takes into account the EVANGELICAL scale and falls to statistical insignificance when a report of an intense religious experience is added. The Pentecostals it would seem are Conservative Protestants whose experience of rebirth was particularly intense. The intensity may add a special element to their religious behavior that inclines them to pray more often, attend church more frequently, and engage in church-related activities more habitually. Other Conservative Protestants—or at least their leaders—may find such constant activity impressive but also embarrassing. Some would think of them perhaps not as heirs of the classic Reformation so much as heirs of Anabaptist enthusiasm. However, their enthusiasm would appear to be linked to biblical faith, the born again experience, and the tradition of winning a convert for Jesus, which are at the core of the Conservative Christian sensibility.

They are also much more likely to report a close relationship with God. Fifty-seven percent say they work with God as partners (25 percent for the rest of the Conservatives. Eighty-two percent say they look to God for strength and support (56 percent), and 89 percent believe that God watches over them (77 percent). Again, when the EVANGELICAL scale is taken into account, the correlation between partnership with God and Pentecostalism declines from .18 to statistical insignificance. The core elements of Conservative Christianity produce a much stronger relationship with God for Pentecostals, it would seem, than for other Conservative Protestants. Whether this level of intensity is religiously appropriate or not is doubtless a matter of the taste.[5] However, it apparently leads to the Pentecostals being more willing to forgive those who have hurt them then are the rest of the Conservative Protestants—74 percent versus 53 percent. Yet again the EVANGELICAL scale accounts for the difference. This analysis turns out to be not unlike the previous one in which Conservative Protestants were compared with Mainline Protestants. The variables that seemed to account for the difference between Conservative Protestants and Mainline Protestants are the same ones that account for the differences between the Pentecostals and other Conservatives. The Pentecostals are really Bible Christians, Super Bible Christians.

They are, in conclusion, like the other Conservative Christians—only more so: more devoted to the Bible, more likely to report a rebirth, more likely to proselytize, more likely to accept predetermination, more likely to be pessimistic, more likely to be orthodox, more likely to be (extremely) devout in their religious practice, more likely to read the Bible frequently, more likely to claim a close relationship to God. Most of these phenomena are a result of their stronger commitment as gauged by the EVANGELICAL scale. If the Conservative Christians claim fidelity to the Reformation, then the Pentecostals are even more devoted to the Reformation—if it were not for the embarrassment (as some of the other Conservatives see it) of the glossolaliac enthusiasms. Some of those other conservatives who know a bit of history might remember what Luther did to the Anabaptists of Munster.

MORALITY

Pentecostals are likely to support traditional sexual morality even more vigorously than are the other Conservative Christians. Sixty-two

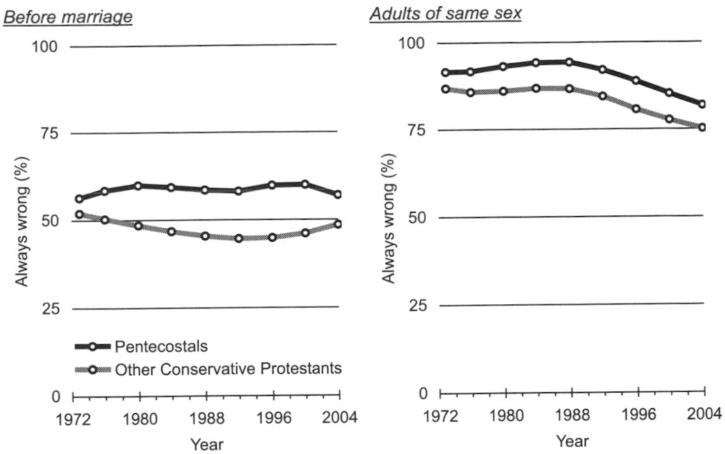

Figure 11.1 Attitudes about sex by year and type of denomination: Conservative Protestants. Data-smoothed using locally estimated regression.

percent of them think that premarital sex is always wrong compared with 47 percent of Conservative Protestants. Eighty nine percent reject sex among those in their middle teens as opposed to 82 percent of the other Conservative Protestants, and 92 percent disapprove of homosexual sex in comparison with 84 percent of the rest of the Conservative Protestants. Moreover, as figure 11.1 shows, the opposition of the Pentecostals has *increased* while that of the rest of the Conservative Protestants has decreased somewhat. No sexual revolution for the Pentecostals! While both groups have diminished their opposition to homosexual sex, nine out of ten Pentecostals think it is always wrong. The same proportion believes that the homosexual orientation is something that is chosen rather than inherent while two-thirds of the other Conservative Protestants believe that it is a matter of choice. The gay rights movement has a long way to go before it makes progress among the Pentecostals.

So too does the pro-choice movement. While 23 percent of the other Conservative Protestants are willing to admit legal abortion when a woman's health is judged to be seriously endangered, only 12 percent of the Pentecostals have reservations about seriously endangering a mother's health. More than a third of the other Conservative Protestants thing that abortion should be legal when a single woman does not want to marry—which makes them consistently pro-choice on the Rossi scale—16 percent of the Pentecostals accept the possibility of legal abortion under such circumstances. More than four of five, in other words, are consistently pro-life. On the critical moral issues in the political climate of the beginning of the twenty-first century, the Pentecostals, a tenth of the Conservative Protestants, come close to fitting the stereotype that many Americans apply to the Conservative Protestants.

One of us, along with Celi Scalon, has studied the Evangelical movements in Brazil (Scalon and Greeley 2003). We commented that on issues of doctrine and morality, the Brazilian Protestants lived more closely to the Catholic ideal than did Brazilian Catholics. In the present context it could be said that American Pentecostals are in many respects closer to the Catholic ideal than are American Catholics *and* to the ideal of Conservative Christianity than are other American Conservative Christians.

Moreover, they tend to abstain on other issues that matter to Conservative Christians. Seventy percent of them don't smoke compared to 65 percent of other Conservative Protestants, and 65 percent of them don't drink alcoholic beverages versus 47 percent of the rest of Conservative Protestants. Eighteen percent are engaged in a nonmarital sexual relationship compared to 23 percent of their fellow Conservative Protestants.

They are also more likely to believe that sinners must be punished (59 percent versus 35 percent) and to reject the notion that morality is a personal matter (35 percent versus 29 percent). Finally they are more inclined than our other Conservative Protestants to support pornography laws that would make it unavailable even to adults (63 percent versus 53 percent), to reject sex education in public schools (32 percent versus 22 percent), and to oppose birth control information for teenagers in public schools (26 percent versus 21 percent). As we remarked earlier the last two items of moral conviction, once controversial in American society, have become much less so.

Pentecostal Christians are not only more committed to their religion than are other Conservative Christians (and the latter, we must remind the reader, are strongly committed) they are also sterner moralists. They are, with the exception of enthusiastic glossolalia, the kind of people in both faith and morals that the leaders of the other

Conservative Christian denominations would like their members to be *and* that those who scapegoat Conservative Christian would like to believe are typical "evangelicals" or "fundamentalists."

FAMILY, MORALE, ENTERTAINMENT, AND POLITICS

In some matters of family structure, the Pentecostals continue outdo the rest of the Conservative Protestants. Forty-six percent approve of spanking children in comparison and they are lower on the FEMINISM scale than are Conservative Protestants—76 percent versus 80 percent. However, when the comparison is made over time as in figure 11.2, the Pentecostals lean more to feminism as measured by the FEMINISM scale than do the rest of the Conservative Protestants in recent years. They have also caught up with their fellow Conservatives in their willingness to vote for a woman president if their party should nominate one. They are four percentage points more likely to have been divorced and four percentage points less likely to endorse the traditional model of marriage. For the first time, then, we see that the Pentecostals are not hyper-Christians but slightly dissident. For all practical purposes the numbers are virtually the same, but we have come to expect a gap between Pentecostals and other Conservative Christians.

Their enthusiastic version of Conservative Christianity does not affect their propensity to report that they are "very happy" or that their marriage is "very happy"—36 percent and 66 percent respectively. They are also equally likely to claim satisfaction with their family life—46 percent. However, just as the Conservative Protestants were somewhat lower on measures of job and financial satisfaction than Mainline Protestants, so are the Pentecostals somewhat less likely than the rest of the Conservative Protestants to claim "very great" satisfaction with their jobs and their finances. On job satisfaction 46 percent of the Pentecostals claim very great satisfaction compared to 51 percent of the others. On financial satisfaction the proportions were 24 percent of the Pentecostals and 31 percent for the rest. We were able to account for the differences between Conservative Protestants and Mainline Protestants by taking into account the somewhat lower levels of education for the former; this does indeed account for the somewhat lower level of job satisfaction among the Pentecostals

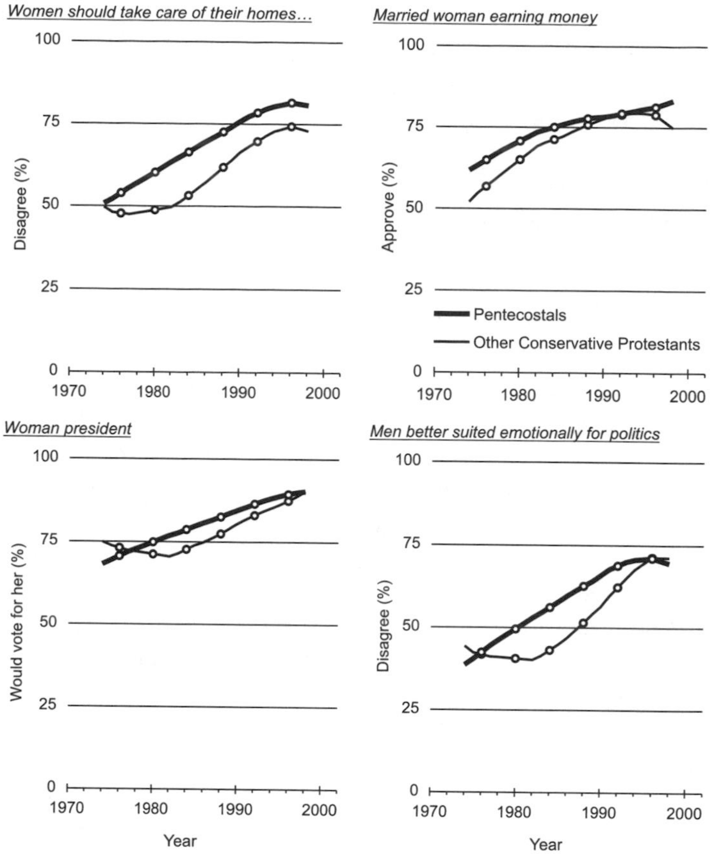

Figure 11.2 Feminism scale items by year and type of denomination. Data-smoothed using locally estimated regression.

in comparison with other Conservative Protestants. The same phenomenon exists when the subject is satisfaction with finances. The .05 negative correlation between being a Pentecostal and financial satisfaction is reversed to .05 positive correlation when lower levels of education are taken into account. Given their educational attainment (28 percent of them attended college opposed to 34 percent of other Conservative Protestants), Pentecostals are more satisfied with their finances than are other Conservative Protestants.

They are no more likely than others to enjoy bluegrass music or country and western music, but substantially more likely (55 percent to 22 percent) to enjoy gospel music. They are also more likely (27 percent to 18 percent) to have attended automobile races last year. They have the same predisposition to watch PBS ever day, a fact that may well astonish the network.

However, the biggest surprise in this analysis is how the Pentecostals vote. One would expect that, since they are super-Conservative Christians, they would be more likely to vote for Republican candidates than Democratic in the presidential elections. In fact, the opposite is the case. They were more likely to vote for Clinton in 1996 than other Conservative Christians by seven percentage points and for Gore in 2000 by ten percentage points. It does not follow that the majority of them voted for Democrats but only that they were more likely to vote for Democrats than their fellow Conservative Christians. While the differences in the two elections fall short of statistical significance, when they are combined the numbers do become slightly significant.

If the most hyper of Conservative Christians are not as strongly Republican as are other Conservatives—or even as other Protestants—then more reservations arise about the strength of the link between Conservative Christians and Republican voting. The reservations become even stronger when we consider the fact that men and women of a different color vote overwhelmingly Democratic though they have the same religious and generally the same moral values as white conservatives.

In summary, on the variables analyzed in this book, Pentecostals are easily the most conservative of Conservative Christians. But, given this fact, they don't vote the way they should.

TWELVE

Conservative Christians and Catholics

Too Estranged for Alliance

As this volume is being prepared, Conservative Christian leaders (or some of them) are entering a loosely organized group that includes Mainline Protestants, Eastern Orthodox, and Catholics to pursue common interests in what leaders of all denominations see, rightly or wrongly, as an increasing secular and even antireligious society and culture. The Conservative Christians who are involved are apparently not unwilling to sit down with leaders of the Catholic denominations—whatever they might think of the evil and the corruption of the Church of Rome and the validity of its claim to be "Christian." It is argued by some observers of the American scene that there has been an abatement in anti-Catholic attacks. The question remains, however, whether the anti-Catholic sentiments that William Shea has reported (we summarized in chapter 2) still persist.

In 2004 the GSS asked how Americans feel about Catholics in a way that might impinge on this issue:

> *I'd like to get your feelings toward groups that are in the news these days. I'll read the names of a group and I'd like you to rate that group using a feeling thermometer. Ratings between 50 degrees and 100 degrees that you feel favorable and warm toward the group. Ratings between 0 degrees and 50 degrees mean that you don't feel favorable toward the group and you don't care too much for that group*
>
> ■ *[. . .] Catholics*

Catholics receive lower ratings from Jews, those with other religion, and especially, no religion (table 12.1). The difference between Conservative and Mainline Protestants is not statistically significant.

Table 12.1 Feeling thermometer readings for attitude toward Catholics by religion

Religion	Mean	*N*	Standard Deviation
Conservative Protestant	60	201	21.5
Afro-American Protestant	57	53	25.8
Mainline Protestant	61	200	21.9
Catholic	80	210	20.7
Jewish	53	9	18.0
Other	50	25	12.8
No religion	51	126	19.4
Total	63	824	23.4

SOURCE: General Social Survey, 2004.

Among Protestants, women and Midwesterners have more favorable views of Catholics while those who say the Bible is God's word, literally, have significantly more negative views of Catholics than Protestants who view the Bible as inspired but not literally true.

The same questions were asked before in 1987, 1988, and 1989. Non-Catholics had slightly but significantly warmer feelings toward Catholics back then—the scores were 4.3 points higher in the late 1980s. Moreover, Catholics offer significantly warmer judgments about Jews and Protestants than vice versa, which hints that ill feelings across religious lines have not gone away and indeed may not be going away.

In the 2004 General Social Survey three items were added to measure anti-Catholic sentiments:

To what extent do you agree or disagree with the following statements

- *[Strongly agree/agree/neither agree nor disagree/disagree/strongly disagree]*
- *A) The statues and images in Catholic churches are idols.*
- *B) Catholic rosaries and holy medals are superstitious.*
- *C) Catholics are not really permitted to think for themselves.*

Only one-third of non-Catholics reject the slur that Catholics are not permitted to think for themselves. Approximately the same proportion do not reject the charge that the Rosary is superstitious and accept the allegation that the statues, medals, and Catholic devotions are a form of idolatry. The highest scores on measures of anti-Catholicism are those of Conservative Protestants (evangelical, fundamentalist, and Pentecostal), Southerners, and those with no religion. Mainline Protestants have somewhat lower scores.

In 1991 the then-editor of a Catholic journal requested one of us to review the data then available on anti-Catholic sentiments. There were no such data, so he commissioned a "pretest in force" survey by Knowledge Network to determine whether slurs which were pervasive in the early nineteenth-century and early twentieth-century America had some credibility at the beginning of the twenty-first century. He was especially interested in the historic charges that Catholics could not think for themselves and engaged in superstitious devotional behavior. (For a treasure trove of anti-Catholic bigotry, see Shea 2002).

He summarized the findings in a paper at the conference and suggested that three of the twelve measures—idolatry, superstition, not thinking for oneself—were appropriate for further research. Since it did not seem likely that anyone was going to rise to the bait and fund a national study based on the pretest, he commissioned (and paid for) the inclusion of the three best items (high response rate, adequate distribution) in the 2004 General Social Survey. While the responses are certainly adequate evidence that anti-Catholic slurs still have wide acceptance in American society,[1] they are only the first step in a necessary study of this last great bigotry in the United States.

For the sake of simplicity we will address in this chapter two of the slurs—Catholics are not permitted to think for themselves and the Rosary is a superstitious devotion. We make two assumptions based on the "rules of the game" currently practiced by officially approved minority groups (among which American Catholics are definitely not listed): If the vast majority of a minority group says that a statement about them is not true, they have the right to interpret the statement as a slur. Women may legitimately object when it is said that they are not qualified to be scientists or mathematicians. Jews may object when it is said that they are more avaricious than others. African Americans may object when others aver that they are not good workers. Hispanics may object when it is said that they are not truly committed to becoming Americans. In each case it must be presumed that those under assault know falsehoods about themselves when they hear them. Hence if four out of five American Catholics say that they can too think for themselves (and leaders of the worldwide church complain that they do too much thinking for themselves), then the claim that they cannot is a slur. It is a repetition of the slur when a critic says that he knows better. Similarly if four out of five American

Catholics insist that praying the Rosary is not superstitious, then to say that it is superstitious is a slur. The proper measure of the absence of bigotry is whether a respondent says that she is willing to disagree strongly or disagree somewhat with the slur.

Thus while more than three-quarters of the Catholic respondents deny both that they can't think for themselves and that the Rosary is a superstition, only 37 percent of other Americans are willing to concede the point and reject (either "strongly" or "somewhat") the slur about Catholics not thinking for themselves and only a third are inclined to dismiss the charge that the Rosary is superstitious.

About a third of Americans who are not Catholic accept the two slurs, another third refuse to either agree or disagree and a final third reject them. Denial of Catholic freedom to think correlates significantly only with two variables—South and Conservative Christian (of a battery including age, gender, education, income, party affiliation, political ideology). When the same battery is applied to the Rosary, women are more likely to reject the charge that the Rosary is superstitious and Southerners and Conservative Protestants continue to be less likely than other Americans to reject it. However, only the correlation with Conservative Protestants is fairly large, −.18. When the two variables are entered into both equations the South becomes statistically insignificant.

There are statistically significant differences between Conservative Protestants and Mainline Protestants in their attitudes towards Catholics. Thirty-four percent of the conservatives reject the assertion that Catholics cannot think for themselves as do 43 percent of Mainline Christians. Note that the majority of American Protestants do not reject the charge. Similarly the majority does not reject the charge that the Rosary is superstitious—only 36 percent do so. However, the difference between the Mainline and the Conservatives continue to be striking—and statistically significant. Forty-one percent of the Mainline reject the charge that the Rosary is superstitious compared to 28 percent of the Conservative Christians.

Finally, among the Conservative Protestants, the Pentecostals are even more inclined to accept the anti-Catholic stereotypes. Only 22 percent reject the premise that Catholics cannot think for themselves (compared to 35 percent of the other Conservative Protestants) and a mere 15 percent deny that the Rosary is a superstition in comparison to 32 percent of the other Conservative Protestants. The latter difference is not quite statistically significant at the conventional level (.08) even though there are only 88 Pentecostals in the sample. While Shea may be correct in suspecting that anti-Catholic sentiments have diminished among conservatives, there can be no question that such sentiments still persist. Moreover, once again the Pentecostals prove themselves to be most fervent of the Conservative Christians.

Despite the variations among different groups, the fact remains that these indicators of anti-Catholic feeling are not unpopular among Americans. Most of the respondents apparently experienced little unease in admitting (in face-to-face interviews) that they do not reject anti-Catholic slurs. Indeed, as often happens with slurs, some who promote them may view them as merely descriptive, not catching their bigotry.

By design, these items parrot clichés one would have encountered in nativist circles a hundred years ago. This dislike of Catholics does not lead to riots or convent burning any more. It does not affect the occupational careers of most Catholics. One encounters discrimination against Catholics only in certain high visibility and high prestige occupations.[1] However, the argument that nastiness went away with the election of John Kennedy is patently not true. It is true that the nastiness is not quite so prevalent among younger and better educated Americans. Nonetheless, only 40 percent of those with graduate degrees dismiss the charges that Catholics can't think for themselves and that their rosaries are superstitious.

Where does this sentiment come from? Perhaps it has always been here, imported from England with the Puritans and lurking beneath the surface of American culture ever since, not as virulent as it used to be, but still alive and occasionally breaking out in the reactions of some Americans and some American media. There are a fair number of Americans who just don't like Catholics. Maybe they never will. One cannot make that judgment with any great confidence until the measures introduced in this project are repeated in years to come. Given the general feeling that anti-Catholic prejudice disappeared with the election of John Kennedy, it does not seem likely that such replication is likely to occur. It is also useful to note that there are statistically significant correlations between scales measuring intolerance for the civil liberties of homosexuals and racists (permitting to teach in a college, to lecture, and to have their books in the library) and anti-Catholic sentiments—a scale combining the three measures: .14 for homosexuals and .09 for racists. Those who respect the civil liberties of such disparate groups are also inclined to respect Catholics. Thus there is evidence that there is at least a taint of intolerance in anti-Catholic reactions.

One should not be surprised by these findings. Anti-Catholic sentiments are deeply imbedded in American culture. The nation was founded by religious activists who not only defined their religious dissent as opposition to the English religious establishment but also considered occasional mildness in that establishment's commitment to fighting for the Protestant cause among its failings. They are less virulent today than they used to be. Are they less widespread? These findings, short of analysis over time, suggest that they may not be. They persist, perhaps, as a latent hostility on the limen of consciousness of many, perhaps most, Americans.

Is there anything Catholics can do? Stop saying the rosary? Demonstrate that they can think for themselves? Persuade their leaders to be more moderate in their public statements? Avoid crises like the sexual abuse scandals? Be nice to everyone?

It seems to us that it is unlikely that there is much Catholics can do about the anti-Catholic mean-spiritedness in American society. They just have to live with it, realizing that it is always a potential danger. It is, to use someone else's metaphor, as American as cherry pie.

What does this imply for a possible political alliance between Catholics and Conservative Protestants? They may share a disdain for abortion and would like to see public funding for church schools. But the lack of warm feelings and the reluctance to renounce bigotry would make any alliance problematic. The Reformation casts a long shadow, and in its darkest recesses bad feelings lurk.

THIRTEEN

Conclusions

We began this study of Conservative Christians with the intention of exploring the social and demographic condition of these Christians and with the hope of ascertaining whether conservative religious belief necessarily correlated with conservative political orientation. We discovered that approximately a fifth of white Americans belong to the denominations that might legitimately be categorized as conservative. Roughly half of that fifth were strictly "evangelical" in the sense that they believed in the literal, word-for-word inerrancy of the Bible.

There were some demographic differences between them and the Mainline Protestants (who seemed to be the most appropriate comparison group). The Conservative Protestants were more likely to be from the South and somewhat less likely to have pursued a college education. But these differences were not large. The political cartoonists' images of uneducated "rednecks" from the South miss their mark badly; it is not only offensive but inaccurate.

RELIGION

We reported that the Conservative Christians are in a certain sense the heirs of the original Reformers as they claim to be. They are significantly more likely—though not unanimously so—to insist on the literal word-for-word interpretation of scripture, they are likely to say that they had undergone the born-again experience, and that they had tried to convert others to the following of Jesus. They also tended to accept predetermination, to reject evolution, to be stern and strict morally, to be more devout, and have a more personal spirituality than Mainline Protestants. Like the demographic differences, however, these differences were not so great as to make the Conservative Christians unique.

We showed that their striking growth over the last several decades was the result of higher birth rates—one more child per family on average—and increased ability to retain their membership. It was not the result, as has been so often claimed, of conversions from Mainline Protestant denominations.

POLITICS

We discovered that Conservative Protestants are only six percentage points more likely to vote Republican and to identify as Republicans and political conservatives. As such they added very little to a Republican base. The problem for the Democrats politically is not to win over the Conservative Christians but rather to cope with the fact that approximately three out of five white Protestants tend to vote Republican, a very large base that is difficult for the mixtum-gatherum Democratic coalition to overcome. We also concluded that while religion is important in all elections and has been more important recently, so is social class more important recently too. Three out of five working-class Conservative Christians tend to vote Democratic, more indeed than working-class Mainline Protestants.

On sexual matters, the conservatives are more likely to disapprove of premarital sex (though not by much), extramarital sex, and homosexuality than Mainline Protestants. Yet in their own personal lives, they are more likely to be in partnership relationships and cohabitation relationships than members of the Mainline denominations. Conservatives were also more likely to admit infidelity in the course of a marriage. We wondered in passing why the leaders of the Conservative denominations, so eager to denounce threats to the institution of the family, seem disinclined to criticize these relations (about which they cannot be ignorant), which are either fornication or adultery by their own moral standards. Homosexuals, it would seem, threaten the family but not infidelity or living in sin.

On abortion issues, the large majority of Conservative Christians were not consistently pro-life. Large majorities, for example, were willing to tolerate abortion when the health of the woman was in jeopardy or she had been raped. Indeed, even the majority of conservatives who believed in the literal word-for-word interpretation of the Bible was not consistently pro-life. Neither abortion nor homosexuals are the "value" issues that the leaders or the Conservative Christians would have us believe—yet there are millions of Conservative Christians for whom they are important issues.

The cultural style of the Conservative Christians is somewhat different than that of the Mainline. They are less likely to attend opera and classical music concerts and more likely to go to NASCAR events and to enjoy bluegrass and gospel music. They are equally likely to watch news on PBS every night. Within the Conservative denominations, the Pentecostals are in fact the super-Conservatives, more likely to believe in literal interpretation, more likely to oppose abortion and homosexuality, more likely to be born again. However, they are also more likely that other Conservatives or Mainline Protestants to identify as Democrats.

There still exists among the Conservatives—and even more among the Pentecostals—remnants of the anti-Catholicism that has historically been part of their perspective.

Thus we have established that Conservative Christians are somewhat different from the rest of Americans, but even on issues like abortion and homosexuality and voting behavior not all that different from other American Protestants. There is a whiff of fact behind some stereotypes but no basis for the venomous denunciations that one hears so often. Those white Conservative Christians who believe in word-for-word literalism and would deny abortion even to women whose health is thought to be endangered are a little more than 2 percent of the American population—hardly a mass of barbarians at the gate.

Does the religious conservatism of biblical Christianity therefore still relate to conservative politics, albeit at a lower level of correlation than we might have expected?

The answer to that questions is "yes," but only if you want to exclude Afro-American Christians from the ranks of the religiously conservative. But that is a groundless exclusion. Their "Evangelical" credentials are as good as anyone else's, in some cases marginally better. It would be very hard among a mixed group of Conservative Christians to discern race without peeking to use only information about doctrinal, devotional, or major moral stands. Afro-American Protestants are even marginally more likely to believe in literal, word-for-word inerrancy of the Bible. Moreover, belief in the Bible correlates for them, just as it does for Conservative Christians in predominantly white denominations, strongly with political commitment and voting patterns, *though in the opposite directions*! Bible Christians in Afro-American denominations are even more likely to vote Democratic than are other African Americans while Bible Christians in other conservative denominations are more likely to vote Republican than other members of their denominations who take a less traditional approach to scripture. Belief in biblical literalism actually *stretches* the political difference between African American and white Conservative Christians.

Who is to say which evangelicalism is superior to the other?

As we explained earlier, Conservative Christianity appears to be a motor, a driving force behind political movements whether of the right or left—abolition, prohibition, prairie populism, the civil rights movement, and now the movement to "restore" America to what it used to be. The proper question for social science is not whether Conservative Christianity is the motor but for which bandwagon it has provided the motor. We suggest that in this case the bandwagon is occupied by white Protestants who are not only resisting modernity but also fighting the powerful federal government and secular humanism—seen often as a combination.

This movement, however, fits the paradigm of the civil rights movement (and perhaps the prohibition movement). While claiming support of a large group of people (among which it has some supporters but not all of the group), it is in fact a minority within a minority within a minority within a minority. The largest minority is Conservative Christians, within that group are those that believe in the literal interpretation of the Bible, within that group those who, let us say, oppose abortion even when a woman's health is in danger, and finally within that group, the leadership and the activists who agitate for the view that they claim to represent—and in some part do represent.

A sensible observer will always wonder how well those one observes on the television screen actually represent the various ascending minorities. It is part of the American political game for the person in the spotlight to claim the largest possible constituency. However, the aforementioned sensible observer will resist the impulse to attribute to a large group of fellow Americans the claims being made by the self-anointed spokesperson. In the case of the Conservative Christians this impulse has often prove irresistible. They make such a wonderful inkblot.

So those zealous Conservative Christians who try to use their smoke and mirrors to enforce their convictions on the media, school districts, courts, and local governments have every right to create whatever illusions they find useful. If others, such as many American liberals, buy into these illusions it's their own fault.

In conclusion, what advice might one add to that currently inundating the Democratic party.

1. Try to arrange that you don't have to run against an incumbent who has managed to portray himself as a wartime president.
2. Try not to lose your gender gap advantage because your own candidate cannot present a credible national security strategy.
3. Try to remember that poor and working-class Conservative Christians share attitudes on equality that are closer to yours than you realize and vote your way when you give them cause to.
4. Try to understand that Catholics lean your way, that they do not vote as their bishops tell them to do, and that they are more likely to vote Democratic than others who hold the same views—whether we are talking about the economic agenda, the social agenda, or the military agenda. Call it loyalty. They like that.

As for the advice that you should not be ashamed of religion and that you should try to spark a dialogue with pro-life supporters, these suggestions can do no harm but won't help much either.

Economic justice is back on the table. The consequences of injustice waded in the streets of New Orleans in the aftermath of Hurricane Katrina in September 2005. More broadly, we note that for the last thirty years American productivity has gone up but real income has not (except for the brief span from 1996 to 1999). The fruits of productivity are not going to workers.[1]

You need a better issue?

Get economic justice right, and the Conservative Christians held back by economic injustice will back you.

CULTURE

We strove to discover whether religious faith brings more happiness to Conservative Christians. We found that frequency of church attendance is the predictor of happiness and not denominational affiliation.

In our experience most of those who stereotype the Conservative Christians do not know any of them. Their image of these denominations is shaped by their experience of TV clergy, the statements of some of the Conservative Christian leaders, the campaigns of the various activist organizations (during election campaigns), and solemn statements issuing from national meetings of the Conservative Christians. Such seemingly unusual spokespersons give rise to the assumption that all Conservative Christians are religious fanatics. Leaving aside for the present discussion the fact that not a few American secularists think that anyone with religious faith is mentally unbalanced, such criteria would not be applied to activists from other organizations—though only the most naïve would think that activists speak for all or even a majority of their alleged constituencies.

We suggest, as an alternative that does not involve stereotyping a fifth of Americans, that one ought to begin with the assumption that Conservative Christians are men and women of very strong religious faith who are in most respects like other Americans and then observe how this model fits the data. To quote Christian Smith at the end as we did at the beginning,

> Most of those who disparage evangelicals in general terms really don't know what they are talking about. In fact, many don't have significant personal relationships with enough ordinary evangelicals to inform their views of what evangelicals are actually like. So, often they are left to base their views on media reports, organizational newsletters, ideas about what evangelicals should be like based on the few things they think they do know, and the general sense about evangelicalism they pick up from others like themselves. From a sociological perspective, these people are working with too small and too biased a sample to be able to draw valid, generalizable conclusions. They need, in sociological jargon, to "increase their N" and address their "sampling biases."

Appendix

Regression results for models of vote and party

	Vote		*Party*	
	All	Conservative Protestants	All	Conservative Protestants
Republican vs. Democrat Religion (relative to Catholic)				
Conservative Protestant	.6005*	—	.6059*	—
	(.0819)		(.0899)	
Carter candidacy	−.4095*	—	.0346	—
	(.1027)		(.1075)	
Clinton candidacy	.0604	—	.2367*	—
	(.1123)		(.1124)	
Afro-American Protestant	−1.7903*	—	−1.1882*	—
	(.1234)		(.1120)	
Mainline Protestant	.6130*	—	.9478*	—
	(.0528)		(.0550)	
Jewish	−.8099*	—	−1.0015*	—
	(.1150)		(.1495)	
Other religion	−.5632*	—	−.1410	—
	(.1492)		(.1558)	
No religion	−.4570*	—	.0046	—
	(.0798)		(.0818)	
Family income (logged)	.2573*	.1963*	.0466	−.0545
	(.0376)	(.0842)	(.0439)	(.0878)
1980s	.0757	.1349	.1910*	.2460*
	(.0522)	(.1030)	(.0553)	(.1046)
1992+	.1574*	.3201*	.2642*	.3902*
	(.0613)	(.1212)	(.0601)	(.1209)
Education	.0978*	.2235*	.2645*	.3381*
	(.0222)	(.0466)	(.0239)	(.0458)
Advanced Degree	−.5123*	−.3752	−.6723*	−.2294
	(.0851)	(.2020)	(.0970)	(.2019)

	Vote		Party	
	All	Conservative Protestants	All	Conservative Protestants
Union member	−.6045*	−.7100*	−.7630*	−.7897*
	(.0543)	(.1151)	(.0597)	(.1257)
Abortion attitude	−.0442*	−.0807*	−.0253*	−.0616*
	(.0126)	(.0252)	(.0128)	(.0239)
1988+	−.1842*	−.1765*	−.1536*	−.1373*
	(.0205)	(.0390)	(.0186)	(.0329)
Woman	−.1463*	−.4055*	−.1324*	−.2353*
	(.0438)	(.0908)	(.0410)	(.0749)
1992+	−.2623*	.2024	−.2821*	−.0182
	(.0844)	(.1537)	(.0728)	(.1378)
Lives in South	.0619	.0276	−.3574*	−.4508*
	(.0718)	(.1283)	(.1121)	(.1681)
1984+	.0716	−.0250	.2649*	.1245
	(.0974)	(.1545)	(.1292)	(.1850)
Lives in Suburb	.2878*	.2141*	.2620*	.2371*
	(.0510)	(.0994)	(.0556)	(.1008)
Election				
1972	.2040	1.7266*	.0466	.8044
	(.2792)	(.5306)	(.2846)	(.5229)
1976	−.4892	.4230	.0674	.8029
	(.2782)	(.5398)	(.2871)	(.5047)
1980	−.5098	.1077	−.5162*	.0754
	(.2829)	(.5138)	(.2599)	(.4527)
1984	−.2265	.8696	−.4490	.1577
	(.2742)	(.4833)	(.2571)	(.4527)
1988	.4877	1.4038*	.3420	.8369
	(.2760)	(.4926)	(.2469)	(.4398)
1992	−.4107*	.0870	.0132	.3326
	(.1212)	(.2380)	(.1111)	(.2177)
1996	−.7404*	−.3634	−.1052	.2762
	(.1203)	(.2311)	(.1134)	(.2098)
Constant	−.6967*	−.9980*	−1.2352*	−.8579*
	(.2377)	(.4215)	(.2119)	(.3805)
3rd Party / Independent vs. Democrat				
Religion				
Conservative Protestant	.3891	—	.1202	—
	(.2490)		(.0639)	
Carter candidacy	−1.0408*	—	.1430	—
	(.3650)		(.0865)	
Clinton candidacy	.0078	—	.1620	—
	(.2623)		(.0987)	

(continued)

Appendix (*continued*)

	Vote		*Party*	
	All	Conservative Protestants	All	Conservative Protestants
Afro-American Protestant	−1.4837*	—	−.7956*	—
	(.2102)		(.0631)	
Mainline Protestant	.3105*	—	.3009*	—
	(.0939)		(.0432)	
Jewish	−.6896*	—	−.4351*	—
	(.2429)		(.1027)	
Other religion	−.1396	—	.5569*	—
	(.1946)		(.1047)	
No religion	.3421*	—	.7288*	—
	(.1157)		(.0592)	
Family income (logged)	−.2372*	.0685	.0424	.1228
	(.0870)	(.2007)	(.0266)	(.0639)
1980s	.5011*	−.0450	−.0278	−.1530
	(.1168)	(.2786)	(.0371)	(.0807)
1992+	.3964*	.3174	−.0505	−0.511
	(.0972)	(.2223)	(.0354)	(.0902)
Education	.1445*	.1687*	.1295*	.0705
	(.0387)	(.0816)	(.0205)	(.0378)
Advanced degree	−.4406*	−.6396	−.3796*	.0627
	(.1379)	(.3841)	(.0837)	(.1861)
Union member	−.0204	−.1773	−.4047*	−.5617*
	(.1161)	(.2464)	(.0513)	(.1120)
Abortion attitude	.0501	.0461	.0053	−.0332
	(.0339)	(.1012)	(.0112)	(.0222)
1988+	−.1079*	−.1115	−.0776*	−.0160
	(.0382)	(.1078)	(.0166)	(.0328)
Woman	−.1483	−.9879*	−.2997*	−.4092*
	(.1018)	(.2973)	(.0377)	(.0739)

Appendix (*continued*)

	Vote		*Party*	
	All	Conservative Protestants	All	Conservative Protestants
1992+	−.3693*	.6131	.0648	.3274*
	(.1395)	(.3464)	(.0709)	(.1351)
Lives in South	−.6442*	−.1886	−.1970*	−.2875*
	(.1772)	(.3278)	(.0754)	(.1190)
1984+	.5060*	−.1327	.0959	−.0490
	(.2252)	(.3866)	.0960)	(.1576)
Lives in Suburb	.1532	.3232	.2054*	.3388*
	(.0851)	(.2043)	.0465)	(.0943)
Election				
1972	.7560	2.3772*	−.4972*	.1983
	(.4581)	(1.0199)	(.1750)	(.4232)
1976	−.4153	.5632	−.4815*	.3103
	(.4634)	(1.1123)	(.1744)	(.4166)
1980	−.1134	1.7008	−.3622*	.8065*
	(.4630)	1.1401)	.1779)	(.3922)
1984	−2.5995*	.5899	−.4745*	.6018
	(.5191)	(1.2483)	(.1796)	(.3966)
1988	−1.8540*	.7299	−.1555	.8177*
	(.4849)	(1.1754)	(.1608)	(.3777)
1992	1.3950*	2.5876*	−.0160	.5070*
	(.2425)	(.7128)	(.1017)	(.1875)
1996	.9559*	2.1820*	.0461	.5551*
	(.2396)	(.7224)	(.0968)	(.1879)
Constant	−2.7417*	−4.3713*	.1278	−.3641
	(.3212)	(.7655)	(.1391)	(.3312)
Valid cases	17,953	4,082	27,477	6,827

* $p < .05$.

Notes

INTRODUCTION

1. We are outsiders twice over—Roman Catholic academics.

2. For purposes of data analysis we identify Conservative Christians by their denominational preferences (see our methodological appendix for details). In the text we frequently refer to "Conservative Christians"—with or without quotes—when we are referring to the broader notions about religion in contemporary American society and politics. We reserve the term "Conservative Protestants" for our precise references to data based on our classification of denominations.

3. As our colleague Sidney Verba once remarked all stereotypes are 30 percent true—that's where they come from.

4. Afro-American Protestants are members of the historically black churches such as the Church of God in Christ and African Methodist Episcopal church. Most are African American, and half of African American adults list an Afro-American Protestant denomination as their religion.

5. We will present evidence later that many blue-collar white Conservative Protestants also vote Democratic.

6. One of us wrote a data-based essay about Southern Baptists in *Religion as Poetry* that reported that many of the images of that denomination in academic and media culture are wrong.

7. We are in fact members of a denomination that many Conservatives write off as an apostate church. Some would deny that we have any right to claim to be Christians. Some would suggest, as in a series of popular novels, that Jesus will be vaporize us along with Jews, Moslems, atheists, agnostics, secular humanists, and mainline Protestants when he returns at the time of the Rapture. We don't agree. We do assert, however, that we disagree respectfully. We will not belittle their beliefs, much less belittle them.

8. We interrupt the narrative time and again in what follows in order to interject the exact wording of the questions we analyze. We do that, not out of some academic formalism, but as insurance against spin and intellectual laziness. Researchers have documented numerous instances in which subtle wording dif-

ferences between questions have profound effect on the distribution of answers. So we keep those words ever before us and the reader.

9. The many topics we explore in this book barely scratch the surface of this remarkable data resource. Public access to the data is facilitated by a Web site maintained by the University of California, Berkeley, Survey Research Center and its Computer-assisted Survey Methods program. Its Web address is http://sda.berkeley.edu. Web pages at that address will direct interested users in how to discover all the questions ever asked and to make tabulations of the sort we report in this book. It also has facilities for making charts and for doing multivariate analysis.

CHAPTER 2

1. Shea's book contains a rich collection of Conservative Christian attacks on Catholicism. Little has changed since the Reformation in these assaults.

2. One of the more interesting movements within Conservative Christianity is that of the premillennial dispensationalists (Weber 2004), a group that believes that it is able to anticipate the return of Jesus on the basis of a careful reading of the Book of Revelation. They find seven different "dispensations" in the scriptures and believe that the end time is at hand. Before the final battle between the Christ and the Anti-Christ, the good (born again) will be "raptured" up to heaven and a time of great tribulation will follow which the raptured will have escaped. Before the end time, Israel must have its own nation, a red heifer must be slaughtered, and a new temple built in Jerusalem. Weber points out that their alliance with Israel is peculiar because while the Israeli government has praised their commitment to Israel, they have made common cause with some of the more radical Israeli movements that the government opposes. The movement crosses denominational lines within Conservative Christianity and is opposed by many theologians and leaders within the conservatives. However, their insistence on the literal interpretation of the Bible has won them considerable praise.

3. In Greeley's research on Southern Baptists, 57 percent believed in word-for-word inspiration.

4. One of us usually responds "yes, but it doesn't quite mean the same thing as you mean." If the Conservative Christian presses for an explanation—which usually does not happen—then the Catholic will try to explain the difference and thus reopens the "sola gratia" question of the Reformation. With some luck it might then be possible to go on to a discussion of the implacable quality of God's love.

5. Instead of complaining about the "sects" Catholic leaders might be well advised to cease their prating about "evangelization" and actually engage in some of it.

6. We ran four ordered logistic regressions with frequency of reading the Bible as the dependent variable. In the first one, we restricted the sample to Protestants and used dummy variables to distinguish Afro-American and Mainline Protestants from Conservatives. Both coefficients were statistically significant.

Second we added EVANGELICAL to the equation as a third independent variable. The EVANGELICAL coefficient was large and significant; neither the dummy variable for Afro-American nor the one for Mainline was significant. In the third and fourth regressions we broadened the sample to include Catholics, necessitating a third dummy variable for denomination. The third only included the three dummy variables for denominations; all were significant. The fourth added EVANGELICAL to the third. evangelical was once again highly significant, neither the dummy variable for Afro-American nor the one for Mainline was significant, but the one for Catholic was still significant. We will follow this template throughout the rest of the chapter as a means of discerning the explanatory power of the EVANGELICAL scale.

7. The items are arranged in the order of the factors that emerge.

8. A "factor" is a cluster of strongly interrelated variables.

9. The third item was not repeated in the 1998 ISSP so the parts of the analysis that use the "predetermination" item only pertain to 1991. However, restricting our attention to the first two items and using the first two items alone yields the same substantive conclusions about the extent of denominational differences among Protestants and how much they depend on the EVANGELICAL scale.

10. Catholics are indistinguishable from Mainline Protestants on this and the other items in this scale.

11. Afro-American Protestants are a statistically insignificant one-fourteenth of 1 standard deviation more theistic than Conservative Protestants.

12. Each item has five response options: yes, definitely; yes, probably; can't choose; no, probably not; no, definitely not. We gave these answers scores of 2, 1, 0, −1, and −2, respectively.

13. We list the items in order from largest to smallest denominational difference. Consult the GSS Web site for the order of the items on the questionnaire.

14. The African American difference appears among Catholics and people with no religion as well. African American Catholics score 2.3 points higher than other Catholics on the God-in-action scale; African Americans with no religion score 3.1 points higher than others with no religion.

15. As before, we list the items in descending order of denominational differences, not in the order they appear in the questionnaire.

16. God's forgiveness also prompts Catholics to oppose capital punishment.

17. Forty percent of Catholics say that conscience is very important while only 32 percent say the teachings of the Church are important.

18. As do 15 percent of Catholics.

19. Attempts to reduce this difference to sociodemographic differences are futile. Gender, marital status, region, and education have no effect on the moral absolutism item. Nor do church attendance or political views have a significant relationship.

20. On the first two, see Hays (1957); on the latter, see Morris (1980).

21. We had to recalibrate the EVANGELICAL scale for this analysis because the question about converting others was not in the 1991 ISSP.

22. In fact, education does not explain any other denominational difference reported in this chapter, either.

CHAPTER 3

1. As before, our data on Conservative Protestants exclude members of largely conservative Afro-American Protestant congregations.

2. The voting question in the GSS refer to the past of course. So the pre-Reagan era is covered in the 1972–1980 GSSs, the Reagan era in the 1982–1991 GSSs, and the current era in the 1993–2004 GSSs.

3. There is also a statistical advantage of pooling elections. While Conservative Protestants, Mainline Protestants, and Catholics are numerous enough to get statistically reliable information from a single election's surveys, the margins of error for Afro-American Protestants, Jews, people of other religions, and those with no religion grow smaller the more data we combine.

4. When we published similar calculations in the *New York Times* on 1 September 2004, we got a lot of mail inquiring why we used Mainline Protestants as the counterfactual; our correspondents seemed to think that asking what would happen if the Conservative Protestants voted as the average voter does made more sense. We remain convinced that other Protestants are the appropriate reference group for Conservative Protestants, but for the sake of those who would prefer a less credible general counterfactual we note that 1.6 percentage points grows to 2.4 if we credit the entire 10 percentage-point difference between Conservative Protestants and the electorate as a whole to the Republican base. Even granting a dubious impact score of 2.4 points, the so-called "Evangelical base" is not an electoral lock.

5. Manza and Brooks (1997) show a persistent effect of religion on American presidential elections but, the 1960 election aside, few changes from election to election over the whole span from 1964 to 1992.

6. The rest described themselves as politically moderate. The question actually allows people to place themselves on a 7-point scale from "extremely liberal" to "extremely conservative," but we set aside the modifiers for now.

7. That is not to say that election outcomes are more predictable. The near-perfect balance between Democrats and Republicans, liberals and conservatives, makes it hard to say who will win a particular election.

8. Less obvious from the figures is the significantly lower turnout rate among independents. That is, for some people, "independent" is another label for nonpolitical, antipolitical, or apolitical—a point first made by the authors of *The Myth of the Independent Voter* (Keith et al. 1992).

9. The most important point to make is that Afro-American Protestants are doctrinally at least as conservative as the group we call "Conservative Protestants," but they are the most liberal of America's religious groups. This point is so important that we give it its own chapter (see chapter 4).

10. All incomes reflect the purchasing power of the dollar in 2004 (the latest available data on purchasing power).

11. See Hout, Brooks, and Manza (1993) and Larry Bartels (2005), "Partisan Politics and the U.S. Income Distribution."

12. It is a scene in *Fahrenheit 9/11*. Then-governor Bush made the remarks at the annual Alfred E. Smith dinner hosted by the Cardinal Archbishop of New York, 17 October 2000.

13. The index fails to meet statistical criteria for a proper scale, so we enter these items separately in the multivariate analysis.

14. They are also important for party identification, though the party relationship is not quite as dramatic as the vote relationship.

15. Wedge issues do not divide African American voters. Eighty-nine percent of the members of Afro-American Protestant denominations vote for Democrats regardless of their views on abortion and gay sex. Multivariate models that include abortion and gay sex items show that African Americans in Conservative Protestant denominations and African American Catholics are significantly less likely than whites of the same religion to vote Republican.

16. The 1960 election was truly exceptional. John F. Kennedy's candidacy took the Protestant-Catholic divide to heights not seen again.

17. The coefficient for church attendance in our multivariate model intensified from a statistically insignificant .06 in the 1972–1976 elections, to a significant but not very consequential .22 in the 1980–1988 elections, to the significant and more substantial .36 in the 1992–2000 elections. The church attendance variable we used is a recode of the GSS categories worked out by Tom Smith (1998) that reflects the probability of attending in a typical (nonholiday) week (with a theoretical range from 0 to 1.00 and an actual range from .005 to .94). The outcome in our multivariate analysis is the log-odds of voting Republican compared to Democrat (the other votes are treated in separate equation). A coefficient .36 means that yearly attenders average 8 or 9 percentage points more Democratic than weekly attenders of the same religion.

18. In 1998, card 16 mistakenly contained the phrase "I strongly agree people should take care of themselves"—the phrase that was (correctly) printed on card 15 in all years. We have no evidence that suggests that this error affected our results.

19. Our statistical model of partisan voting, appended to this chapter, classifies red states as those that Bush won by five percentage points or more in 2000 (AL, AK, AZM, AR, CO, GA, ID, IN, KS, KY, LA, MS, MT, NB, NC, ND, OK, SC, SD, TX, UT, VA, WV, WY) plus TN, blue states as those that Gore won by five percentage points or more in 2000 (CA, CT, DE, DC, HA, IL, MD, MA, NJ, NY, RI, VT, WA), and battleground states as those in which neither candidate had a five-point margin over the other (FL, IA, ME, MI, MN, MO, NV, NH, NM, OH, OR, PA, WI).

20. The abortion issue also accounts for 52 percent of the different voting preferences of Conservative and Mainline Protestants.

21. The host of the program correctly identified Hout as a professor of sociology at the University of California, Berkeley, and affiliate of its Survey Research

Center, but she did not inquire about his religious affiliation. For his part, Hout mostly kept to the statistics and made no attempt to represent a Catholic point of view.

CHAPTER 4

1. These are our original calculations from the American National Election Studies (NES). We defined low income as a family income below $20,000 and the religious categories in the same way we have for our calculations based on the GSS. The NES data are available at the same Web site as the GSS, that is, http://sda.berkeley.edu.

2. We had not. For the *Times* article, we excluded African Americans. Our practice here, of course, is to separate Conservative Protestant denominations from Afro-American Protestant denominations. Although some African Americans identify with a Conservative Protestant denomination, they amount to just 5 percent of Conservative Protestants. So even if we had included African Americans in the Conservative Protestant calculations we would not have reached different conclusions.

3. We got virtually the same results using party identification instead of vote.

CHAPTER 5

1. The Supreme Court majority said that Mr. Newdow did not have the right to sue because he did not have legal custody of his daughter, and her mother (who did have custody) opposed the suit.

2. The GSS always has a higher turnout rate than we find in official statistics for several reasons: people who participate in elections are also more likely to participate in surveys, the GSS excludes institutional populations that tend to have lower turnout, and people who did not vote sometimes say they did.

3. Both are significantly below average in the value they place on item C—"inner spiritual peace."

4. Ignore for a moment the possibility that some people worry about inequality precisely because they feel that riches are too often amassed by fraud and manipulation and not enough by effort and focus on the freedom part.

5. See, for example, the review of Thomas Frank's *What's the Matter with Kansas?* by Anatol Lieven in the *London Review of Books* (2 December 2004).

6. Catholics and Jews (not shown) have significantly more pride in America's achievements in arts and literature than do Protestants (see Greeley 2000).

7. All of these adjustments are made using an ordered logistic regression model appropriate for this kind of survey items.

8. On this particular issue, Catholics are joined by Jews and secularists in preferring the communal solution.

9. The term "living wage" was coined by John Ryan, a Catholic priest and sociologist whose 1906 dissertation at Catholic University was entitled "A Living Wage." Father Ryan advocated for the concept through the Progressive Era. Though he lost that round, he was "the New Deal's Ambassador to Catholics" in

the 1930s (Dolan 1992). Ryan's inspiration was *Rerum Novarum,* Pope Leo XIII's encyclical on working conditions, issued in 1891. *Reum Novarum* crafted a distinctive Catholic view of social justice that critiqued both socialism and capitalism, endorsed both the right to private property and the right of workers to organize, and the responsibility of governments to take action to redress economic injustices where and when they occur.

10. We have already seen one version of these differences; we described them a few paragraphs above. The only difference between this model and the results above is the case base; the results in table 5.1 all use only the 922 cases with valid data on all variables. Above we used every case we could for each calculation.

11. The religious differences in assessments of the extent of economic inequality in the country fail to rise to the level of statistical significance.

CHAPTER 6

1. We are not the first sociologists to make this point. Smith (1998) emphasized it in *American Evangelicalism.*

2. We found no evidence of substantial trends in any of these compositional variables and distinguishing habits and activities.

3. Kappa is not a correlation coefficient and can take values outside the −1 to 1 range.

4. The GSS vocabulary quiz consists of ten words. Respondents read a card containing the word to be defined and five possible synonyms. They pick the word from the list that they think comes closest to the meaning of the vocabulary word. All respondents get the same ten words. The score is the number of correct answers ("don't know" is considered wrong, not missing).

5. Eighty-four percent for Catholics and Jews. Closest to the Conservative Protestants are Afro-American Protestants at 58 percent.

CHAPTER 7

1. This chapter draws extensively on our article in the September 2001 issue of *American Journal of Sociology* and a precis we published in *Christian Century.* Some passages may appear in similar form both here and in those sources.

2. Because nearly 80 percent of adults practice the religion they were raised in or one that is very similar to it, we use peoples' religious origins to reach further into the past than the data would otherwise permit. We classify the denominations people mention in response to the questions "What religion were you raised in? [to Protestants]: What denomination was that?" according to Smith's schema. We date these answers according to the year the person turned sixteen years old.

3. Some scholars have registered dissent from the "excessive liberalism" argument before. Most importantly, Roof and McKinney (1987) noted that higher fertility and a younger age distribution give conservative denominations a demographic advantage. Robert Wuthnow (1993) and Darren Sherkat (1998) also took note of the demography of denominations. While these authors have, to varying degrees, presented data that established the plausibility of the demographic fac-

tor alongside other explanations, none were able to quantify the relative contributions of demography and switching to Mainline decline.

4. We reported the technical details of our demographic calculations in the September 2001 issue of the *American Journal of Sociology* (see Hout, Greeley, and Wilde 2001).

5. Of the remainder, nearly all—71 percent—stayed in the Mainline tradition, but 2 percent now consider themselves "interdenominational" or "nondenominational."

6. The differences to date, especially for the youngest cohorts we are projecting at the end of the time series, may differ more in timing than in final numbers of births. We have taken the differential timing in older cohorts into account in making our projections, but if some Mainline women's delays result in foregone births, we may be underestimating the contemporary difference somewhat.

7. Two does not suffice because, even in a country like the United States, some children die before they reach an age where they can reproduce themselves. The "extra" one-tenth of a child in the average is what it takes to offset that mortality given the mortality level we find in the United States. If all infant and child mortality were eliminated, then the average number of births per couple needed for replacement would be exactly 2.0.

CHAPTER 8

1. We include Catholics in this chapter because they had at one time attitudes on sexual matters as stern as those of the Conservative Protestants.

2. And 22 percent of Catholics.

3. The other two items in the EVANGELICAL scale are not asked often enough to be useful in accounting for sexual attitudes.

4. So called because they are those Conservative Protestants who believe in the literal word-for-word inspiration of the Scriptures.

5. As do 62 percent of Catholics.

6. And Catholics five percentage points.

7. In the 1992 General Social Survey a majority of Catholics say that they do not believe that all homosexual sex is always wrong. Note that in most of the matters discussed in this chapter Catholics are the least likely to be Puritans.

8. This is the official teaching of the Catholic Church as it has been propounded in recent years.

9. Though Catholics have changed their minds on this issue rapidly.

10. And 68 percent of Catholics despite the Church's teaching on birth control.

11. The abortion for "any reason" was not part of Rossi's original battery and does not fit the requirements for a Gutman scale.

12. And 70 percent of Catholics.

13. Thus the *New York Times* attributed G. W. Bush's reelection in 2004 to a concern for "moral values" though it was an important consideration to only 20 percent of the electorate. The myth is just too useful to succumb to contrary evidence.

14. Since weekly church attendance for Catholics could be considered the equivalent to Protestant biblical literalism, we add that 7 percent of Catholics who go to church every week and oppose abortion when a woman's health is in danger are less than 2 percent of the total American population.

15. The issue of whether the responses to such questions are valid is beyond the scope of the present book. We accept the conclusions of Laumann et al. (2000) that there is solid reason to believe that most respondents tell the truth.

16. For Catholic men the fidelity rate is 96 percent and for Catholic women 97 percent.

CHAPTER 9

1. The 1980 and 1982 estimates are less than 1 percent, but Brooks cautions that the question in those two years was different from the question used in all other years of the time series.

2. "Feminist" is not a popular label. Only 12 percent of the men and 28 percent of the women in the United States apply the word to themselves—5 percent of the Conservative Protestant men and 14 percent of the women.

3. The GSS Board of Overseers revised the feminism scale in the late 1990s. Only the fourth item is part of the new feminism scale. The first three items were last asked in 1998.

4. For the purposes of presentation, the data are smoothed using locally estimated regression methods (see Hout et al. 2001 for an exposition on these methods.)

5. Emotional (inter)dependence also helps Catholic marriages, but neither factor matters for the marital happiness of Afro-American or Mainline Protestants.

6. The ISSP practice of limiting replication to two-thirds of a repeat study thwarts our efforts to measure change here.

7. Readers inclined to judgmental language might infer from this finding that the experience of fornication made one more open to abortion. We strongly caution against such an inference since both may be related to some prior cause such as a basic rejection of certain elements of the Conservative Christian sexual ethic.

CHAPTER 10

1. Some context and switching problems interfere with accurate measurements of the time trend in happiness. Smith (1990a) has identified these problems, and we follow his recommendation to drop some forms in a few years and to leave the 1972 and 1985 data out of the time series.

2. We pool the two surveys together for this part of the analysis to increase the case basis for multivariate analyses; there were only 251 Afro-American Protestants and 62 Jews in the 2000 GSS.

3. The three numbers only sum to 99 percent instead of 100 percent because we rounded each percentage independently.

4. Technical analyses indicate that this is the optimal coding of the attendance categories for our purposes (for details see Hout and Greeley 2003). We refer to this scale as "frequency of attendance" to distinguish it from "probability of attendance."

5. Our statistical model is nonlinear so our language must be somewhat imprecise here.

6. In each pair we list the happier person first.

7. Cronbach's alpha for the scale is .91.

8. We tried several expressions for this relationship. The zero-order relationship between belief in God and happiness is significant but not linear. People who believe sometimes but not at other times are less happy than believers, agnostics, and atheists.

9. These remarks apply to the trend lines that remove sampling fluctuations that occasionally yield observed percentages that contradict our generalizations.

CHAPTER 11

1. Many scholars maintain that "speaking in tongues," as reported by Luke, was different from the usual Pentecostal manifestations today in that the apostles spoke in their own language and the foreigners in Jerusalem heard them in their languages.

2. Mostly those who identify with the Assembly of God, Holiness Churches, and explicitly Pentecostal denominations.

3. We are unaware of any other research on Pentecostals using probability samples. Unfortunately there is nothing in our data that enables us to discuss the enthusiastic experiences that are at the heart of these churches. However, we can study the correlates of the Pentecostal faith and compare them with the other Conservative Christians.

4. This is an assumption that we cannot actually prove.

5. Neither of us are part of the charismatic movement within Catholicism. Truth to tell, the enthusiasms of the charismatics sometimes makes us feel edgy. We can understand why some more moderate Conservative Christians would have the same reaction. Yet if it works for some people, then why should others tell them to fix it?

CHAPTER 12

1. See, for example, Alba and Abdel-Hady's (2005) analysis of the rolls of the American Academy of Arts and Sciences.

CONCLUSION

1. See, for example, Hout et al. (1997) or Fantasia and Voss (2003, 15–16).

References

Alba, Richard. 2005. "Gallileo's Children: Italian Americans' Difficult Entry into the Intellectual Elite." *Sociological Quarterly* 46: 3–18.

Alwin, Duane F., and Robert M. Hauser. 1975. "The Decomposition of Effects in Path Analysis." *American Sociological Review* 40: 37–47.

Bartels, Larry. 2005. "Partisan Politics and the U.S. Income Distribution." Working paper. Department of Politics. Princeton University.

Binder, Amy. 2002. *Contentious Curricula: Afrocentrism and Creationism in American Public Schools*. Princeton: Princeton University Press.

Biswas-Diener, Robert, Ed Diener, and Maya Tamir. 2004. "The Psychology of Subjective Well-Being." *Daedalus* 133 (spring): 18–25.

Brooks, Clem, 2002. "Religious influence and the Politics of Family Decline Concern: Trends, Sources, and U.S. Political Behavior." *American Sociological Review* 67: 191–211.

DiMaggio, Paul, John Evans, and Bethany Bryson, 1996. "Have Americans' Social Attitudes Become More Polarized?" *American Journal of Sociology* 102: 690–755.

Dolan, Jay P. 1992. *The American Catholic Experience*. South Bend, IN: University of Notre Dame Press.

Duncan, Otis Dudley. 1966. "Path Analysis: Sociological Examples." *American Journal of Sociology* 72: 1–16.

———. 1969. "Contingencies in Constructing Models for Causal Analysis: An Illustration." *Sociological Methodology* 1: PAGE NOS

———. 1970. "Paths, Partials, and Partitions." *Sociological Methodology* 2: 38–47.

Duncan, Otis Dudley, and Robert W. Hodge. 1963. "Education and Occupational Mobility." *American Journal of Sociology* 67: 629–644.

Fantasia, Rick, and Kim Voss. 2003. *Hard Work: Remaking the American Labor Movement*. Berkeley: University of California Press.

Frank, Thomas. 2004. *What's the Matter with Kansas?* New York: Metropolitan Books.

Goodman, Leo A., 1991. "Measures, Models, and Graphical Displays in the Analysis of Cross-Classified Data." *Journal of the American Statistical Association* 86: 1085–1111.

Greeley, Andrew M. 1977. *The American Catholic: A Social Portrait*. New York: Basic Books.

———.1996. *Religion as Poetry*. New Brunswick, NJ: Transaction Press.

———. 2000. *Catholic Imagination*. Berkeley: University of California Press.

Greeley, Andrew M., and Michael Hout. 1999. "Americans' Increasing Belief in Life After Death." *American Sociological Review* 64: 813–835.

Harrison, Paul M., 1971. *Authority and Power in the Free Church Tradition*. Carbondale: Southern Illinois University Press.

Hays, Samuel P. 1957. *Response to Industrialism*. Chicago: University of Chicago Press.

Hout, Michael. 1999. "The Terms of the Debate: Abortion Politics in the United States, 1972–1996." *Gender Issues* 17: 3–34.

Hout, Michael, Clem Brooks, and Jeff Manza. 1993. "The Persistence of Classes in Postindustrial Society." *International Sociology* 8: 259–77.

———. 1995. "The Democratic Class Struggle in U.S. Presidential Elections, 1952–1992." *American Sociological Review* 60: 805–828.

Hout, Michael, and Claude S. Fischer. 2002. "Why More Americans Have No Religious Preference: Politics and Generations." *American Sociological Review* 67: 165–90.

Hout, Michael, with Claude S. Fischer, Martín Sanchez Jankowski, Samuel R. Lucas, Ann Swidler, and Kim Voss. 1997. "Inequality by Design: Data, Myths, and Politics." Working paper. New York: Russell Sage Foundation.

Hout, Michael, Andrew Greeley, and Melissa J. Wilde. 2001. "The Demographic Imperative in Religious Change." *American Journal of Sociology* 107: 468–500.

Keith, Bruce E., David E. Magleby, Candice J. Nelson, Elizabeth Orr, Mark C. Westlye, and Raymond E. Wolfinger. 1992. *The Myth of the Independent Voter*. Berkeley: University of California Press.

Kelley, Dean M., 1972. *Why Conservative Churches Are Growing*. New York: Harper and Row.

Laumann, Edward, John H. Gagnon, Robert T. Michael, and Stuart Michaels. 2000. *The Social Organization of Sexuality: Sexual Practices in the United States*. Chicago: University of Chicago Press.

Long, J. Scott. 1997. *Regression Methods for Categorical and Limited Dependent Variables*. Thousand Oaks, CA: Sage.

Manza, Jeff, and Clem Brooks. 1996. "The Religious Factor in U.S. Presidential Elections, 1960–1992." *American Journal of Sociology* 103: 38–81.

Marty, Martin E., 1986. *Pilgrims in Their Own Land: 500 Years of Religion in America*. New York: Penguin Books.

Morris, Aldon D., 1986. *The Origins of the Civil Rights Movements*. New York: Free Press.

Roof, Wade Clark, and William McKinney. 1987. *American Mainline Religion: Its Changing Shape and Future*. New Brunswick, NJ: Rutgers University Press.

Scalon, Maria Celi, and Andrew Greeley. 2003. "Catholics and Protestants in Brazil." *America* 189: 20–21.

Schuman, Howard, Charlotte Steeh, Lawrence Bobo, and Maria Krysan. 1997. *Racial Attitudes in America: Trends and Interpretations*. Revised edition. Cambridge, MA: Harvard University Press.

Shea, William M. 2004. *The Lion and the Lamb: Evangelicals and Catholics in America*. New York: Oxford University Press.

Sherkat, Darren E. 1998. "Counterculture or Continuity? Examining Competing Influences on Baby Boomers' Religious Orientations and Participation." *Social Forces* 76:1087–1114.

———. 2001. "Tracking the Restructuring of American Religion: Religious Affiliation and Patterns of Mobility, 1973–1998." *Social Forces* 79: 1459–1492.

Smith, Christian. 1998. *American Evangelicalism: Embattled and Thriving*. Chicago: University of Chicago Press.

———. 2000. *Christian America? What Evangelicals Really Want*. Berkeley: University of California Press.

Smith, Tom W. 1979. "Happiness: Time Trends, Seasonal Variations, Inter-survey Differences, and Other Mysteries." *Public Opinion* Quarterly 42: 18–30.

———. 1990. "Classifying Protestant Denominations." *Review of Religious Research* 31: 225–245.

———. 1990a. "Timely Artifacts: A Review of Measurement Variation in the 1972–1989 GSS." GSS Methodological Report No. 56. Chicago: NORC.

———. 1998. "A Review of Church Attendance Measures." *American Sociological Review* 63: 131–136.

———. 2003. "American Sexual Behavior: Trends, Socio-demographic Differences, and Risk Behavior." GSS Topical Report 25. Chicago: National Opinion Research Center.

Stouffer, Samuel A. 1955. *Communism, Conformity, and Civil Liberties*. Garden City, NY: Doubleday.

Steensland, Brian, Jerry Z. Park, Mark D. Regnerus, Lynn D. Robinson, W. Bradford Wilcox, and Robert D. Woodberry. 2000. "The Measure of American Religion." *Social Forces* 79: 291–318.

Swidler, Ann. 2002. *Talk of Love*. Chicago: University of Chicago Press.

Tracy, David. 1981. *The Analogical Imagination*. New York: Cross Roads.

Waite, Linda J., and Maggie Gallagher, 2000. *The Case for Marriage: Why Married People Are Happier, Healthier, and Better-off Financially*. New York: Doubleday.

Wilcox, W. Bradford. 2004. *Soft Patriarchs, New Men: How Christianity Shapes Fathers and Husbands*. Chicago: University of Chicago Press.

Wuthnow, Robert. 1993. *Christianity in the 21st Century*. New York: Oxford University Press.

Index

abortion, 52, 121–26, 179–80; circumstances of pregnancy and support for, 122–26; Pentecostals and, 167–68; as political issue, 52–55; Republican votes and, 53, 54

affirmative action, 60–62

African Americans: attitudes toward, 59–61 (*see also* racism); denominational differences among, 95–96. *See also* race

Afro-American Protestants, 4, 8, 37–38, 189n4. *See also specific topics*

alcohol use, 100–102

assisted suicide, 58

atheists, civil liberties and academic freedom of, 63, 64

beliefs, religious. *See* religious beliefs

Bible: frequency of reading, 72, 73; influence on daily life, 30–31; as sole rule of faith, 14; views of, 15–16, 56, 73 (*see also* biblical literalism); as word of God, 12–13, 15–16, 18

Bible Christians, 115–16, 120, 124–26, 166. *See also* biblical literalism; Pentecostals

Biblical Christianity, 13

biblical literalism, 56, 74, 156–57; education and, 36–37. *See also* Bible Christians, inerrancy

blacks. *See* African Americans

"born again" experience, 16–18

Bryan, William Jennings, 57

Bush, George H. W., 68

Bush, George W., 39, 44, 53, 66, 92

Carter, Jimmy, 2, 53

Catholics: attitudes toward, 172–77; and Conservative Christian proselytization, 16–17; contrasted with Protestants, 20; idolatry, superstition, and free thinking among, 173–75; opposition to, 12, 13. *See also* Reformation

censorship, 33. *See also* civil liberties

childbearing, 96–98, 147

church: importance of one's, 30–31; versus one's own conscience, 31;

church attendance, 56, 153–56, 160

church organizations, central, and local congregations, 31–32

civil liberties, threat to, 62–64

class gap in voting, 40–41

clergy, 112

Clinton, William Jefferson, 2, 50, 51, 54, 68, 89; morality and, 32–33; Pentecostals and, 171; personal liberty and, 78

cohabitation, 128–30

conscience, personal, versus the Church and God's law, 31, 33

Conservative Christian growth, 103–5; and the demographic explanation, 104–11; future changes in rate of, 111–12

Conservative Christianity: nature of, 1; as religious movement, 1

Conservative Christians, 178–79, 189n2; demonization of, 4, 74–75; insider versus outsider portraits of, 1–2; relationships with others, 16; self-perception, 1; social portrait of, 91–102. *See also specific topics*
Conservative Protestants, 189n2; ancestry, 93–96; geography, 92, 93; portion of Protestants who are (*see* Conservative Christian growth). *See also specific topics*
Conservative-to-Mainline conversion, diminishing, 108–9
Conservative vs. Mainline Protestants, 6–8, 37. *See also specific topics*
conversion, 16–17, 164; from Conservative to Mainline Protestant denominations, 108–9
coping, belief as an aid in, 26, 27
cultural life and interests, 101, 170–71, 180, 183
"culture wars," 109–11

Darwinism, 3, 34. *See also* evolution
democracy, American: satisfaction with, 81–82
Democratic party, advice to, 182
Democratic votes, 179; by race and denomination, 72–73. *See also* politics, partisan pattern in; Republican votes
"demographic imperative," 106
devil, belief in, 23, 24
divorce, 146
Dole, Bob, 68
duties and responsibilities, 29–32

economic inequality, 84–87, 90
economics, 182; and the limits of market, 84–89. *See also* income; socioeconomic indicators
education: and belief in Bible versus evolution and science, 36; religion and, 98–100
egalitarian views, 84–85; and the presidential vote, 89–90
employment, 98, 169–70
end-of-life issues, 58
entertainment, 101, 170–71, 180
ethnicity: religion and, 93, 94. *See also* race
EVANGELICAL scale, 19, 20, 22. *See also specific topics*
Evangelicals, 15, 183
evil, belief in, 20, 28
evolution, 3, 34–36, 56–57

faith, 14, 28
family, 137; extended, 148. *See also* marital relations and marital paradigms
"family decline," 136–37
family status, religion and, 96–98
family values, 96, 125, 126, 136
feminist attitudes, 138–40, 145, 169, 170. *See also* gender roles
"feminist revolution," 136, 145, 148
fertility rates, 96–98, 106–8
financial satisfaction, 169–70
First Amendment, 76–77. *See also* free speech
forgiveness, 29–30
Frank, Thomas, 39–40
free speech, threat to, 62–64, 76–77
freedom: assessments of, 77–81; importance of different kinds of, 80, 81; quality of, 77–82; religious, 76
Fundamentalism, 14, 18
"fundamentalist" denominations, 6
Fundamentals, The, 12, 14–15

gay rights, 53–55, 58–59. *See also* homosexuality
gender roles, 138–41. *See also* marital relations and marital paradigms
Genesis, 12–14
geography: political, 64–65; religion and, 92, 93
God: experience of, 27–28; images of, 20–22; relationship with, 20–22, 26–27, 165–66
Gore, Al, 50, 51, 171
government, limits of, 84–89
gun ownership, 101

happiness, 150–53, 157–59, 161; attendance at religious services and, 153–56, 160; biblical literalism and, 156–57; how religious affiliation affects,

155–56; and the millennium, 152–57; Pentecostals and, 169–70; September 11 and, 157–58; trends in, since 1970s, 158–61
health care, national spending on, 51
heaven and hell, belief in, 23, 24
homosexuality, 63, 64, 115, 118–20, 132–33; Pentecostals on, 167. *See also* gay rights
human nature, 20

immigrants, 93, 94
income, family, 48–50, 98–100. *See also* financial satisfaction
income disparities, 84–87, 90
inerrancy, 12–13, 15–16, 18, 36–37

Kennedy, John F., 44, 176
Kerry, John F., 44, 51, 92
Koukl, Greg, 67

law, morality and, 33–34
leisure activities, 101, 170–71, 180
liberalism, reaction against "excessive," 103–4, 109–10, 112, 195n3. *See also* Democratic votes
liberals, pointing fingers at Conservative Protestants, 74
lifestyle, 100–102, 170–71, 180
Liturgical Christianity, 13

Mainline Protestants, 6–9; and the Reformation, 12, 14, 18, 28–29, 37. *See also* *specific topics*
marital relations and marital paradigms, 141–48
marital status, 96, 97
marriage: cohabitation with spouse before, 128–30; and happiness, 152
maternity leave, 147
McCarthy era, 62
McGovern, George, 53
Midwest politics, 40
miracles, belief in, 23, 24
missionaries, 16–17
Moore, Roy (judge), 76
morality, 32–33, 40; law and, 33–34. *See also under* Pentecostals

National Association of Evangelicals, 15
national pride and nationalism, 82–84, 90
9/11 terrorist attacks and happiness, 157–58

occupations, 98, 99
orthodoxy, 18. *See also* Fundamentalism

parenting, 145, 147
partnership revolution (sexual behavior), 127–32
patriotism. *See* national pride and nationalism
Pentecostals, 162–63; attitudes about sex, 166–67; attitudes toward Catholics, 175–76; family, morale, entertainment and politics, 169–71; morality, 166–69; religion, 163–66
Perot, H. Ross, 50
physician-assisted suicide, 58
political geography, 64–65
politics, 65–68, 179–82; class, economics, and, 48–52, 66; moral values as political issues, 52–55; partisan pattern in, 44–48; race and, 69–72. *See also* voting; *specific presidential candidates*
pornography, 120–21
prayer in schools, 57
predestination / predetermination, 22
premillennial dispensationalists, 190n2
promiscuity, 127, 128, 132–34. *See also* partnership revolution
proselytization, 16–18, 164
Protestant denominations, 6; breakdown by religion category, 8; diminishing Mainline (*see* Conservative Christian growth). *See also specific denominations*
punishment of sinners, 32
Puritans, 32

race, 71–72; "directs" religious impact, 72–74; religion and, 93, 94. *See also* African Americans
racial ancestry of Conservative Protestants, 93–96
racism, masked, 59–63
Reagan era, 53

Reformation, 31, 32; Conservative Christians and, 12–16
religions, prevalence of various, 7
religiosity, 29–31, 178–79; and happiness, 153–55, 160; race and, 72–74. *See also* Bible; church attendance; spirituality
religious beliefs, 23–24. *See also specific topics*
religious feelings, 155, 156
religious organizations, 6
religious stories, 73–74
Republican identification, 44–45, 50, 72; by religion, 45–46; by year, 46, 50
Republican votes, 179; by family income and political era, 48–50; geography and, 64–65; Pentecostals and, 171; by political era, 47–48, 51–54; by political views, 47–48; by religion, 42, 43; by support for unions and social spending, 51, 52. *See also* Democratic votes; voting
Rosary, as superstitious devotion, 173–76

salvation, 16
same-sex marriages, 53–54
science: morality and, 34; versus religion, 34–35. *See also* Darwinism
segregationist attitudes, 59, 61
September 11 terrorist attacks and happiness, 157–58
sex, 113, 134–35, 179; extramarital, 115, 117–18; Pentecostals and, 166–68; premarital, 114–16, 167; teenage, 115–17. *See also* homosexuality; promiscuity
sexual revolution, 113, 114, 116, 117; and the partnership revolution, 127–32
Shea, William M., 3, 12–14
sin, belief in, 20
sinners, 32–33
Smith, Christian, 183
Smith, Tom W., 6
social class, values, and voting, 40–41
social justice, 86, 182. *See also* economic inequality
socioeconomic indicators, religion and, 98–100
sociology, 5
Specter, Arlen, 66
spirituality, 24–29. *See also* religiosity
suicide, assisted, 58
supernatural subjects, beliefs about, 23–24

taxes, attitude toward, 85, 88–89
tobacco use, 100–102
Tracy, David, 20

United States. *See* national pride and nationalism

voting: beliefs, practice, and, 55–56; moral values, material interests, and, 40; partisan pattern in, 44–48; by religion, 39–44. *See also* Democratic votes; Republican votes

Wilcox, W. Bradford, 137, 144
women. *See* gender roles; marital relations and marital paradigms
work ethic, Protestant, 86
worldview, 19–22